Cocoon 2 Programming: Web Publishing *with* XML *and* Java

Cocoon 2 Programming: Web Publishing *with* XML *and* Java™

Bill Brogden
Conrad D'Cruz
Mark Gaither

San Francisco · London

Associate Publisher: Richard Mills
Acquisitions and Developmental Editor: Tom Cirtin
Editor: Linda Stephenson
Production Editor: Leslie E.H. Light
Technical Editor: John-Brian Vyncent
Graphic Illustrator: Jeff Wilson, Happenstance Type-O-Rama
Electronic Publishing Specialist: Maureen Forys, Happenstance Type-O-Rama
Proofreaders: Monique van den Berg, David Nash, Nancy Riddiough, Emily Hsuan, Laurie OConnell, Yariv Rabinovich
Indexer: Nancy Guenther
Cover Designer: Carol Gorska/Gorska Design
Cover Illustrator/Photographer: Akira Kaede, Photodisk

Library of Congress Card Number: 2002109624

ISBN: 0-7821-4131-5

Manufactured in the United States of America

10 9 8 7 6 5 4 3 2 1

SOFTWARE LICENSE AGREEMENT: TERMS AND CONDITIONS

The media and/or any online materials accompanying this book that are available now or in the future contain programs and/or text files (the "Software") to be used in connection with the book. SYBEX hereby grants to you a license to use the Software, subject to the terms that follow. Your purchase, acceptance, or use of the Software will constitute your acceptance of such terms.

The Software compilation is the property of SYBEX unless otherwise indicated and is protected by copyright to SYBEX or other copyright owner(s) as indicated in the media files (the "Owner(s)"). You are hereby granted a single-user license to use the Software for your personal, noncommercial use only. You may not reproduce, sell, distribute, publish, circulate, or commercially exploit the Software, or any portion thereof, without the written consent of SYBEX and the specific copyright owner(s) of any component software included on this media.

In the event that the Software or components include specific license requirements or end-user agreements, statements of condition, disclaimers, limitations, or warranties ("End-User License"), those End-User Licenses supersede the terms and conditions herein as to that particular Software component. Your purchase, acceptance, or use of the Software will constitute your acceptance of such End-User Licenses.

By purchase, use, or acceptance of the Software you further agree to comply with all export laws and regulations of the United States as such laws and regulations may exist from time to time.

Reusable Code in This Book

The author(s) created reusable code in this publication expressly for reuse by readers. Sybex grants readers limited permission to reuse the code found in this publication or its accompanying CD-ROM so long as the author(s) are attributed in any application containing the reusable code and the code itself is never distributed, posted online by electronic transmission, sold, or commercially exploited as a stand-alone product.

Software Support

Components of the supplemental Software and any offers associated with them may be supported by the specific Owner(s) of that material, but they are not supported by SYBEX. Information regarding any available support may be obtained from the Owner(s) using the information provided in the appropriate read.me files or listed elsewhere on the media.

Should the manufacturer(s) or other Owner(s) cease to offer support or decline to honor any offer, SYBEX bears no responsibility. This notice concerning support for the Software is provided for your information only. SYBEX is not the agent or principal of the Owner(s), and SYBEX is in no way responsible for providing any support for the Software, nor is it liable or responsible for any support provided, or not provided, by the Owner(s).

Warranty

SYBEX warrants the enclosed media to be free of physical defects for a period of ninety (90) days after purchase. The Software is not available from SYBEX in any other form or media than that enclosed herein or posted to www.sybex.com. If you discover a defect in the media during this warranty period, you may obtain a replacement of identical format at no charge by sending the defective media, postage prepaid, with proof of purchase to:

SYBEX Inc.
Product Support Department
1151 Marina Village Parkway
Alameda, CA 94501
Web: http://www.sybex.com

After the 90-day period, you can obtain replacement media of identical format by sending us the defective disk, proof of purchase, and a check or money order for $10, payable to SYBEX.

Disclaimer

SYBEX makes no warranty or representation, either expressed or implied, with respect to the Software or its contents, quality, performance, merchantability, or fitness for a particular purpose. In no event will SYBEX, its distributors, or dealers be liable to you or any other party for direct, indirect, special, incidental, consequential, or other damages arising out of the use of or inability to use the Software or its contents even if advised of the possibility of such damage. In the event that the Software includes an online update feature, SYBEX further disclaims any obligation to provide this feature for any specific duration other than the initial posting.

The exclusion of implied warranties is not permitted by some states. Therefore, the above exclusion may not apply to you. This warranty provides you with specific legal rights; there may be other rights that you may have that vary from state to state. The pricing of the book with the Software by SYBEX reflects the allocation of risk and limitations on liability contained in this agreement of Terms and Conditions.

Shareware Distribution

This Software may contain various programs that are distributed as shareware. Copyright laws apply to both shareware and ordinary commercial software, and the copyright Owner(s) retains all rights. If you try a shareware program and continue using it, you are expected to register it. Individual programs differ on details of trial periods, registration, and payment. Please observe the requirements stated in appropriate files.

Copy Protection

The Software in whole or in part may or may not be copy-protected or encrypted. However, in all cases, reselling or redistributing these files without authorization is expressly forbidden except as specifically provided for by the Owner(s) therein.

Contents at a Glance

Contents

Acknowledgments

I would like to thank the following people for their help: As always, my wife, Rebecca, my unfailing support for many years. My fellow LANWrights, Inc. employees Ed Tittel and Dawn Rader for their guidance and editorial expertise, respectively. Cheryl Applewood for her help early in the project. Tom Cirtin and Leslie Light of Sybex for constructive criticism and discussion. The many active developers of the Apache Cocoon project and the participants on the users and developers mailing lists.

—Bill Brogden

First and foremost, I would like to acknowledge my parents, Wilma and (late) Albert D'Cruz for their role in shaping my life and career. The following for helping me with issues related to the writing of my chapters: Andreas Hartmann (`www.cocooncenter.org`) for his advice on an example I created, Andrew Oliver of The Triangle Java Users Group for his unwavering support of the Apache Project and a sounding board for my ideas on Cocoon usage, and Meredith Norris (IBM) for helping me surmount some obstacles in getting an example completed on time. My friends and colleagues who encouraged me through the project. A special thank you to my co-authors for their fresh insights and guidance. Cheryl Applewood and Dawn Rader for showing me the ropes in the publishing world. Tom Cirtin and Ed Tittel for taking care of roadblocks and challenges along the way.

—Conrad D'Cruz

I extend my deepest gratitude and thanks to Ed Tittel for his continued friendship, his overwhelming generosity, his steadfast support, and his Sunday night dinners and 9-ball games. Thanks to my co-authors for their patience and understanding. Thanks to the constant voices on the developers mailing lists. Many thanks to my family for believing in me and supporting me through good and bad times. Thanks to my brother, Paul, for his timely guidance and unwavering resolve. Thanks to Scott Bean for being a great friend and great business partner. Lastly, a special thanks to Mikiel Featherston. With his supreme belief in me as a human and a golfing buddy, through holes-in-one and chilly dips, his continued challenging of my faith, through rainbows and floods, and his pure undeniable joy, through crushing football tackles and fumbles, he continues to inspire me. Now, if he could only putt!

—Mark Gaither

Introduction

The technology for production of Internet applications has undergone rapid evolution in the last few years. One of the most dramatic trends has been the rise and standardization of XML as the most widely accepted method of creating and describing content. This has come about by extraordinary vision and collaboration among the creators and users.

XML is a simplified form of the Standard Generalized Markup Language (SGML), which has been a standard for document markup for some time. SGML is very complete, but much too complex to become a useful tool for everyday programmers. The other descendant of SGML is HTML, but HTML went in the direction of describing the appearance of documents rather than the content. Furthermore, when using HTML, you must stick to a given markup scheme. XML is designed as a language for creating your own specialized markup languages, so it is easy to adapt to just about any type of data.

In 1996, the World Wide Web Consortium (W3C) started the design effort that led to the first XML standard. Jon Bosak from Sun Microsystems was one of the main participants, so it is not surprising that most of the early software tools for working with XML were in Java. As a Java programmer, you have access to an awesome array of tools that just keeps on growing.

Since that first standard, XML-related projects have sprung up like mushrooms after a rain. It seems like everybody can find an application for XML in their particular problem domain. Odds are that no matter which industry you work in, some formal or informal group is attempting to standardize an XML vocabulary for you.

Many of these projects have led to standards endorsed by the W3C. In fact, the last time we looked, the W3C had more than 14 XML-related standardization efforts going on. However, a number of significant approaches have become *de facto* standards outside the normal standards bodies.

The Amazing Cocoon Project

The first version of Cocoon (now referred to as Cocoon 1) got started in 1998 by a group of programmers who had worked on several Java projects as part of the Apache Software Foundation. Stefano Mazzocchi took the lead and developed a simple servlet that used one of the first XSL processors to reformat XML formatted documents for the Web. Cocoon 1 grew and acquired enough utility that it was used at a number of websites, but it had some architectural weaknesses.

Cocoon 2, which is the version this book covers, was a major redesign with a much more general and flexible architecture. It also draws on a number of other projects at the Apache Software Foundation. In fact, a large number of open-source Java projects working with XML-formatted data have found that Cocoon is exactly what they needed as a framework.

Version 2.0.1 was the release when we started the book and version 2.0.2 came along as we were midway through. We have not attempted to cover any features that are not in the release version 2.0.2. These versions are stable enough for commercial website development and there are already a number of public Cocoon-driven sites.

If there is one problem with Cocoon, it is that it has an inspiring effect on programmers, so there is a continuous ferment of suggestions for the next versions. There will probably be another major redesign with 2.1. Your best bet is to select a version and stick with it.

There are so many XML-related initiatives in the world of programming these days that it would be impossible to catalog them. However, due to the stability of the basic XML standard as maintained by the W3C, Cocoon programmers will be well positioned to take advantage of the latest developments.

Support for the Book

LANWrights will be maintaining a website for the book at:

```
www.lanw.com/books/cocoonbook/
```

That site will probably be running on Cocoon by the time you read this. We will be posting any errata and revisions to the code samples.

Sybex has published all the code used in this book on their website at `www.sybex.com`. Search for this book using the title, author or the book number (4131) and click the Downloads button. Once you have accepted the license agreement, you'll be able to download any of the code listed in this book, organized by chapter.

Before we go any further, let's clarify a few things. Nothing in this book is going to teach you XML, XSLT, or any other Xwhatever basics. You will need to be comfortable with XML 1.0 2nd edition, including namespaces. We provide an overview of XSLT, CSS, and other technologies used by Cocoon, but you will need other reference books for complete coverage of these subjects.

You should also be familiar with Java 1.3 or 1.4 and the servlet API. If you don't already have a servlet-capable web server, you should plan on getting one. Currently, the most commonly used servlet engine among Cocoon users is Tomcat.

Contacting the Authors

We would be delighted to hear from readers with suggestions, reports of errors in the text, or your Cocoon-related announcements.

You can contact Bill Brogden at `wbrogden@bga.com`; his personal web page is at:

`www.bga.com/~wbrogden/`

You can contact Conrad D'Cruz at `conrad.dcruz@netswirl.com`; his website is at:

`www.netswirl.com`

You can contact Mark Gaither at `mark@markgaither.com`; his website is at:

`www.markgaither.com`

Chapter 1

The Cocoon 2 Architecture

- The Challenges of Web Publishing
- The Challenges of Web Content Management
- Content Management Systems to the Rescue
- The Original Cocoon Project
- Architecture of the Cocoon 2 Framework

Solutions for web publishing abound and have been rapidly evolving to fill the needs of both developers and their customers. All of these solutions come down to systems for managing content and serving it up on the Web upon request in a format easily accessible to a variety of users.

This chapter introduces the Cocoon framework by defining the original design goals and architecture of Cocoon 1 and studying the areas where the framework fell short. The chapter also provides an overview of the Cocoon 2 architecture and lays the foundation for developing robust web applications using the framework. In the course of this chapter and the rest of the book, we highlight the benefits that the Cocoon framework brings to most web-publishing efforts and why most projects benefit from it.

So why Cocoon 2? Because it's a flexible, powerful solution based on XML—the language of the Web—and related technologies. It is part of the Apache Project, making it fully capable of managing content and presentation for large-scale web publishing.

To fully understand Cocoon's place in the scheme of things, however, we must take a brief look at the origins of the World Wide Web and the technologies that supported the adoption of the Web as the *de facto* standard for information repositories around the world. Ever since the mid-1990s, the popularity of the Web has helped to shape the evolution of strategies for business. This chapter emphasizes the associated problems that came about and the issues that have created challenges for technical and business organizations as they tried to adapt to the constantly changing needs that were created by the Web.

Finally, we take a look at the challenges of developing and maintaining web applications and the impact those challenges have had on development teams. We list the features of a good publishing framework and define the additional requirements of a true content management system (CMS). We also list the most popular open-source publishing frameworks currently available and provide references for each.

The Challenges of Web Publishing

The TCP/IP network called the Internet had been in use since the late 1960s by an exclusive group of individuals affiliated with the government, academia, research institutions, and technology companies. The costs and complexity associated with using this network prevented the average person from understanding and using it as a tool for increasing personal productivity. In 1992, the adoption of the Hypertext Markup Language (HTML), derived from the more complex Standard Generalized Markup Language (SGML), caused a lot of excitement in the technology and business communities. The complexity of using the Internet was abstracted by the creation of a network of servers that could be used for publishing documents based on HTML and its parent, SGML. This network of information servers came to be known as the World Wide Web.

Any document could be marked up using a set of standardized tags and published to a web server. A remote client browser application could access this document, interpret the tags, and then display the information. The web developer predefined the format of the document and changing the presentation involved modifying the markup tags in the document. Vendors began providing their web server applications and browsers for free and this resulted in the proliferation of web technologies. The ease with which a developer could mark up a document and the availability of tools for the nontechnical content developer made HTML a very popular language for web publishing. HTML soon came to be the *lingua franca* of the Web.

Dynamic Presentation and Browser Wars

With the adoption and increasing popularity of HTML came the inevitable battle among vendors for control of the standard. In a move to protect their installed bases, vendors began to support nonstandard tags and server configurations. Developing content for consumption within an intranet was slightly less complicated, because most organizations exercised some control over the browser versions deployed within their enterprises. As time went by, the number of browser vendors increased, as did the versions of a particular browser. The nightmare had only just begun for content developers.

HTML was an excellent mechanism for authoring and rendering static information pages with graphical images, but it had some serious limitations. It did not address dynamic presentation or provide any way for the application to access data from external sources. Dynamic presentation and browser customization was made possible by the introduction of support in HTML for scripting languages like JavaScript and VBScript. Server-side technologies, such as the Common Gateway Interface (CGI), Java Servlet technologies, and a few others, enabled dynamic data to be displayed in browsers. Prior to the introduction of these technologies, the website was a tool for information distribution and was only used to support the marketing functions of an organization. Not long after dynamic content made its way into browsers, the industry presented strategies and products to help organizations make money on the Web. Up until that time, only the big companies could afford to conduct business electronically with expensive and proprietary technologies based on the Electronic Data Interchange (EDI) standard. The new web applications allowed even the smallest players to get into the electronic commerce arena.

Enterprise Applications and Dynamic Data

Web application servers became more sophisticated and could now perform multiple tasks, such as serving up information pages customized for a particular browser and embedding data extracted from one or more data sources in those pages. The servers allowed users to initiate transactions and execute business processes—for example, making a retail purchase or placing a bid on an auction site. The user did not need to navigate to each business server, extract individual pieces of information, and manually correlate all relevant data. The service provider had to develop an application that collected all the data behind the scene and presented the user with an integrated and unified web page with the data requested.

The web browser paradigm abstracted the complexity of the organization's technical infrastructure by presenting the results of all operations in the form of a web page with some dynamic presentation data objects. The web server was promoted from the old role of a static electronic brochure to a dynamic catalog of the organization's products and services. It now provided online service delivery and managed user sessions and transactions. It also provided a front end for managing user relationships and communications with the organization.

Figure 1.1 shows a layout of a web application that interfaces with different enterprise services and data stores. It shows the web server as the repository of all the parts of the web application.

FIGURE 1.1: A typical enterprise web application

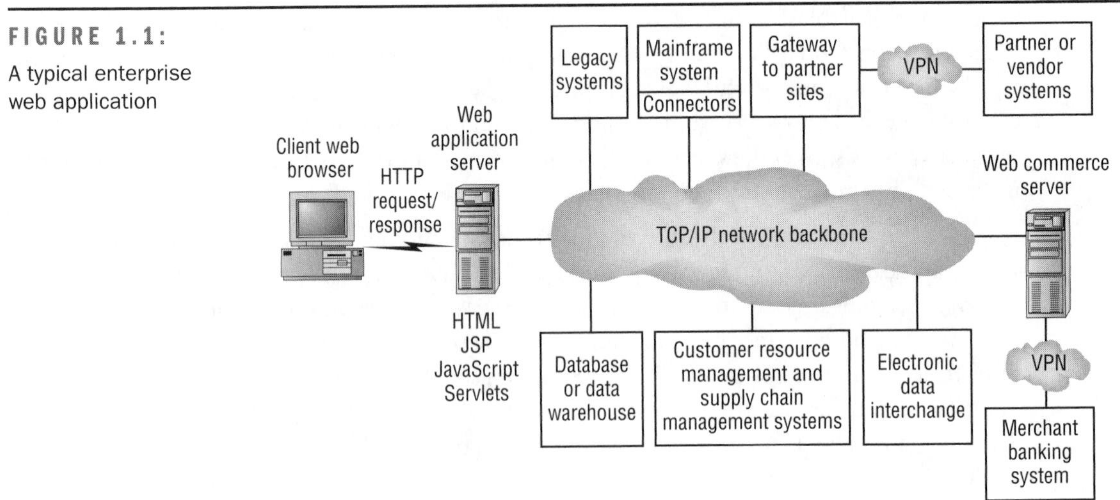

The Challenges of Web Content Management

Figure 1.1 shows the complexity and needs of a typical web application. This section looks at the challenges facing web application developers. It discusses the issues associated with integrating enterprise services as well as the problems associated with managing change, and highlights some of the ways development teams are dealing with these issues.

Integrating and Formatting Data from Multiple Sources

One critical issue that presented a challenge when developing web applications that interfaced with enterprise applications and legacy systems was that data in most enterprises was not available in a single, easy-to-use format. The data had to be extracted, modified, and reformatted before it was suitable for presentation in a web page. Java offered some relief by providing support for developing complex multitier applications. Technologies like Java Database Connectivity (JDBC), Servlets, and Java Server Pages (JSP) provide a means to seamlessly integrate disparate legacy applications and database systems while sticking closely to the web presentation paradigm—that is, output in the form of HTML pages.

This was a double-edged sword and highlighted another critical issue: In an HTML page, content and presentation are so closely tied together that it is difficult for external applications to extract the data embedded in both static and dynamically generated pages. Both these issues were partially addressed by the adoption of Extensible Markup Language (XML) as the standard for modeling data in enterprise and web applications. The use of XML allowed for separation of content and presentation. Because XML documents are normal text files, Java Servlets can be used to dynamically produce XML instead of HTML. Customized presentation was achieved through the use of either Cascading Style Sheets (CSS) or Extensible Stylesheet Language (XSL).

Change Management and Content Management

All these requirements added to the challenges of designing and implementing web applications. As the size and complexity of applications increased, the two issues that moved to the forefront were content management and change management. Content management deals with managing all the objects and parts that go into building the complete application. The use of Java and XML technologies enables the developer to produce robust and easily integrated building blocks for the application. Change management addresses the issues associated with modifying or enhancing the application after it is in production. Some organizations have very stringent requirements, which dictate that changes happen frequently and must be implemented very quickly. This not only includes changes to the dynamic data on the enterprise systems but also how the data gets presented on the pages.

Tighter integration between the web application pages and the enterprise applications or data systems allows for more dynamic data to be available in the final presentation, as in the case of inventory control and purchasing websites. Most content pages have dependencies elsewhere in the same application, or some other application on the same web server, or other applications on remote servers. There is a ripple effect when changes are made to these applications, and often a simple change affects multiple documents, servers, and departments within an organization. The complexity and size of an average dynamic website necessitates either a larger change management team or the automation of the process of change management.

Taming the Web Beast

Most organizations responded to the challenges by increasing the size of the content management team and settling on standardized technologies as the basis for their applications.

An implied challenge was choosing development tools that strictly adhered to the standards and training the entire development team in the use of these tools. Despite all the planning and strategies, content changes rarely could keep pace with the rapidly changing business needs. The limitations of the tools and the change management process often resulted in teams failing in their efforts to manage and maintain web applications. This resulted in a higher cost of ownership, decreased satisfaction on the part of the business sponsors, and an overall reduction in team morale.

Content Management Systems to the Rescue

The Web had proved its potential as a tool for delivery of information and services over the Internet. Organizations of all shapes and sizes quickly jumped on the bandwagon and adopted web strategies. With this came the big push to web-enable products and enterprise applications. Even vendors of proprietary solutions caught the wave and began offering applications designed exclusively for the Web, or at the very least, providing a web front end for their products. The large sites were rich in data and dynamic presentation and created new challenges for the teams designing and maintaining them.

The emphasis was now on teams that were composed of specialists in a particular part of the web application. One such team would specialize in the look and feel of the web pages and the related technologies like HTML and scripting languages. Another team would specialize in integrating enterprise applications into the web application. Newer technologies and standards were hastily put together to support the development and maintenance of large websites. However, this strategy came with its own set of problems. The size of the teams increased and the people-management aspects became a big issue. There were also problems of bridging the training and knowledge gap between teams.

Separation of Concerns

There were sections of the web application that included pieces that mixed the two functions. For example, Java Servlets provided the means to integrate with enterprise applications but would also be used to create the dynamic output to the client. This placed additional pressures on the application integrators because they now had to be concerned with graphical user interface issues. One of the design goals of Java Server Pages (JSP) was to separate content from presentation. However, this came up short and only added to the confusion of the development teams. JSP put additional pressures on the presentation developers because they now had to learn the syntax of Java and had to deal with programming issues. An interim solution was to create cross-functional teams in which members were trained in presentation and application programming, but this was a very expensive solution. There was a need for a solution that would allow the separation of the three areas: content, logic, and presentation.

Web-Publishing Frameworks and CMSs

A web search on the term *content management system* (CMS) reveals a long list of products and frameworks that advertise an easy way to manage the large quantities of information and the services that an enterprise has to offer to its customers. Several of the products and organizations use the term *content management systems* interchangeably with other terms like *content-publishing frameworks*, *web-publishing frameworks*, and *XML-publishing frameworks*.

This section provides a general definition of CMSs that encompasses all the design requirements of a good system. The definition highlights the features of the system that address and solve the challenges created by the surge in the popularity of the Web as a vehicle for delivering information and services. We also name a few of the products available and then shift our focus to the Cocoon architecture. We have chosen to focus on this one framework because it is currently one of the most powerful publishing systems and has the potential of becoming a CMS.

Defining CMS

A CMS is a framework that allows the creator or owner of an information delivery application to effectively manage all the pieces that go into building that application and that define formal processes that support the entire lifecycle of an application. CMSs and web-publishing frameworks offer solutions to most of the common business problems discussed earlier that are associated with developing and maintaining large web applications. They address the issues of rapid application development that offer flexibility in the look and feel as well as added functionality. Using a CMS as the central focal point for web application development strategy allows an organization to produce flexible and scalable applications in a cost effective and timely manner.

A CMS also allows seamless integration of tools and strategies that enable the creation of routine maintenance or upgrades, and the eventual retirement of the application. The CMS integrates data from multiple applications and services and provides a flexible mechanism to format the output and present it to the user. The technologies and strategies might be standards-based or proprietary. The systems that have the term *web* in the name support the standard web technologies and, at the very minimum, use HTML and the Hypertext Transfer Protocol (HTTP). In addition to supporting the Web, the frameworks can support alternative delivery mechanisms, such as dedicated client applications, whether they are stand-alone windows, fat clients, or Java applets embedded in web pages. They also support the integration of the output into another application framework such as Web Services. A few of the products satisfy only a subpart of the definition and might rely on proprietary technologies for the management and delivery of the information and services. Some of the frameworks include specific technologies in the product name itself, such as XML, to emphasize support of the standards for formatting and presenting documents and data. This focuses on technologies that are standards-based and products that are part of the open-source development paradigm.

Web Server Versus CMS

Some of the products attempt to classify regular web information servers as CMSs. This might not be a wrong classification, because creating and managing websites that serve up HTML and images is not trivial given the potential size to which the website can grow. Change management in websites is a significant issue because hyperlinks in HTML pages create interdependencies and any process that enables an easy maintenance strategy needs to get honorable mention. However, the term *content management* is more encompassing and addresses systems and processes for managing information in many different formats and access to enterprise services from multiple sources.

Choosing a framework that offers all the features of a CMS for a website with static HTML content might be overkill, especially if the content is not expected to change over time and the pages do not need to integrate data from external applications. The complexity of configuring and maintaining such HTML content sites using a CMS cannot be cost-justified in the long run. There are several commercial or open-source web servers that are more cost effective and suited for simple websites serving up static HTML pages and images with a little dynamic presentation using scripting languages like JavaScript or VBScript.

A Brief Review of Open-Source CMS Offerings

The following are brief descriptions of some of the open-source CMSs that are currently available and the web addresses of the organizations that support the development of each. It is not a comprehensive list, and their appearance is not meant to be an endorsement over any other open-source products.

XPS Extensible Publishing System from Wyona is an application that uses XML and Java technologies to manage documents and images on the server. Wyona supports XPS at `www.wyona.org`.

eZ Publish From eZ Systems, eZ Publish is advertised as an information management system with the data residing in a database. eZ Publish is created and maintained by eZ Systems at `http://developer.ez.no`.

Zope Developed by the Zope community, Zope enables teams to collaborate in the creation and management of dynamic web-based business applications. Zope is offered by the Zope community at `www.zope.org`.

Cofax Created by the Content Object Factory, Cofax is advertised as a web-based text and multimedia publication system. Cofax is available from the Content Object Factory at `www.cofax.org`.

Midgard From the Midgard Project, Midgard is defined as a toolkit for building dynamic applications for powering e-business and information management processes. Midgard is available at `www.midgard-project.org`.

MMBase MMBase offers a flexible solution for creating and maintaining big websites easily. MMBase can be found at `www.mmbase.org`.

OpenCms From the OpenCms Project, OpenCms is advertised as a Java-based web CMS and emphasizes the ease of creating and publishing web content. OpenCms can be found at `www.opencms.org`.

Why Choose Open-Source Projects?

As stated earlier, we emphasize the open-source frameworks that are helping shape the field of content management. Open-source systems are popular with most enterprises because of the lower costs of ownership. These systems are based on standardized technologies and are vendor independent. Most of the systems have a process for soliciting needs and requirements using a community process. The features invariably are based on needs that solve real problems and not on what a vendor decides is good for you. The developers of the frameworks are professionals in the field who have solved the content management challenges in their work environment. They bring a wealth of knowledge and experience from their careers to the development of these systems.

The Original Cocoon Project

The Cocoon Project started as an attempt to organize and control the documentation of all the projects being run under the Apache umbrella project. The first iteration was simple and was based on proposed technologies that had not yet been standardized. As the technologies evolved, the framework evolved along with it to utilize the new standards and include more developer requirements. The project recently released the second generation of the product, Cocoon 2, which offers more flexibility and features. We start with the first release, Cocoon 1, and examine the design goals, successes, and drawbacks.

Cocoon 1—a Simple Solution

By design, Cocoon 1 (C1) was based on the open technologies adopted by the Apache Software Foundation and utilized existing frameworks. C1 was a publishing framework that was written completely in Java. It was based on technologies standardized by the Worldwide Web Consortium (W3C), such as Document Object Model (DOM) parsing, XML for formatting data, XSLT for transforming data and merging XML documents, and Extensible Stylesheet Language (XSL) for presentation.

Cocoon was originally a very simple Java Servlet with approximately 100 lines of code and the format for the documents was XML. It used the IBM XML4J parser for parsing of XML documents and the LotusXSL parser for transforming the XML file using an XSL stylesheet. The next chapter goes into the details of the technologies that are the building blocks of the application, but we mention each of them in this section. The framework was defined with the adopted standard at that time. When the need arose for a server engine that would utilize XSL for transforming XML documents, the project was formally adopted by a vote on the jserv-dev mailing list and named the Cocoon Project under the Apache umbrella.

The Cocoon 1 Architecture: Strengths and Drawbacks

The Apache Avalon Project is part of the Jakarta Project and was an effort to allow developers of open-source projects to collaborate and share code easily. It created a common extensible framework and a set of pure Java components that could be extended to create new applications. C1 was based on the Apache Avalon framework and continued to have a simple structure with very little code. It was primarily used to demonstrate the importance of XSL and XML in web-based publishing. The Apache Xerces parser replaced the XML4J parser and the Apache Xalan parser replaced the LotusXSL parser. As the number of developers grew and additional requirements were added to the design goals, the simple servlet evolved into a complete XML-based publishing system. The framework was adopted widely and was used in production websites all over the world. The strengths of the framework were its simplicity and the fact that it was based on existing, popular frameworks.

However, the framework was based on XML technologies that were still in their infancy. The available parsers were based on the DOM and had several critical architectural issues. Performance was an issue because of the use of the DOM parser, which parses the XML document and creates a tree in memory. This also created greater demands on the server resources when multiple documents had to be served up to several concurrent users.

These drawbacks were not unique to the Cocoon Project and were based on the limitations of the technologies available at that time. Developers of other XML-based applications were experiencing similar problems. The W3C is the body that introduces, regulates, and adopts standards for the Web. To address the problems associated with XML, several new standards were proposed and adopted.

One of new standards addressed how XML documents would be parsed using inline Simple API for XML (SAX) events, which would eliminate the need for creating the object model in memory on the application server. Another change involved splitting up the XSL standard to address three different areas: XSL Transformations (XSLT), Formatting Objects (XSL:FO), and XPath for defining subparts of an XML document. Armed with these new standards, the Cocoon developers embarked on a two-year project to redesign the framework that solves the architectural problems of Cocoon 1 while adding new and interesting features that expanded the system's capabilities.

Architecture of the Cocoon 2 Framework

This section describes the Cocoon 2 framework and analyzes each of the features that the improved system has to offer. We place emphasis on the features and strengths that make it a good CMS for developing versatile web applications.

An XML-Publishing Framework

Cocoon 2 (C2) is a powerful XML-publishing framework based on XML and XSLT. As previously stated, the C1 architecture was based on DOM processing of XML documents. The C2 architecture is based on pipeline processing of SAX events, which results in better scalability and improved performance of web applications deployed in the framework. (More details on pipelined processing will be in the next section, and details of SAX and XSLT are covered in Chapter 3.)

A centralized configuration system makes the tasks of creation, deployment, and maintenance of applications a lot easier for the developer team. C2 has a powerful caching system that is based on a flexible design in which the components can be dynamically configured. This prevents the components and rules from being hard-coded in the C2 system itself. When a user request is received, the caching system checks to see if the requested Universal Resource Indicator (URI) is available in the cache and delivers the cached content instead of sending the request through a pipeline for processing. This feature also results in better performance when serving static content.

Flexible Content Aggregation

The C2 framework continues to be available as a Servlet but is designed to be an abstract engine not tied to a particular platform or application server. This Servlet can connect to any existing Servlet engine or most web application servers. C2 allows the developer to create custom protocol handlers, which enables the application to connect to external sources that can be accessed and retrieved with a standard URI. Cocoon can also call itself recursively using the `cocoon://<some URI>` protocol. The C2 Servlet does not need to be invoked by name to be used but can be mapped to a name that will be referenced directly in the URI being invoked on the server. Thus, if `some-page.xml` were the resource being requested from `yourserver`, the URI would be as follows:

```
http://yourserver/cocoon/some-page.xml
```

In addition to the Servlet interface, C2 offers a command-line interface for running a batch process to create static content, which can then be cached, in the caching mechanism previously described. Pregeneration of parts of a website that will be static for the life of the application results in marked improvement in the overall performance of the application. Static generation of content can be used to handle content like Scalable Vector Graphics

(SVG) rasterization or for applying stylesheets to XML documents. The features and functions of the C2 system make it very easy to manage static content. With C2, developers can easily aggregate content from many sources.

Pipelines and Components

The C2 architecture is based on component pipelines. The concept of pipelines is similar to that used in the Unix operating systems. The difference is that in Unix, the elements in the pipelines were all bytes; in C2, the elements in the pipeline are all SAX events created by parsing XML documents. There are three types of pipeline elements, or *components*:

- Generators
- Transformers
- Serializers

Generators take a requested URI and produce SAX events. Transformers consume SAX events and produce other SAX events. Serializers consume SAX events and produce a response. Generally in C2, a pipeline is made up of one generator, zero or more transformers, and one serializer. At the very minimum, a Cocoon pipeline consists of a generator and a serializer Figure 1.2 shows a typical Cocoon pipeline with a generator followed by a transformer and a serializer for different types of output responses. It shows the SAX events that are produced and consumed by each component in the pipeline.

The generators, transformers, and serializers have been developed and donated to the C2 Project. These components are classes developed in Java, and all the basic ones come with the C2 distribution. The components can be extended to create new components, which inherit the basic behavior from the base component and add features of their own.

FIGURE 1.2:
A Cocoon pipeline

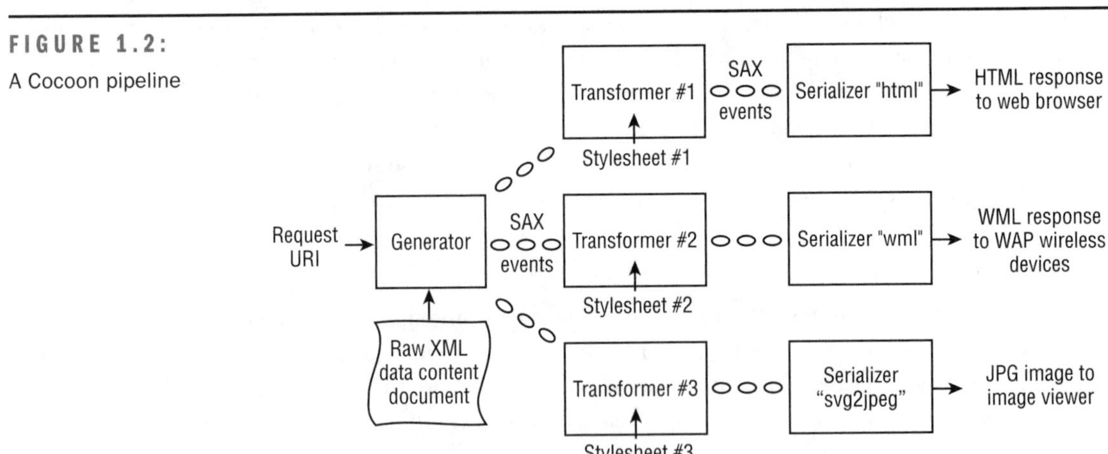

The following are the names of generators in C2. The names listed are the actual class names of the components in the framework.

`FileGenerator` is a parser, which reads a file or Uniform Resource Locator (URL) and produces SAX events.

`DirectoryGenerator` takes a directory listing as input and converts it to an XML format from which it produces SAX events.

`ServerPagesGenerator` generates XML and SAX events from XSP pages.

`JSPGenerator` takes a JSP page as input and generates the XML and SAX events.

`VelocityGenerator` takes the Velocity language templates as input and converts them to XML and generates SAX events.

The following are the names of the transformers in C2. The names listed are the actual names of the components in the framework.

`XSLTTransformer` takes a stream of SAX events as the input and transforms the events based on a given XSLT stylesheet.

`XIncludeTransformer` processes the `xinclude` namespace and includes external sources by adding their SAX events into the existing SAX stream.

`i18nTransformer` transforms SAX events in the pipeline using the i18n dictionary and a language parameter provided to it.

The following are the names of the serializers in C2. The names listed are the actual names of the components in the framework.

`XMLSerializer` takes the SAX events as input and generates an XML response as the output.

`HTMLSerializer` convert SAX streams in the pipeline into standard HTML output for web browsers.

`TextSerializer` produces text responses from text-based SAX events. This is useful for when the output does not have to be formatted and is mostly composed of non-XML text as in Cascading Style Sheets (CSS), Virtual Reality Modeling Language (VRML), and code text.

`PDFSerializer` creates an Adobe Portable Data Format (PDF) response stream using the Apache FOP (Formatting Output Processor). The Apache FOP uses the XSL:FO SAX events in the input stream.

`SVG2JPGSerializer` takes SVG SAX events in the input stream and, using Apache Batik, creates an output stream in JPEG format.

Introducing the Cocoon Sitemap

The Cocoon sitemap is the configuration document that defines the pipelines and components available for use by web applications. The sitemap lets the C2 system match the incoming URI to a particular pipeline that processes the request and creates the desired output responses. The pipelines in turn define the components that produce the static or dynamic output.

The sitemap is an XML file and complies with all XML syntax and notations. An example sitemap is shown in Listing 1.1. We have chosen a simple example to launch the discussion of sitemaps and lay the foundation for an understanding of detailed sitemaps. An actual sitemap for most web applications will have additional code sections, which are discussed in subsequent chapters of this book. For now we provide only the most important sections to help you understand the concepts. We then dissect the sitemap and explain each section in detail.

Listing 1.1 A Sample Sitemap

```
<?xml version="1.0"?>
<map:sitemap xmlns:map="http://apache.org/cocoon/sitemap/1.0">
  <map:components>
    <map:generators default="file"/>
    <map:transformers default="xslt"/>
    <map:serializers default="html"/>
  </map:components>
  <map:pipelines>
    <map:pipeline>
      <map:match pattern="hello.html">
        <map:generate src="hello-page.xml"/>
        <map:transform src="hello-htmlstylesheet.xsl"/>
        <map:serialize type="html"/>
      </map:match>
      <map:match pattern="hello.wml">
        <map:generate src="hello-page.xml"/>
        <map:transform src="hello-wmlstylesheet.xsl"/>
        <map:serialize type="wap"/>
      </map:match>
    </map:pipeline>
  </map:pipelines>
</map:sitemap>
```

All the elements in the sitemap must belong to the same XML namespace. The code fragment shown below defines the namespace `http://apache.org/cocoon/sitemap/1.0` for the sitemap and assigns it to the prefix `map`:

```
<map:sitemap xmlns:map="http://apache.org/cocoon/sitemap/1.0">
```

The sitemap defines the components and pipelines available to the application as child elements of the `sitemap` element. The following code fragment from Listing 1.1 highlights the `components` element and defines the components that are available for use in the Cocoon system.

```
<map:components>
  <map:generators default="file"/>
  <map:transformers default="xslt"/>
  <map:serializers default="html"/>
</map:components>
```

The code defines the default components that are available within Cocoon. The element `generators` has an attribute named `default` and denotes the default generator for the server. The value of the default attribute is `"file"` and designates the component `FileGenerator` as the default generator for the system. The next element is `transformers` and the `default="xslt"` attribute sets the default transformer to be the component `XSLTTransformer`. Finally, the `default="html"` attribute of the element `serializers` sets the `HTMLSerializer` as the default serializer.

A sitemap can define more than one pipeline for processing as shown in the following:

```
<map:pipelines>
  <map:pipeline>
    <!--pipeline #1 code goes here -->
  </map:pipeline>
  <map:pipeline>
    <!--pipeline #2 code goes here -->
  </map:pipeline>
      ...
  <!-- additional pipeline elements defined -->
      ...
</map:pipelines>
```

For simplicity, Listing 1.1 shows the `pipelines` element as having only one pipeline child element.

Matching the URI to a Pipeline

Within the pipeline there are one or more match blocks, which define the actual processing path for a given request. The following code fragment shows the pipeline with the match elements in our code listing.

```
<map:pipeline>
  <map:match pattern="hello.html">
    <!-- match elements for processing the request -->
```

```
    </map:match>
    <map:match pattern="hello.wml">
      <!-- match elements for processing the request -->
    </map:match>
      ...
    <!-- other match blocks -->
      ...
  </map:pipeline>
```

Once again, for simplicity, the `pipeline` element is shown to contain only two match elements. The pattern attribute of the `match` element is a string name of the resource being requested by the client in the URI. C2 matches the incoming request URI to the specific match element in the sitemap. The first match pattern for the pipeline is shown in the following code fragment.

```
<map:match pattern="hello.html">
  <!-- match elements for processing the request -->
</map:match>
```

When the server receives a request from the client for the URI, `http://yoursever/coccon/hello.html`, Cocoon matches the requested resource in the URI (`hello.html`) with the pattern attribute of the `match` element and invokes this path in the pipeline.

If the server received a request of the type `http://yourserver/cocoon/hello.wml`, Cocoon will match the requested resource (`hello.wml`) to the pattern attribute of the `match` element and invoke the appropriate path as highlighted below.

```
<map:match pattern="hello.wml">
  <!-- match elements for processing the request -->
</map:match>
```

We have kept the example sitemap very simple and have shown only two paths for processing within the pipeline. In reality, an XML document might need to be consumed by many more types of applications. In that case, the `pipeline` element will have several more match blocks, one for each type of output response that will be generated. Within each match block there will be a generator, transformer, and serializer for processing the request and generating the response.

Processing the Requested URI

Once the incoming URI is matched to a pipeline, C2 begins processing the request by processing each element within the pipeline. The elements within the match block specify the generator, transformer, and serializer that make up a processing path within the pipeline and create the specific response to the input URI. The actual components used for each step of the processing were specified in the components element of the sitemap as discussed earlier. The following code fragment shows the match block for the resource matching the pattern `hello.html`.

```
<map:match pattern="hello.html">
  <map:generate src="hello-page.xml"/>
  <map:transform src="hello-htmlstylesheet.xsl"/>
  <map:serialize type="html"/>
</map:match>
```

The code fragment that follows shows the match block for the second match element in the pipeline, which services requests for the resource `hello.wml`.

```
<map:match pattern="hello.wml">
  <map:generate src="hello-page.xml"/>
  <map:transform src="hello-wmlstylesheet.xsl"/>
  <map:serialize type="wap"/>
</map:match>
```

The `generate` element has an attribute `src`, which specifies the source file that is the input of the generator component. It should be noted that for the given pipeline, the `generate` element is the same for both match elements, and the same XML document is the input for both paths in the pipeline. This is highlighted in the following code fragment.

```
<map:generate src="hello-page.xml"/>
```

This XML document contains all the raw data for a particular section of the web application. For large web applications, the raw content will be appropriately segmented into different XML documents, each pertaining to some subpart of the whole application. For the purposes of this discussion the input file `"hello-page.xml"` represents a particular piece of a web application.

Each match element uses the same transformer component to customize the presentation for the target client application. In each case, the transformer uses a different XSLT stylesheet specified in the attribute `src` to transform the SAX events. In our example sitemap, the first match element is using a stylesheet that formats the output for presentation in an HTML browser as shown in the following code fragment.

```
<map:transform src="hello-htmlstylesheet.xsl"/>
```

In the second pipeline, the transformer is using a stylesheet for creation of content for handheld wireless devices and is shown in the code fragment that follows.

```
<map:transform src="hello-wmlstylesheet.xsl"/>
```

The final stage of the pipeline is the serializer, which takes the SAX events from the transformer and creates the output response that will be streamed to the target client application. The serializer has an attribute named `type` that specifies the format of the output response created by the pipeline. In the case of the first pipeline, the attribute `type="html"` specifies that the output response will be an HTML document for display in a web browser and is shown in the following code fragment.

```
<map:serialize type="html">
```

The serializer in the second pipeline has an attribute `type="wap"` and creates the response for wireless devices as shown in the following code fragment.

```
<map:serialize type="wap"/>
```

This concludes the description of the sitemap and the basic features of Cocoon. In a real application, the sitemap contains many pipelines and each pipeline has multiple match blocks to handle the generation of responses in many different formats. We introduce advanced features and elements of the sitemap in the rest of the book as we develop applications for the framework. As stated earlier, C2 is a powerful framework for content aggregation, which is enabled and supported by the features of the C2 sitemap. The developer can assign different namespaces to the different content sources and aggregate the output content into one document.

Integrating Business Services

Cocoon supports XSP as the language for business logic. Cocoon has a built-in XSP processor that evaluates and compiles XSP code embedded in XML files. The syntax of XSP is very similar to XML, but it allows the developer to embed Java code within the pages. This concept is very similar to JSP, which had special tags to mix Java code with HTML. XSPs can be used to separate out business logic from an XML document or they can be used to aggregate content from other applications and services. Cocoon also supports the extended Structured Query Language (SQL) XML tags for use in XSP pages. This enables the Cocoon application to have direct access to data in a relational database, and the final output of the database query is formatted in XML. We develop sample applications in subsequent chapters to demonstrate the use of XSP for integration of SQL data and integration with other Java applications.

Separation of Presentation, Content, and Logic

The C2 architecture supports strong separation of presentation, content, and business logic. This allows web development teams to be demarcated along functional tasks and responsibilities. Content developers create raw XML files without concern for how the content will be used. These XML files can also be created dynamically by external applications or XSLT transformations of documents. Another team of developers can create XSP logic sheets that integrate business logic into the application. Cocoon can aggregate the data from a combination of raw XML files or the output of these logic sheets. Finally, a team focused on the presentation aspects of the application can create the stylesheets used for transformation of the data into the final output. Individual teams can then have separate processes for managing the creation of their deliverables.

The next chapter provides additional details of the sitemap and provides examples of how to use the sitemap, components, and pipelines. We also lay the foundations for building powerful web applications using all the features of Cocoon.

Summary

This chapter took a brief look at the history of the Web and how web applications have evolved from simple static HTML pages to very complex applications that integrate with enterprise systems. As the Web revolution spread, enterprise web applications that had a mix of dynamic data, content, and presentation became popular. We followed the evolution of technologies that enabled creation of very complex and sophisticated frameworks and the evolution of content publishing from simple static HTML pages to highly integrated web applications based on XML that can have a flexible look and feel.

To manage the design, implementation, and maintenance processes and resources, it became imperative that there be some level of separation between presentation, content, and logic elements of the applications. This enabled the demarcation of teams based on skills, roles, and responsibilities.

There are a plethora of systems available, each supporting a set of technologies and a methodology for the creation and management of web applications. These range from simple and inexpensive web servers that serve up HTML documents to very complex and expensive enterprise web application servers. We looked at some of the requirements and design goals of publishing frameworks as well as those of content management systems and highlighted examples of the open-source CMSs available.

The Cocoon 1 framework started out as a simple document-management system but evolved into an advanced web-publishing framework, albeit with some drawbacks. The Apache Project redesigned and released the enhanced version, Cocoon 2, which solved many of the performance and configuration problems of the original framework.

Cocoon 2 is a powerful XML-publishing framework based on XML and XSLT. The following are the salient features of the Cocoon 2 framework:

- A centralized configuration system
- A powerful caching system
- Support for flexible content aggregation
- Support for separation of presentation, content, and logic

The sitemap is the central configuration mechanism that utilizes pipeline processing of XML documents. It uses prefabricated components such as matchers, generators, transformers, and serializers to process SAX events dynamically. It is an extensible framework and supports creation of custom components that extend the basic functionality of the system.

The next chapter expands on the concepts covered in this chapter by designing web applications that demonstrate the features of the Cocoon 2 framework.

Chapter 2

Uses of Cocoon

- Setting Up Cocoon for Application Development
- Two Simple Applications
- Interfacing with a Database
- Site Serving Mobile Devices
- A Menu-Driven Site
- Rendering Scalable Vector Graphics

In this chapter we create several examples that demonstrate the different features of Cocoon 2. We start with providing the steps for setting up the Cocoon environment for creating applications and then test it with a simple Hello Cocoon example.

Cocoon offers two ways to access dynamic data from a relational database. One example shows how to use the SQLTransformer and another demonstrates the use of XSP and ESQL.

The power of the Cocoon 2 pipeline can be leveraged to serve content to many different types of devices. In our example, the Cocoon 2 pipeline serves up pages that will be accessed using a WAP emulator.

The Cocoon 2 pipeline can also be used to create a menu-driven website. Using the `matchers` and `tokens`, we will create an example to demonstrate menu navigation.

Scalable Vector Graphics (SVG) is an industry standard that enables creation of XML files that represent two-dimensional graphical objects. The Cocoon 2 pipeline in our examples demonstrate how to render the graphics in a web browser.

The sitemap is the most important part of designing and deploying applications for Cocoon 2.0, and we expand on significant parts of the sitemap as we present the applications.

Setting Up Cocoon for Application Development

To manage the development and deployment process in Cocoon 2, it is very important to have the proper file organization structure for the application. We provide some best practices for organizing and managing the directory structure for typical Cocoon 2 applications in this chapter. However, we encourage you to adapt your best practices to meet your own needs in the Cocoon 2 environment.

A robust Cocoon application benefits from using subsitemaps to develop the application. The subsitemap is just a `sitemap.xmap` file; there is no construct or file named "subsitemap." This chapter defines all applications in subdirectories of the Cocoon directory. The subsitemap file resides in the subdirectory holding the rest of the application files. We will use the Hello Cocoon example to describe a recommended format for the directory structure for the applications.

For Cocoon to read and compile both the main sitemap and the subsitemaps correctly, one change needs to be made to the sitemap element of the `cocoon.xconf` file in the main Cocoon application directory. The two significant attributes of the sitemap element that determine the reloading of the sitemap are as follows:

```
check-reload
```

```
reload-method
```

The `check-reload` attribute is used by Cocoon to determine if the sitemap is reloaded when changes are made to it during runtime. The following are the two values of `check-reload` and the resulting action taken by Cocoon:

`check-reload="no"` The sitemap is generated only once when Cocoon is launched at startup.

`check-reload="yes"` The sitemap is regenerated if changes are made during runtime.

The `reload-method` attribute tells Cocoon how the sitemap will be regenerated when changes are made to it during runtime. The following are the two values for `reload-method` and the resulting action taken by Cocoon:

`reload-method="asynchron"` When the sitemap changes, the next request causes the sitemap to be regenerated in the background. The current request and any other request that comes before the regeneration is complete are served with the old sitemap.

`reload-method="synchron"` When the sitemap changes, the next request causes the sitemap to be regenerated and the request will not be serviced immediately. After the regeneration is complete, the request that launched the regeneration and all subsequent requests will be serviced with the new sitemap.

The Cocoon documentation recommends the following settings for a development environment: `reload-method="synchron"` and the `check-reload="yes"`. Listing 2.1 shows the sitemap element of the `cocoon.xconf` file for a development environment.

Listing 2.1 The sitemap element definition in *cocoon.xconf* for a development environment

```
<sitemap file="sitemap.xmap" reload-method="synchron" check-reload="yes"
logger="sitemap"/>
```

The Cocoon documentation recommends the following settings for a production environment: `reload-method="asynchron"` and the `check-reload="no"`. Listing 2.2 shows the sitemap element of the `cocoon.xconf` file for a production environment.

Listing 2.2 The sitemap element definition in *cocoon.xconf* for a production environment

```
<sitemap file="sitemap.xmap" reload-method="asynchron" check-reload="no"
logger="sitemap"/>
```

To use subsitemaps, a few changes must also be made to the main sitemap, which resides in the main Cocoon directory. We cover each change that pertains to a particular example in this chapter. We will now continue with setting up the directories and file hierarchies within the Tomcat installation.

For simplicity, all the applications have been placed within the webapps hierarchy of the tomcat directory. Below the cocoon directory is a directory named c2, which is used to organize all the applications used in this chapter. Figure 2.1 shows the directory structure for organizing the Hello Cocoon example, which is a very small Cocoon 2 application.

FIGURE 2.1: Directory structure for organizing the Hello Cocoon example

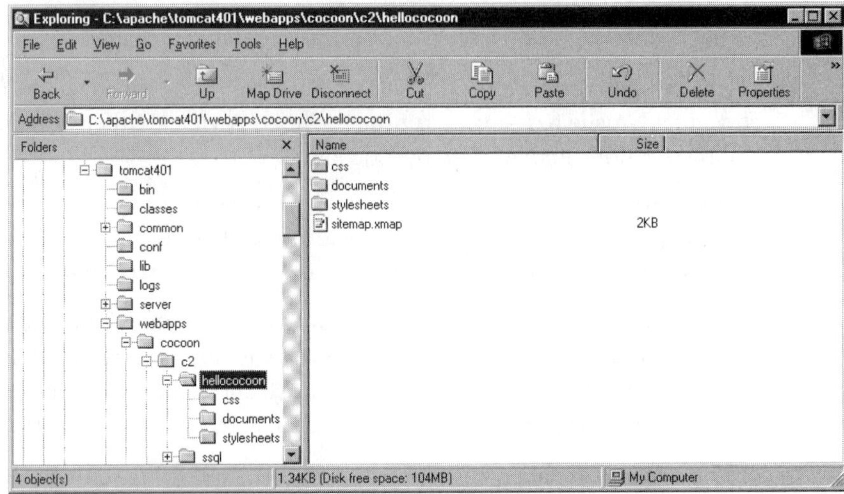

Figure 2.1 also shows three subdirectories under the hellococoon directory: css, documents, and stylesheets. The css subdirectory holds any cascading stylesheets that will format the HTML that is sent to the browser. The documents subdirectory will hold all the XML content files. The stylesheet subdirectory holds all the XSL stylesheets to be used by the Transformers in the Cocoon 2 pipeline. One more item that can be seen in the hellococoon directory is a sitemap.xmap file, which is the subsitemap for this particular application. The main sitemap.xmap file is always present in the cocoon directory.

The css directory holds two cascading stylesheets, default.css and menu.css, which could be used to style the final presentation in the browser. For this example, they are not used in the pipeline and are used as placeholders. Figure 2.2 shows the contents of the css subdirectory.

The documents subdirectory holds two XML content files: hellococoon.xml and hello-page.xml. Figure 2.3 shows the contents of the documents subdirectory.

The stylesheets subdirectory holds three XSL stylesheets: simple-page2html.xsl, simple-sql2html.xsl, and tx_xml2html.xsl. Figure 2.4 shows the contents of the stylesheets subdirectory.

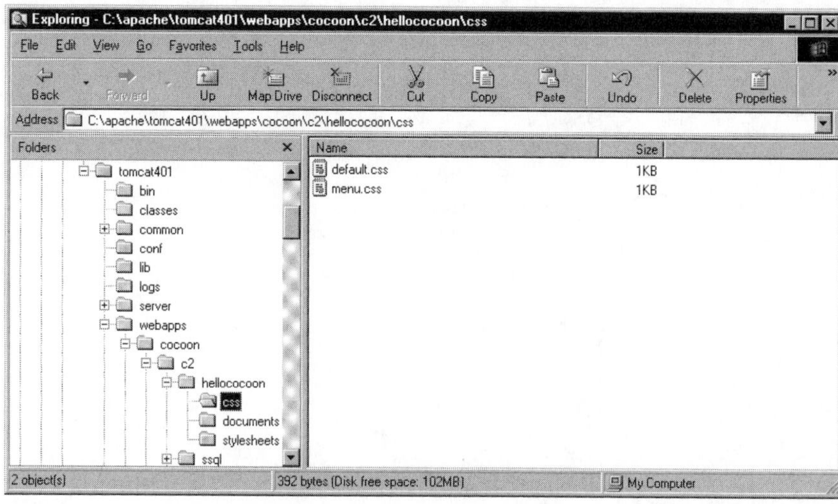

FIGURE 2.2: The contents of the `css` subdirectory

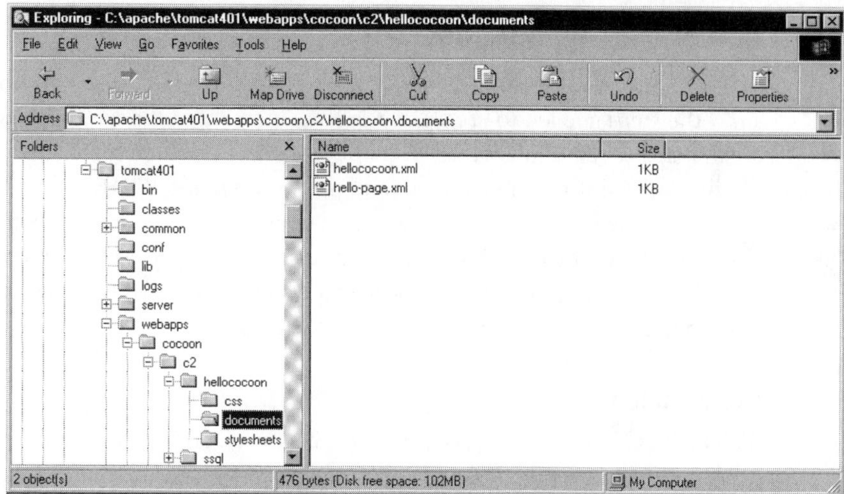

FIGURE 2.3: The contents of the `documents` subdirectory

When analyzing and designing a Cocoon 2 application, we separate content from logic and presentation. The directory structure scheme shown provides a convenient way of organizing the elements of an application in these three broad categories.

This is the minimum set of requirements needed to start designing and implementing Cocoon 2 applications. We will now describe each of the examples and the elements that make it up.

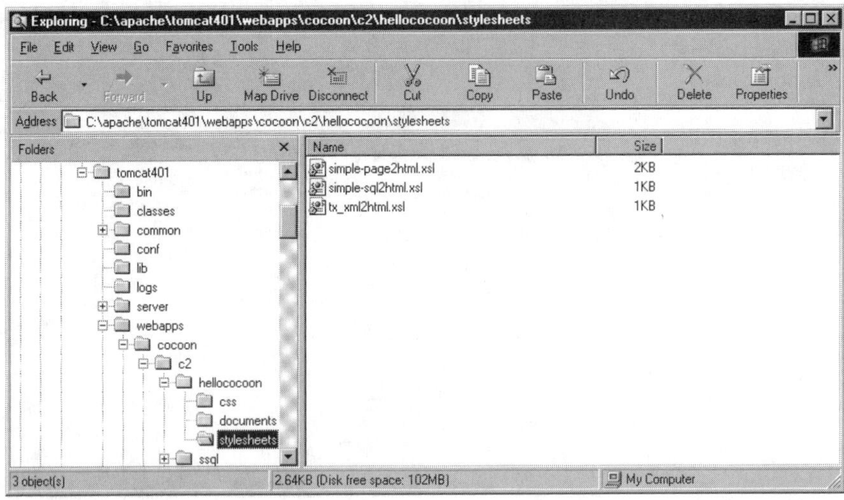

FIGURE 2.4: The contents of the stylesheets subdirectory

Two Simple Applications

We will start by creating two simple applications, Hello Cocoon and Business Card, which show the steps needed to create and use subsitemaps. This section expands on the discussion of sitemaps covered in Chapter 1, "The Cocoon 2 Architecture." Both examples show how to modify the main sitemap to work with the subsitemaps. These examples also demonstrate how to use the `generate`, `transform`, and `serialize` components to create a working application. The content source files and the transformation stylesheets have been kept simple to help the reader step through the working examples while following along as the chapter describes the structure of a Cocoon 2 application.

Hello Cocoon

The Hello Cocoon example is the easiest Cocoon 2 application for demonstrating how the sitemaps and the Cocoon pipeline work. We begin by describing the parts of the main sitemap that will service the incoming request. In this example (see Listing 2.3), the application responds to a simple URI request of the type `http://<serveraddress>:port_number/cocoon/hellococoon`.

Listing 2.3 The *<map:pipeline>* element in the main sitemap

```
<map:pipeline>
  <map:match pattern="hellococoon">
```

```
      <map:mount uri-prefix="hellococoon"
                 check-reload="yes"
                 reload-method="synchron"
                 src="c2/hellococoon/"/>
    </map:match>
  </map:pipeline>
```

We have shown only one match pattern in the main sitemap—"hellococoon". Within the match block, the <map:mount> element is used to mount the subsitemap. The following are the required attributes and their functions in the mount element:

uri-prefix="hellococoon" defines the pattern that will be removed from the URI after the cocoon root. The resulting URI is passed on to the subsitemap.

src="c2/hellococoon/" defines the subdirectory below the cocoon directory where the subsitemap is located.

Figure 2.1 shows the directory structure for this example, including the location of the subsitemap.

The other two attributes define the parameters for regeneration of the subsitemap when changes are made to it. They have the same names and values as the attributes of the sitemap element in the cocoon.xconf file discussed under the check-reload="yes" and reload-method="synchron" headings.

We will now define the subsitemap and the resources that it uses during runtime when the application is invoked. We focus only on the pipelines section of the subsitemap, because that is what is most relevant to this discussion. We have presented detailed analyses of the rest of the sitemap elements in other chapters of this book. Listing 2.4 shows the pipelines definition of the subsitemap.

Listing 2.4 The *<map:pipelines>* element of the subsitemap

```
<map:pipelines>

  <map:pipeline>
    <map:match pattern="">
      <map:generate src="documents/hello-page.xml"/>
      <map:transform src="stylesheets/tx_xml2html.xsl"/>
      <map:serialize type="html"/>
    </map:match>
  </map:pipeline>

</map:pipelines>
```

The subsitemap in Listing 2.4 shows that the `<map:pipelines>` element is made up of only one Cocoon 2 pipeline in our simple example. The pipeline has only one `match` block, which matches the request being sent down from the main sitemap. This match element in the sitemap defines that the pipeline will service only the resulting URI that was sent down from the main sitemap. In our example of the main sitemap, the resulting URI is `""`.

The input of the `generator` component is the source XML file `hello-page.xml` located in the `c2/hellococoon/documents` subdirectory. Listing 2.5 shows the contents of the simple content file.

Listing 2.5 The content XML file, *hello-page.xml*

```
<?xml version="1.0"?>
<page>
 <title>Hello Cocoon 2.0</title>
 <content>
  <para>
   Congratulations, new user!!  This is your first Cocoon application!
  </para>
  <para/>
  <para>Welcome to the fascinating world of Cocoon</para>
 </content>
</page>
```

The next stage of the pipeline is the transformer component with an `src` attribute that specifies the XSLT stylesheet that will be used to transform the output SAX events from the generator stage of the pipeline. Listing 2.6 shows the XSLT stylesheet `tx_xml2html.xsl` file, which is located in the `c2/hellococoon/stylesheets` subdirectory.

Listing 2.6 The XSLT stylesheet file, *tx_xml2html.xsl*

```
<?xml version="1.0"?>
<xsl:stylesheet version="1.0" xmlns:xsl="http://www.w3.org/1999/XSL/Transform">

  <xsl:template match="page">
   <html>
    <head>
     <title>
      <xsl:value-of select="title"/>
     </title>
    </head>
    <body bgcolor="white">
     <xsl:apply-templates/>
    </body>
   </html>
  </xsl:template>
```

```
    <xsl:template match="title">
     <h1 style="color:black; text-align: center">
          <xsl:apply-templates/>
     </h1>
    </xsl:template>

    <xsl:template match="para">
     <p align="center">
      <i><xsl:apply-templates/></i>
     </p>
    </xsl:template>
  </xsl:stylesheet>
```

The final stage of the pipeline is the `serializer` component, which will produce the HTML output for a web browser. Figure 2.5 shows the output of the Hello Cocoon example in a web browser.

FIGURE 2.5: The output of the Hello Cocoon example

In this example, we provided a detailed explanation of each major section of the application to provide some guidelines for the development of a Cocoon 2 application. Subsequent examples will highlight only the relevant sections of the sitemap and subsitemap and display the final output in the browser of the target device.

Business Card

In this example we have created an XML content file that models an online business card or contact information card. This example will demonstrate matching two different URI strings using two distinct pipelines in the sitemaps. Listing 2.7 shows the `<map:pipeline>` element of the main sitemap in the `cocoon` directory.

Listing 2.7 The <*map:pipeline*> element for the vcard example

```
<map:pipeline>
  <map:match pattern="vcard">
    <map:mount uri-prefix="vcard"
               check-reload="yes"
               reload-method="synchron"
               src="c2/vcard/"/>
  </map:match>

  <map:match pattern="vcard/**">
    <map:mount uri-prefix="vcard" check-reload="yes"
      reload-method="synchron" src="c2/vcard/"/>
  </map:match>
</map:pipeline>
```

The first `match` element makes an exact match for the pattern "vcard" while the second `match` element will match a pattern "vcard/**". Cocoon will then remove the `uri-prefix` and pass on the remaining URI to the pipeline that will be serviced by the subsitemap.

Listing 2.8 shows the `<map:pipeline>` element of the subsitemap for the business card example.

Listing 2.8 The <*map:pipeline*> element of the subsitemap for the business card example

```
<map:pipeline>
  <map:match pattern="">
    <map:generate src="documents/vcard.xml"/>
    <map:transform src="stylesheets/vcard_two.xsl"/>
    <map:serialize type="html"/>
  </map:match>

  <map:match pattern="**">
    <map:generate src="documents/vcard.xml"/>
    <map:transform src="stylesheets/vcard_one.xsl"/>
    <map:serialize type="html"/>
  </map:match>
</map:pipeline>
```

The subsitemap will service each of the pipelines as defined in the main sitemap. Note that the two pipelines differ only in the XSLT stylesheet that is used by the `transformer` component in each pipeline.

Listing 2.9 shows the content XML file `vcard.xml`.

Listing 2.9 **The content file, *vcard.xml***

```
<?xml version="1.0"?>
<vcard>
  <name>
    John Doe
  </name>
  <company>
    Acme Supplies, Inc.
  </company>
  <address>
    101 Acme Blvd.
  </address>
  <city>Smallsville</city>
  <state>Ohio </state>
  <zip>43532</zip>
</vcard>
```

Figure 2.6 shows the output of the URI request, `http://<serveraddress:port_number>/cocoon/vcard`, which is serviced by the first pipeline.

Figure 2.7 shows the output of the URI request, `http://<serveraddress:port_number>/cocoon/vcard/two`, which is serviced by the second pipeline.

In this example, we saw how two pipelines can be used to service two different URIs. Within the subsitemap each of the pipelines used a different transform stylesheet to produce different output from the same content files.

FIGURE 2.6: The output of the application invoked by the URI `http://192.168.1.3:8080/cocoon/vcard`

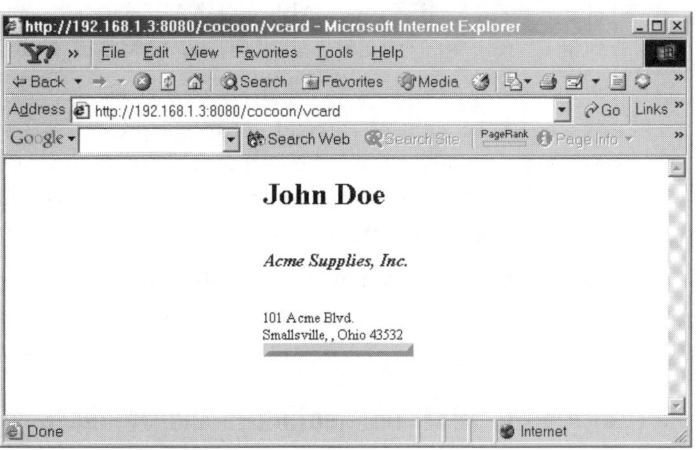

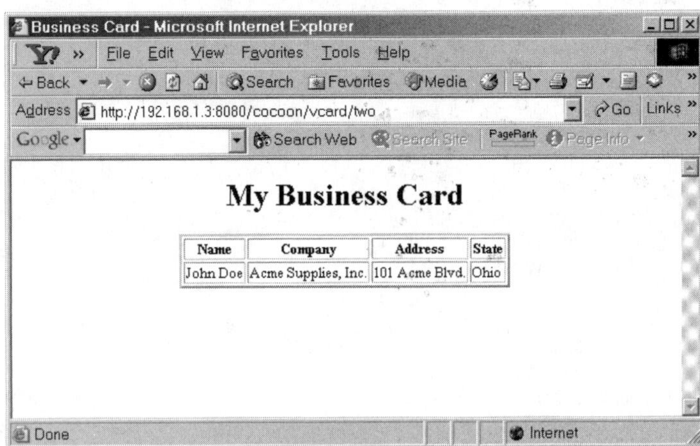

FIGURE 2.7: The output of the application invoked by the URI, `http://192.168.1.3:8080/cocoon/vcard/two`

Interfacing with a Database

Cocoon can access data stored in a variety of schemes, such as local filesystems, network-based data sources, Lightweight Directory Access Protocol (LDAP), native XML databases, and relational database management systems (RDBMS). To demonstrate the features of the Cocoon system, we have chosen to demonstrate data access using an RDBMS system, which is the most cost-effective and widely deployed scheme at the present time. The Apache Xindice project is a native XML database. Native XML databases are useful if the data to be stored is already in XML format. Although XML databases are slowly becoming popular, most of the current applications use relational databases. Details of the Xindice project can be found at `http://xml.apache.org/xindice`.

In this section, we will step through setting up a Cocoon 2 application that reads from a relational database and presents the output table to the browser. We have chosen MySQL, an open-source database, which can be downloaded from `www.mysql.org` along with the JDBC (Java Database Connectivity) driver for the database.

Installation and configuration of the database will not be covered in this section. For more information, consult the documentation at `www.mysql.org` or see *Mastering MySQL 4* (Sybex, 2002).

Setting Up the JDBC Connection to the Database

After you install MySQL, create a simple database with one table named `emp`. For simplicity, the table will have only two columns—`name` and `address`—both of type `varchar (20)`.

In order for Cocoon to access a database server, the JDBC driver needs to be configured in the application as follows:

1. Install the `mysql.jar` file in the `lib` subdirectory under `tomcat`.
2. Create a `jdbc` block in the `cocoon.xconf` file:

```
<jdbc name="mysql_pool">
        <pool-controller min="5" max="10"/>
        <dburl>jdbc:mysql://localhost/mydb</dburl>
        <user>root</user>
        <password></password>
      </jdbc>
```

   In this example, the MySQL database is named `mydb` and is running on a localhost.

3. In the `webapps/cocoon/WEB-INF` directory, add the following code to the `<init-param>` element in the `web.xml` file:

```
<init-param>
  <param-name>load-class</param-name>
  <param-value>

    <!-- For MySQL on localhost -->
    org.gjt.mm.mysql.Driver

    <!-- For JDBC-ODBC Bridge: -->
    sun.jdbc.odbc.JdbcOdbcDriver

  </param-value>
</init-param>
```

The `<init-param>` block will already be present in the `web.xml` file and will contain several `<param-value>` elements for other drivers that Cocoon uses. The JDBC driver will be added to the list of parameters named `load-class`.

Accessing the Databases

There are two ways to access databases from within the Cocoon 2 server:

- Using the SQLTransformer
- Using XSP and ESQL (Extended SQL) logicsheets

We will start by describing an application that uses the SQLTransformer.

Using the SQLTransformer

The `mysql_pool` created in the `cocoon.xconf` file (see step 2 above) is used in the application as shown in the following code, Listing 2.10. It shows the subsitemap for the application.

Listing 2.10 **The subsitemap *<map:pipeline>* element for the *c2sql* application**

```
    <map:pipeline>
     <map:match pattern="">
     <map:generate src="docs/sql-page.xml"/>
     <map:transform type="sql">
<map:parameter name="use-connection"
    value="mysql_pool"/>
      </map:transform>
      <map:transform src="stylesheets/sql2html.xsl"/>
      <map:serialize/>
     </map:match>
   </map:pipeline>
```

Listing 2.11 shows the definition of the SQLTransformer in the `<map:components>` definition of the main sitemap.

Listing 2.11 **The SQLTransformer defined in the main sitemap**

```
<map:transformer name="sql"
   logger="sitemap.transformer.sql"
   src="org.apache.cocoon.transformation.SQLTransformer"/>
```

The first `<map:transform>` element in the subsitemap is the SQLTransformer and it uses a parameter named `use-connection` to establish a connection to the database using `mysql_pool`. The SQLTransformer queries the database and generates XML. The second transformer will transform the output of the SQLTransformer into a format suitable for presentation in the browser.

The input to the generator is an XML file that holds the SQL commands as shown in Listing 2.12.

Listing 2.12 **The SQL commands in *sql-page.xml***

```
<?xml version="1.0"?>
<page xmlns:sql="http://apache.org/cocoon/SQL/2.0">

 <title>Employees in Acme, Inc.</title>
 <content>
  <para>Employees in Acme, Inc.</para>
  <para/>
  <execute-query xmlns="http://apache.org/cocoon/SQL/2.0">
   <query>
        select * from emp
   </query>
  </execute-query>
 </content>
</page>
```

The <page> and the <execute-query> elements both have an attribute that defines the namespace `xmlns="http://apache.org/cocoon/SQL/2.0"`.

The <query> element holds the SQL query that will be executed to perform tasks against the database.

Listing 2.13 shows the configuration of the pipeline in the main sitemap that will call the subsitemap for the c2sql application.

Listing 2.13 The main sitemap *<map:pipeline>* element for the *c2sql* application

```
<map:pipeline>
  <map:match pattern="c2sql">
    <map:mount uri-prefix="c2sql"
               check-reload="yes"
               reload-method="synchron"
               src="c2/ssql/"/>
  </map:match>
</map:pipeline>
```

Figure 2.8 shows the browser output when the SQL application is invoked with the URI `http://192.168.1.3:8080/cocoon/c2sql`.

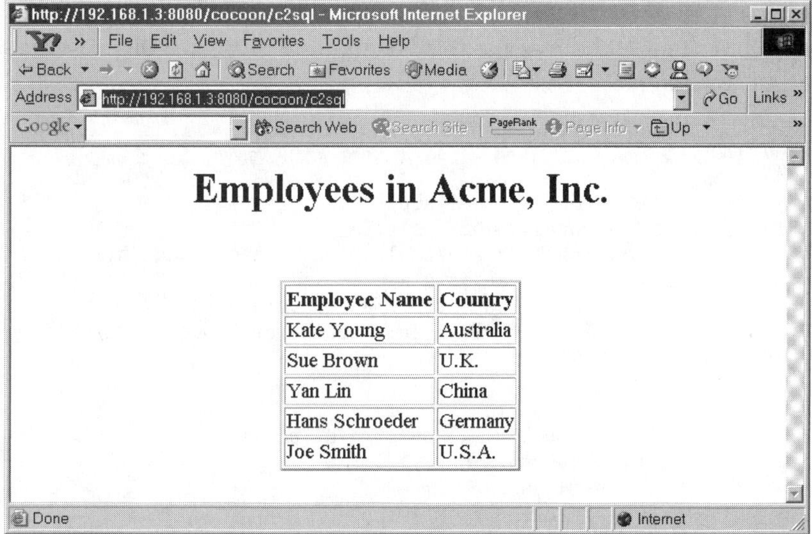

FIGURE 2.8: The output of the SQLTransformer application

Using XSP and ESQL

Another way to access databases is using XSP and ESQL. We will create an extension application that will use the database table, JDBC pool, and JDBC driver from the previous example and demonstrate how to access the database and present the output in a browser.

The `cocoon.xconf` file should be configured to handle ESQL. This is done by defining the ESQL builtin-logicsheet as shown in Listing 2.14.

Listing 2.14 The *<builtin-logicsheet>* definition in *cocoon.xconf*

```
<builtin-logicsheet>
  <parameter name="prefix" value="esql"/>
  <parameter name="uri"
           value="http://apache.org/cocoon/SQL/v2"/>
  <parameter name="href"
value="resource://org/apache/cocoon/components/language/markup/xsp/java/esql.xsl
"/>
</builtin-logicsheet>
```

An ESQL logicsheet is a specialized XSP logicsheet. Logicsheets will be described in detail in Chapter 6, "Introducing XSP Usage," and Chapter 7, "XSP Logicsheets." The ESQL logicsheet defines and performs SQL queries against the database and outputs the results as XML. This output can then be transformed to and formatted for the browser.

Listing 2.15 shows a simple ESQL logicsheet that will access the same database from the last example.

Listing 2.15 The ESQL logicsheet, *acme.xsp*

```
<?cocoon-process type="xsp"?>
<?cocoon-process type="xslt"?>
<?xml-stylesheet href="stylesheets/dynamic-page2html.xsl" type="text/xsl"?>
<xsp:page language="java"
          xmlns:xsp="http://apache.org/xsp"
          xmlns:esql="http://apache.org/cocoon/SQL/v2">
<page>
  <content>
    <esql:connection>
      <esql:pool>mysql_pool</esql:pool>
      <esql:execute-query>
        <esql:query>
          select * from emp
        </esql:query>

        <esql:results>
          <div align="center">
            <h1>List of all Acme, Inc. Employees</h1>
            <br/>
```

```
                <br/>
                <table border="1"
                       cellpadding="2"
                       cellspacing="2" width="500">
                  <tr>
                    <th>Employee Name</th>
                    <th>Location</th>
                  </tr>

                  <esql:row-results>
                    <tr>
                      <td><esql:get-string column="name"/></td>
                      <td><esql:get-string
                              column="address"/></td>
                   </tr>
                  </esql:row-results>
                </table>
              </div>
            </esql:results>

            <esql:no-results>
              <para><em>No records found.</em></para>
            </esql:no-results>

          </esql:execute-query>
        </esql:connection>
      </content>
    </page>
    </xsp:page>
```

The attributes of the <xsp:page> element defines Java as the language for the XSP logic-sheet and establishes two namespaces:

```
xmlns:xsp="http://apache.org/xsp"
```

```
xmlns:esql="http://apache.org/cocoon/SQL/v2"
```

These two attributes let Cocoon associate elements in the ESQL namespace with the ESQL taglib for processing.

In order to use the ESQL logicsheet, the subsitemap should define the <map:generate> element to use the acme.xsp file. Listing 2.16 shows the subsitemap for this application.

Listing 2.16 The subsitemap *<map:pipeline>* element for the *esql* application

```
<map:pipeline>
  <map:match pattern="acme_esql">
    <map:generate type="serverpages" src="docs/acme.xsp"/>
    <map:serialize/>
  </map:match>
</map:pipeline
```

Listing 2.17 shows the main sitemap, which invokes the subsitemap.

Listing 2.17 The main sitemap <*map:pipeline*> element for the *esql* application

```
<map:pipeline>
  <map:match pattern="c2sql/**">
  <map:mount uri-prefix="c2sql"
             check-reload="yes"
             reload-method="synchron"
            src="c2/ssql/"/>
  </map:match>
</map:pipeline>
```

Figure 2.9 shows the browser of the XSP and ESQL application when invoked with the URI `http://192.168.1.3:8080/cocoon/c2sql/acme_esql`.

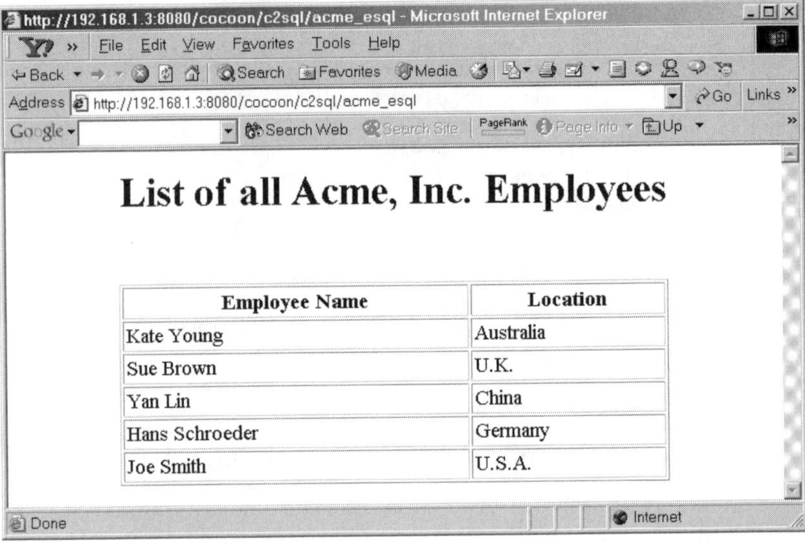

FIGURE 2.9: The output of the XSP ESQL database application

In this example, we saw how Cocoon supports two different techniques for accessing a database using a JDBC connection. Although each technique has its advantages, both can be used effectively to create powerful applications with easy access to dynamic data.

Site Serving Mobile Devices

In this example, we are going to create a simple application that demonstrates how the Cocoon 2 pipeline can be used to serve up content for a device other than a web browser. For this section we downloaded a WAP phone emulator for the Microsoft Windows environment. The simulator we chose was the Wapsody emulator from IBM Alphaworks, which can be downloaded from `http://alphaworks.ibm.com`.

The subsitemap in the `c2/mobile` directory will specify both the XML content file and the stylesheet to format the output for a WAP device. In this case, the WAP device is the mobile phone simulator running on the workstation. Listing 2.18 shows the subsitemap for the mobile application.

Listing 2.18 The *<map:pipeline>* element of the subsitemap for the mobile application

```
<map:pipeline>
   <map:match pattern="">
     <map:generate src="docs/mobile.xml"/>
     <map:transform src="stylesheets/mobilewml.xsl"/>
     <map:serialize type="wml"/>
   </map:match>
</map:pipeline>
```

We highlight the serializer, which is of `type="wml"`. The serializer is defined in the `<map:components>` of the main sitemap and is shown in Listing 2.19.

Listing 2.19 The *wml* serializer defined in *<map:components>*

```
<map:serializer name="wml"
   mime-type="text/vnd.wap.wml"
   logger="sitemap.serializer.wml"
        src="org.apache.cocoon.serialization.XMLSerializer">
<doctype-public>
  -//WAPFORUM//DTD WML 1.1//EN
</doctype-public>
<doctype-system>
  http://www.wapforum.org/DTD/wml_1.1.xml
</doctype-system>
  <encoding>ASCII</encoding>
  <omit-xml-declaration>yes</omit-xml-declaration>
</map:serializer>
```

Listing 2.20 shows the XML content file `mobile.xml`.

Listing 2.20 The *mobile.xml* content file

```
<?xml version="1.0"?>
<page>
 <title>A WML Page</title>
 <content>
```

```
    <para>Congratulations new user!!</para>
    <para>This is your first WML Cocoon page!</para>
  </content>
  <next>
    <para>We hope you are enjoying Cocoon 2.0!!</para>
  </next>
</page>
```

We have defined two distinct pages in the content file to demonstrate the use of the navigation buttons on the mobile device and the simulator. The two sections of the `mobile.xml` file are marked up by the tags `<content/>` and `<next/>`.

Listing 2.21 shows the details of the `mobilewml.xsl` stylesheet used by the transformer to format the output for the WAP device.

Listing 2.21 The *mobilewml.xsl* file

```
<?xml version="1.0"?>

<xsl:stylesheet version="1.0"
   xmlns:xsl="http://www.w3.org/1999/XSL/Transform">

<xsl:template match="page">
  <wml>
    <card id="index" title="{title}">
      <xsl:apply-templates select="content"/>
      <do type="accept" label="Next">
        <go href="#next"/>
      </do>
    </card>

    <card id="next" title="{title}">
      <xsl:apply-templates select="next"/>
        <do type="accept" label="Back">
         <go href="#index"/>
        </do>
    </card>
  </wml>
</xsl:template>

<xsl:template match="para">
  <p align="center">
   <xsl:apply-templates/>
  </p>
</xsl:template>
</xsl:stylesheet>
```

The mobilewml.xsl file, which is the stylesheet used by the transformer, will format each section of the content XML file as shown. There are two cards, one each for the *index* and *next* sections.

Listing 2.22 shows the main sitemap <map:pipeline> element that will launch the mobile site.

Listing 2.22 The *<map:pipeline>* element of the main sitemap

```
<map:pipeline>
<map:match pattern="mobile">
<map:mount uri-prefix="mobile"
           check-reload="yes"
           reload-method="synchron"
           src="c2/mobile/"/>
</map:match>
```

The main sitemap will accept a URI, http://192.168.1.3:8080/cocoon/mobile, and launch the application by calling the subsitemap.

Figure 2.10 shows the index page of the mobile application. Clicking the Next button will bring up the next page of the application (see Figure 2.11). Clicking the Back button will take the user back to the index page.

FIGURE 2.10: The index page of the mobile application

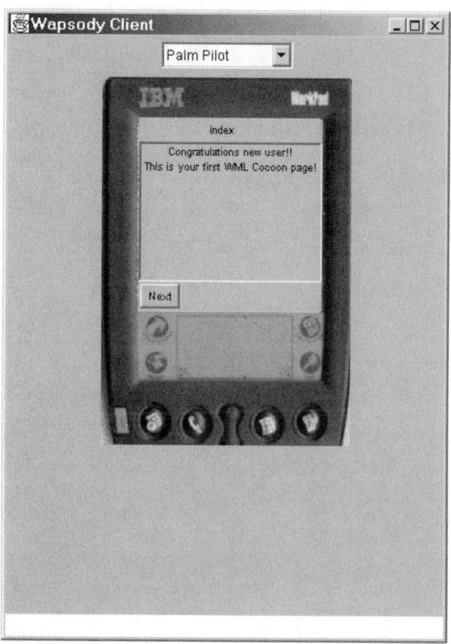

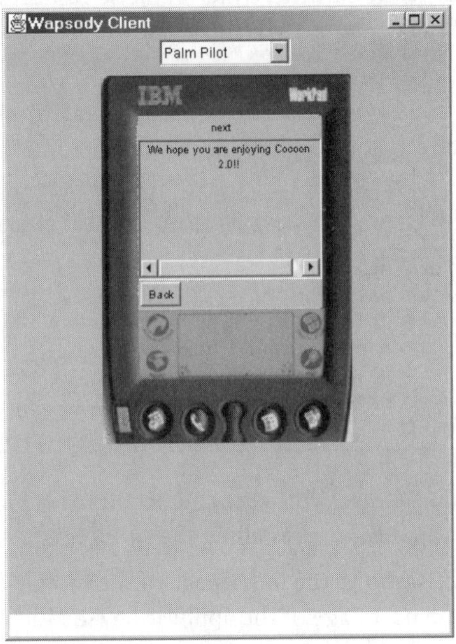

FIGURE 2.11: The next page of the mobile application

In this simple `wml` application, we have demonstrated how to use the Cocoon 2 pipeline to serve up existing XML content for a device other than a web browser.

A Menu-Driven Site

In all the examples that served browser-based clients, the output was presented in a single page. Creating a menu-driven site is just a matter of using dynamic matching in Cocoon 2 pipelines. In this section, we will develop a menu-driven website for a fictional Fortune 100 company—Acme, Inc.—the manufacturer of the finest widgets on the Web.

The `matcher` is a critical component in a Cocoon 2 pipeline and has appeared in all the sitemaps shown in the previous examples. It is very clear that this approach of explicitly defining match patterns for URIs can be used in very small sites but cannot be used to serve up large sites with lots of resources. Dynamic behavior in the Cocoon 2 pipeline is achieved using the `matchers`, `tokens`, and `regular expressions`.

The `<map:pipeline>` element in the main sitemap is shown in Listing 2.23.

Listing 2.23 The main sitemap <*map:pipeline*> element

```
<map:pipeline>

  <!-- match the ACME homepage -->
  <map:match pattern="acme">
    <map:mount uri-prefix="acme"
               check-reload="yes"
               reload-method="synchron"
               src="c2/acme/"/>
  </map:match>

  <!-- match all other ACME pages -->
 <map:match pattern="acme/**">
   <map:mount uri-prefix="acme"
              check-reload="yes"
              reload-method="synchron"
              src="c2/acme/"/>
 </map:match>

</map:pipeline>
```

The URI used to launch the application is `http://192.168.1.3:8080/cocoon/acme`. Both match patterns will match the incoming URI up to this string and then pass the remaining URI down to the subsitemap, which will start processing in one of the pipelines.

Listing 2.24 shows the subsitemap `<map:pipeline>` element for the menu application with the components shown using patterns for a generalized URI.

Listing 2.24 The subsitemap of the menu-driven application

```
<map:pipeline>

  <!-- homepage -->
  <map:match pattern="">
    <map:redirect-to session="false" uri="acme/home/home.section"/>
  </map:match>

  <!-- pages -->
  <map:match pattern="*/*.*">
    <map:generate src="documents/{1}/{2}.xml"/>
    <map:transform src="stylesheets/{3}.xsl">
      <map:parameter name="section" value="{1}"/>
      <map:parameter name="toc-file"
        value="../documents/toc.xml"/>
      <map:parameter name="base-url"
```

```
          value="/cocoon/acme"/>
      </map:transform>
      <map:transform src="stylesheets/menupage.xsl">
        <map:parameter name="section" value="{1}"/>
        <map:parameter name="request-url"
          value="{2}.{3}"/>
        <map:parameter name="toc-file"
          value="../documents/toc.xml"/>
        <map:parameter name="css-stylesheet"
          value="default.css"/>
        <map:parameter name="base-url"
          value="/cocoon/acme"/>
      </map:transform>
      <map:serialize/>
    </map:match>

    <!-- css stylesheets -->
    <map:match pattern="*.css">
      <map:read src="css/{1}.css"
        mime-type="text/css"/>
    </map:match>

  </map:pipeline>
```

In the first `match` block, the default URI is redirected to a pattern that will fit the format of the pattern used in the second `matcher`.

The second `match` block in Listing 2.23 defines a generalized URI pattern—`"*/*.*/"`—to match all incoming URIs. The URI string is tokenized based on this pattern, and the first token represented by the first `"*"` in the pattern will subsequently be available in the pipeline as a variable named *{1}*. The second and third tokens, both represented by `"*"` in the pattern, will be available as variables named *{2}* and *{3}*, respectively.

The use of the variables named *{1}*, *{2}*, and *{3}* are used in the rest of the components in the subsitemap. We will highlight a couple of the occurrences:

```
<map:generate src="documents/{1}/{2}.xml"/>
<map:transform src="stylesheets/{3}.xsl">
```

This sitemap also shows the use of the `<map:parameter>` elements of the transformers for passing in parameters from the sitemap into the application. Parameters are covered in more detail in other chapters of the book.

To leverage the strengths of this design, the code should be organized in a hierarchical structure and all the content documents and stylesheets should adhere to a naming convention. Figure 2.12 shows the directory structure used for this application.

FIGURE 2.12: The directory structure for the Acme menu-driven application

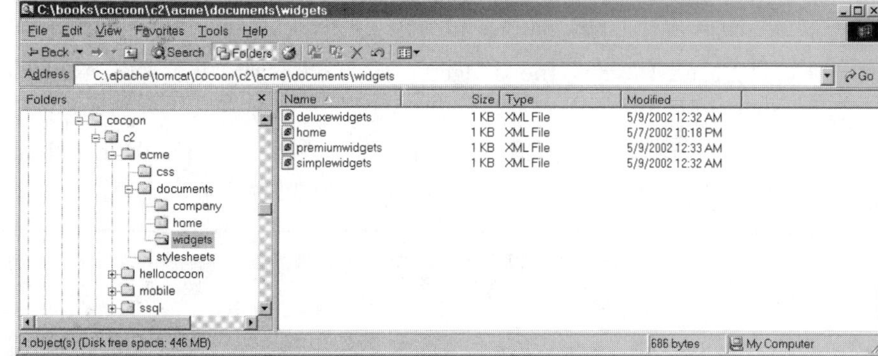

The general structure follows the guidelines presented earlier in this chapter. The figure shows the details of the `documents` directory. The three major sections of the site—Company, Home, and Widgets—each have their own subdirectories within the `documents` directory. The XML content resources for each section are placed within the respective subdirectory.

Figure 2.13 shows the stylesheets used by the transformers. These stylesheets are used to create the dynamic nature of the menu-driven site.

FIGURE 2.13: The `stylesheets` subdirectory

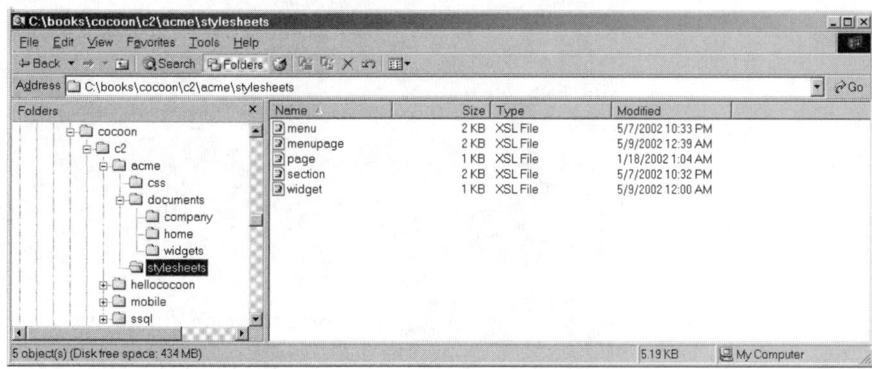

Figure 2.14 shows the subdirectory where the two cascading stylesheets reside, which are used to format the output for display in the browser.

Figure 2.15 shows the home page to be displayed when the user accesses the site. The items in the left navigation bar show the three main sections of the site.

Figure 2.16 shows the Widgets section of the site. It lists the available widget resources sold on the site.

In the interest of space we expand only on the Premium Widget link within the Widgets-RUs section of the site. This is shown in Figure 2.17.

FIGURE 2.14: The css subdirectory

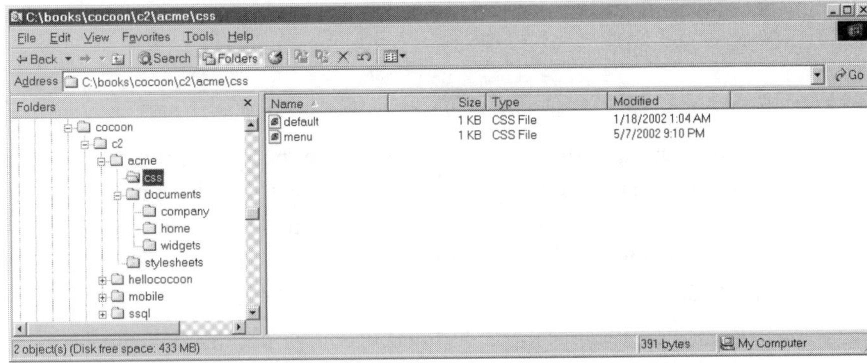

FIGURE 2.15: The main page for the Acme site

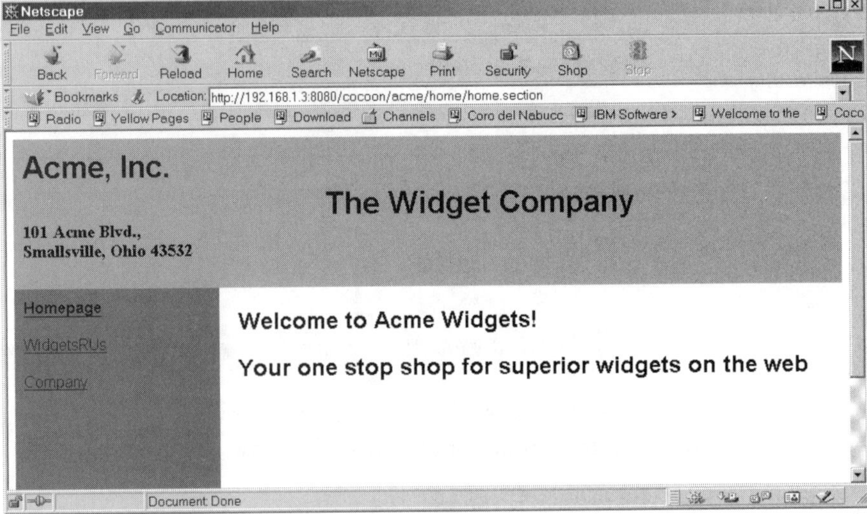

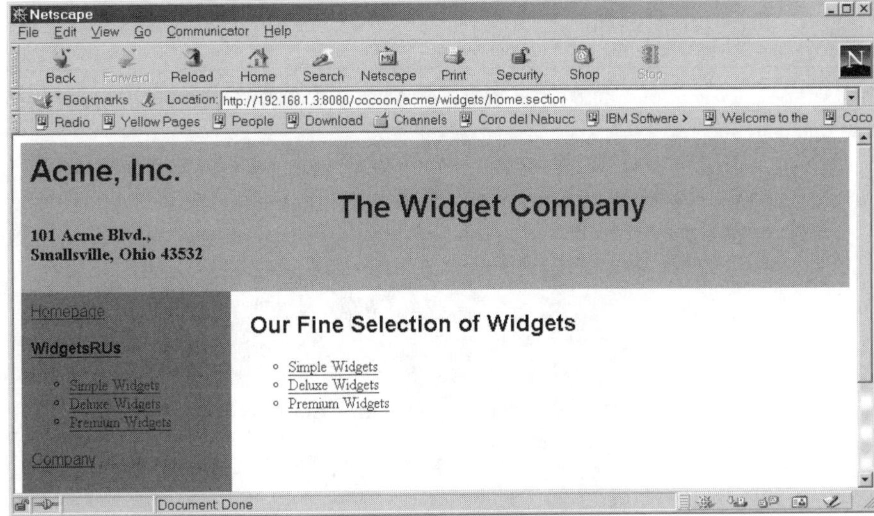

FIGURE 2.16: The WidgetsRUs section

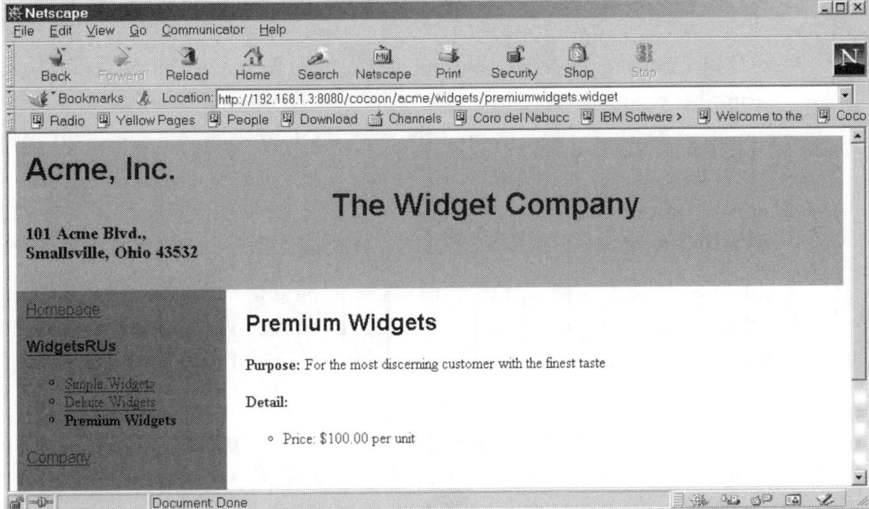

FIGURE 2.17: The Premium Widgets page

Figure 2.18 shows the Company section of the website. It presents the page that has a link to external resources.

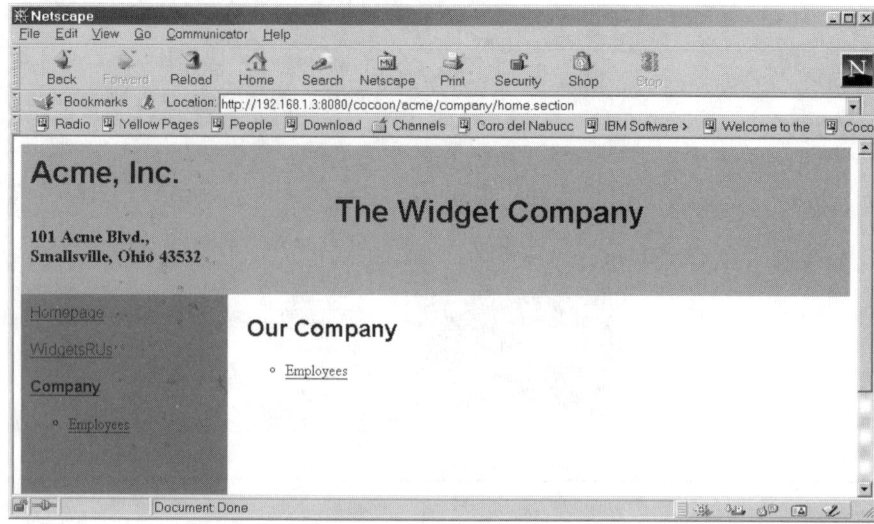

FIGURE 2.18: The Company section

The example presented in this section is a framework that can be expanded to create very complex menu-driven sites. The concepts presented in subsequent chapters provide details on other features of Cocoon 2 that can be used to create powerful sites.

Rendering Scalable Vector Graphics

SVG is a W3C standard that uses XML to define two-dimensional vector graphics. The SVG specification defines the operations that can be performed on shapes, images, and text before being rendered. The complete SVG specification can be found at `www.w3.org/TR/SVG`.

The SVG files are in essence XML files. The content and the markup language are defined in the SVG specification. Using the Cocoon 2 pipeline, this XML content can be processed and displayed in a browser. Describing the SVG specification and the elements used in the rendering process are beyond the scope of this book. We will, however, demonstrate the Cocoon 2 processing steps using simple SVG documents.

A Simple Example

The content of an SVG file defines the objects to be rendered. Listing 2.25 shows the SVG content file for the first example, which displays a welcome greeting in the browser.

Listing 2.25 The *hellococcon.svg* content file

```
<?xml version="1.0" standalone="no"?>
<!DOCTYPE svg PUBLIC "-//W3C//DTD SVG 20001102//EN"
"http://www.w3.org/TR/2000/CR-SVG-20001102/DTD/svg-20001102.dtd">

<svg width="2000" height="400">
<rect x="10" y+"10"
    style="fill:black;"
    width="1000" height="200"/>
  <text x="225" y="125"
    style="fill:white;
    font-size:48pt">
      Hello Cocoon SVG!
  </text>
</svg>
```

This SVG file is an XML file with the following definitions:

SVG Namespace: `www.w3.org/2000/svg`

Public Identifier for SVG 1.0: PUBLIC "-//W3C//DTD SVG 1.0//EN"

System Identifier for SVG 1.0: `www.w3.org/TR/2001/REC-SVG-20010904/DTD/svg10.dtd`

Within a defined drawing area, the example will create a rectangle within which the text "Hello Cocoon SVG!" will be rendered.

The `matcher` of the Cocoon 2 pipeline in the subsitemap that renders this SVG file to the browser is shown in Listing 2.26.

Listing 2.26 The *matcher* in the subsitemap pipeline

```
<map:match pattern="hellosvg">
  <map:generate src="docs/hellococoon.svg"/>
  <map:serialize type="svg2png"/>
</map:match>
```

The Hello page will be serviced by the pipeline when processing starts by generating from the `hellococoon.svg` content file. The serializer that is used in this pipeline is defined in the main sitemap as shown in the following:

```
<map:serializer name="svg2png"
        src="org.apache.cocoon.serialization.SVGSerializer"
        logger="sitemap.serializer.svg2png"
        mime-type="image/png"/>
```

The main sitemap defines the URI that will launch the processing of this pipeline. The `<map:pipeline>` element of the main sitemap is shown in Listing 2.27.

Listing 2.27 The *<map:pipeline>* element of the main sitemap

```
<map:pipeline>
<map:match pattern="svg">
<map:mount uri-prefix="svg"
           check-reload="yes"
           reload-method="synchron"
           src="c2/svg/"/>
</map:match>

<map:match pattern="svg/**">
<map:mount uri-prefix="svg" check-reload="yes"
           reload-method="synchron" src="c2/svg/"/>
</map:match>
</map:pipeline>
```

The URI `http://192.168.1.3:8080/cocoon/svg/hellosvg` launches the application, and the output is shown in Figure 2.19.

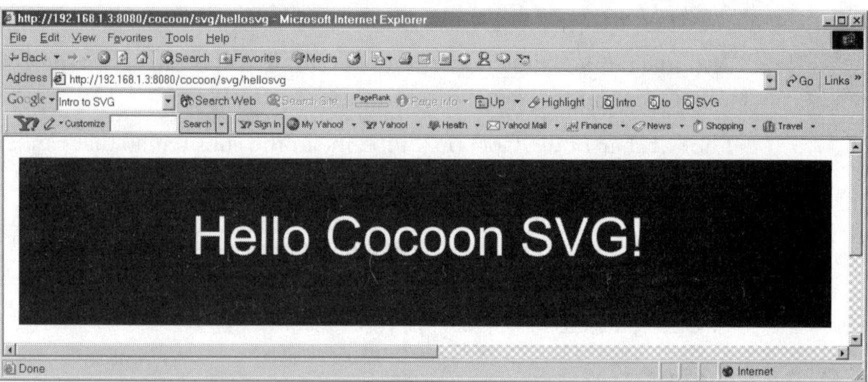

FIGURE 2.19: The `hellococoon.svg` rendered

This simple example shows how an XML content file containing text can be processed by Cocoon and rendered as an SVG file in the browser.

Rendering Complex Graphics

This example shows how graphic objects defined in the SVG format can be rendered and displayed in the browser. The SVG file contains all the markup elements that define the positioning and parameters for the drawing of the graphic objects. We will keep the example simple—define three intersecting circles, each filled in with a distinct color and drawn with a border. Listing 2.28 shows the SVG file.

Listing 2.28 The *circles.svg* file

```
<?xml version="1.0" standalone="yes"?>

<svg width="1000" height="1000">

  <g style="fill:#444">
    <path d="M0,0v250h300v-250z"/>
  </g>

  <g style="stroke:#000;
     stroke-width:4;
     fill:#f0f;
     fill-opacity:0.6">
    <circle cx="100" cy="100" r="80"/>
  </g>

  <g style="stroke:#000;
     stroke-width:4;
     fill:#ff0;
     fill-opacity:0.6">
    <circle cx="200" cy="100" r="80"/>
  </g>

  <g style="stroke:#000;
     stroke-width:4;
     fill:#0ff;
     fill-opacity:0.6">
    <circle cx="150" cy="150" r="80"/>
  </g>
</svg>
```

The SVG file will be rendered in the space defined by the `height` and `width` attributes to the <svg/> element. The three circles will be rendered using the `style`, `stroke-width`, `fill`, and `fill-opacity` defined for each one of them.

The `matcher` in the subsitemap defines the generator and the serializer that will process the request for this application. Listing 2.29 shows the `<map:match>` element of the subsitemap.

Listing 2.29 The *matcher* of the pipeline in the subsitemap

```
<map:match pattern="circles">
  <map:generate src="docs/circles.svg"/>
  <map:serialize type="svg2png"/>
</map:match>
```

Listing 2.27 showed the main sitemap that serviced all SVG resources in this example application. The URI that would launch this application is `http://192.168.1.3:8080/cocoon/svg/circles`. Figure 2.20 shows the rendered image in the browser.

SVG has many more features that can be used in rendering dynamic content. Cocoon 2 makes it easy to use these features to create sites rich in graphics and dynamic images.

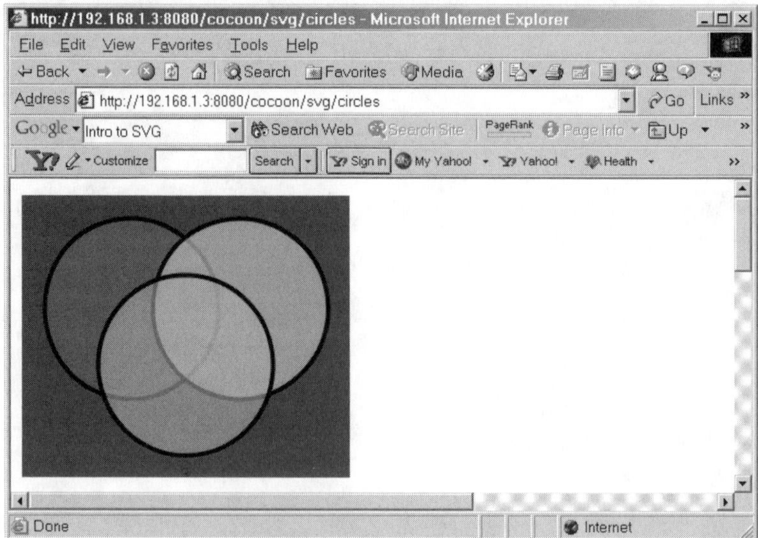

FIGURE 2.20: The `circles.svg` rendered in the browser

Summary

This chapter covered several examples that demonstrated the salient features of Cocoon. To use the power of Cocoon for developing large and dynamic sites, it is necessary to follow simple directory organization rules for storing different resources of the application. We introduced a recommended technique for organizing the applications in a hierarchical structure.

The next step after organizing the resources is to create subsitemaps. The main sitemap processes only the incoming request up to the point of recognizing the application name and then delegating the rest of the processing to the subsitemap. All of the examples used in this chapter used subsitemaps and demonstrated how to demarcate the application between the main sitemap and the subsitemap. The most important area where the processing pipelines differed between the main and subsitemaps was in the `matcher`.

In the simple applications, we reinforced the concepts of a Cocoon 2 pipeline that were described in Chapter 1. A typical pipeline consists of one generator component, zero or more transformer components, and one serializer component.

In the section that demonstrated how a Cocoon 2 application would access a database, we showed two powerful techniques for accessing a relational data store. A SQLTransformer accesses a predefined database using a set of rules defined in an XML file that is the input to the generator component. The XSP and ESQL example leveraged the power of the ESQL taglib to create simple but powerful logicsheets to access and format the data.

In the section on mobile devices, we created an application that used a mobile device simulator to access content on the Cocoon server. This demonstrated the versatility of the application, because the same content could be viewed in a regular web browser using a different transformer.

A menu-driven website allows a user to access content at different levels by navigating through various indexed screens to access the content. The use of `matchers`, `tokens`, and `regular expressions` enables the creation of a powerful menu-driven Cocoon site.

SVG is an industry standard for creating two-dimensional vector graphics using XML syntax. The Cocoon pipeline uses the SVG serializers to render these images in any device capable of displaying SVG images.

Chapter 3

A Review of the Essential Technologies

- Developing Content
- The Avalon Project
- The Document Object Model (DOM)
- Simple API for XML (SAX)
- Developing Logic
- XSL Transformations (XSLT)
- Extensible Server Pages (XSP)
- Developing Presentation
- Extensible Stylesheet Language (XSL)
- Extensible HTML (XHTML)

Chapter 1, "The Cocoon 2 Architecture," described how Cocoon 2 supports a strong separation of the content, logic, and presentation aspects of an application. Cocoon 2 is built upon a collection of XML and Java related technologies that enable this separation of concerns and we review these essential technologies in this chapter. We have subdivided the discussion of the technologies into the three areas of concern to match the functional areas in the Cocoon philosophy, namely: developing content, logic, and presentation.

Our mission in this chapter is to provide a roadmap of the technology skills needed to understand and effectively work with Cocoon 2. This chapter is meant to be an overview of the technologies. An in-depth description of each of the essential technologies is beyond the scope of this book. We do, however, provide references to both printed and online resources that will help you hone your skills and work productively with Cocoon 2.

This chapter is organized as three large sections to reflect the tripartite architecture of Cocoon 2:

- Developing Content
- Developing Logic
- Developing Presentation

The "Developing Content" section deals with technologies that are significant to the representation and management of application content. Chapter 1 mentioned that Cocoon was based on the Avalon framework. This chapter takes a closer look at the Apache Avalon Project. We describe the salient points of the Document Object Model (DOM) and DOM parsing, which was the basis of the Cocoon 1 architecture. We also take a close look at Simple API for XML (SAX) parsing of XML documents, because this is one of the fundamental aspects of processing used by all the components in the Cocoon 2 pipeline.

The "Developing Logic" section looks at XSL Transformations (XSLT) for transformations from one XML document format to another. We briefly mention Extensible Server Pages (XSP) and embedding of business logic in XML. Because XSP is an important technology in the Cocoon 2 architecture, Chapter 6, "Introducing XSP Usage," and Chapter 7, "XSP Logicsheets," are dedicated to an in-depth study of XSP.

The "Developing Presentation" section focuses on the technologies used for the presentation of the output document. We look at Cascading Style Sheets (CSS) and Extensible Stylesheet Language (XSL) from the point of view of presentation templates. We also describe the Extensible Hypertext Markup Language (XHTML).

Developing Content

Cocoon 2 is built on the Avalon framework; a discussion of this framework is essential to understanding the internal architecture of Cocoon. In many of the chapters describing the individual components, we have made references to the components in the Avalon framework that supports them. This section is intended to be an overview of the Avalon Project and not a detailed analysis of the framework.

We then describe the DOM that was the basis of the parser used in the Cocoon 1 architecture. This helps set the stage for a discussion of SAX parsing, which gives the Cocoon 2 architecture its strength, power, and flexibility.

The Avalon Project

The Avalon Project defines a framework and several core components used for developing Java applications. It was originally called Java Apache Server Framework, which was a redesign of an existing project architecture called Apache JServ. The project was initiated to create an environment that would facilitate the development of applications by sharing resources and maximum reuse of code.

The Avalon Project is made up of five subprojects:

- Framework
- Excalibur
- LogKit
- Phoenix
- Cornerstone
- Testlet

We expand on each of the five subprojects as we detail the relevant pieces that play a vital role in the Cocoon architecture.

Framework

The Avalon framework includes the set of interfaces and the default implementations of these interfaces. The interfaces specify the design patterns and rules for the framework as well as their relationship to some of the more commonly used implementations of application components. The framework supports the design of pluggable software modules developed along the stipulated guidelines and encourages code reuse between software projects.

The following is a list of the most important components within the Avalon framework that play a significant part in Cocoon 2.

`ComponentManager` `org.apache.avalon.framework.component.ComponentManager`

The Cocoon class implements this interface and is used to manage all the components configured in the system.

`Component` `org.apache.Avalon.framework.component.Component`

This interface identifies the classes that are components.

`LogEnabled` `org.apache.Avalon.framework.logger.LogEnabled`

This interface is implemented by components that need to provide logging functions.

`AbstractLogEnabled` `org.apache.Avalon.framework.logger.AbstractLogEnabled`

This is an abstract class that defines the behavior for a logger. It implements the `Loggable` interface.

The Avalon Framework draws on the strengths of several patterns and architectural standards for the design of servers. The three main conceptual patterns used are:

Aspect-Oriented Programming (AOP) This is a logical extension of Object-Oriented Programming (OOP) and it provides a means to address issues pertaining to separation of concerns in software development. Because Java does not fully support AOP, this is done using aspect marker interfaces and Component-Oriented Programming (COP).

Component-Oriented Programming This promotes the idea of black-box modules in development. A component is a group of objects that performs a certain function and are replaceable in their entirety by another component that performs the same function.

Inversion of Control This refers to a parent object controlling a child object. The application is designed as a chain of objects in a delegation hierarchy and they perform work by reacting to messages. The framework itself functions as the main program and is responsible for coordinating all application activity.

Multidimensional Separation of Concerns This promotes representing the system using multiple views of the same model; it is implemented by using Java interfaces.

When implementing a system, the developer uses patterns that help in the implementation of the system. There are several architectural standards used and the two most popular ones are:

The Factory Pattern This pattern helps to define an interface that assists in creating objects at run time in situations in which the type of class to be instantiated is not known. In this case, the subclasses decide which object will be instantiated.

The Singleton Pattern In some applications it is necessary to have exactly one instance of a class for the entire application. The pattern defines that the class itself is responsible for ensuring that there is only one instance at any given time. The class receives the request and either provides access to the only instance if it exists or instantiates a new object and provides access to it.

A robust framework encourages and supports the creation of modular and pluggable components that are reusable. The following is a list of guidelines that help to design a good framework:

- All components of a particular type implement the same interface.
- Refactor and redesign code to avoid testing objects to verify their class instance.
- Design methods to have a low number of arguments.
- The size of a method should be small and manageable.
- All base classes at the top of a hierarchy should be abstract.
- Follow strict encapsulation of attributes in classes.
- Use inheritance for defining subclasses.
- The size of a class should be manageable.
- Refactor methods and classes if they do not fit into the inheritance hierarchy.
- Refactor methods if they deal with two different aspects of the same data.
- Avoid using the method `"this"` and redesign the classes to use method calls on instances of objects.
- Methods that share attributes within a class should pass those variables explicitly as parameters instead of accessing them directly.

Excalibur

This subproject defines a set of components that are frequently needed when designing software solutions. Many Cocoon components implement the `Poolable` interface defined in the `org.apache.avalon.Excalibur.pool` package. This interface facilitates the reuse of complex components. Some of the functions covered by the Excalibur components follow:

Command-Line Inspection These are useful for parsing command-line parameters at startup.

Collections These provide high-speed implementations of collections and utilities for performing set operations on a list.

Component Utilities The Container is made up of ComponentManagers and ComponentSelectors that manage the lifecycle of components, which are listed in configuration files.

Concurrent Threading These are the set of thread handling classes and other utilities for managing concurrency issues.

DataSource Management The internal `DataSource` package or the data management resources of a J2EE server can manage data connection pools.

Internationalization Support for internationalization is provided in the `org.apache.avalon.excalibur.i18n` package.

IO Utilities These utilities provide support that is not available in the standard Java utilities, such as FileFilters and advanced copying of bytes and characters.

LogKit Management This is integrated into the Excalibur component management system and controls the functions of the logger.

Resource Monitoring Resources can be monitored actively or passively. In passive monitoring, the container receives events from the resource and passes it on to all registered listeners. In active monitoring, the container polls the monitored resources and looks for changes that occurred in the monitored resource.

Pooling Support This provides implementations for pooling of all components including data sources.

Property Utilities The context object stores all properties as name-value pairs and these utilities can be used to resolve lookup of properties.

Proxy Implementation This provides the JDK 1.3 proxies for applications developed using JDK 1.2.

The following components are listed as optional and are under development:

Cache Support The framework has interfaces and components that support caching. The implementation is modular and allows for different caching algorithms and storage mechanisms to be used.

Container Management This provides the means to manage the state of components deployed within the container.

Optional Package Management These are the utility classes that scan a manifest document and provide information on the optional packages that are available or required.

XML Resource Bundle The supporting classes for this bundle are under development. When complete they will complement the components that provide internationalization to the framework.

Pipelining Support These support the creation of virtual pipelines, which enables processing and operations at each stage of the pipeline.

Thread Pool Management This provides support for managing thread pools.

Source Resolving Components that resolve a URI (Universal Resource Indicator) using any of the protocols that are supported in Java. The SourceFactory interface is used for providing support for custom protocols.

LogKit

A mechanism to perform logging functions is an essential part of any software development framework. It helps the developer get valuable debugging information during the development stages of a project. System administrators have access to valuable operational and configuration data to help debug problems in a running system or for performance enhancement. LogKit is the toolkit for performing logging operations and is available for use by all subprojects and the extensions defined in the framework.

LogKit provides speed and reliability in logging functions and the logger can be dynamically configured. The logging hierarchies are restricted, which makes the LogKit inherently secure. It provides a filter mechanism and has support for multiple listeners for each logged category. It also supports delayed serialization of events. The toolkit has three basic components:

`Logger` This is the client interface to the underlying logging system.

`LogEvent` These are generated by user actions in the `Logger`.

`LogTarget` These consume `LogEvents` by writing to a file or database. Events can also be sent across the network to an instant messaging client, an IRC channel, a syslog server, and so on.

There are five priority levels defined to provide control over the logged events:

DEBUG This level is useful during system development and testing. There are overloaded methods named `debug()` available for use in programs that use this level. The program can test if this level is enabled using the `isDebugEnabled()` method.

INFO This level provides generic information pertaining to user logins, network connections, etc. The overloaded methods named `info()` are available for use by developers. The program can test if this level is enabled using the `isInfoEnabled()` method.

WARN This level provides significant information about conditions that could potentially result in system failure if not rectified. The overloaded methods named `warn()` are available for using this priority level. The program can test for this level using the `isWarnEnabled()` method.

ERROR This level logs non-fatal errors, which do not cause immediate system failure but could be problematic if unattended. Developers can use the methods named `error()` for using this level. The method `isErrorEnabled()` is used to test for this level.

FATAL_ERROR This level logs events indicating that the system has failed and needs administrator intervention to fix the problem and restart the system. The methods named `fatalError()` are available to use this level. The method `isFatalErrorEnabled()` is used to test if this level has been enabled.

For each priority level, the method to use the priority level can take either a string message or a string message and an exception parameter. Listing 3.1 shows an example usage of the priority levels and testing methods of the logger.

Listing 3.1 **Use of Logger Methods**

```
if (logger.isWarnEnabled()) {
  final String message = "Condition occured " + somecondition;

  // throw Exception ex1

  logger.warn(message,ex1);
}
```

The entire logging operation for a particular system can be subdivided into named *categories*. A category is a name, which in turn is made up of named components. A logger is associated with a category when the system is started. LogKit supports a hierarchical logging namespace that supports inheritance of priorities. A logger inherits the priority of the parent logger by default and can explicitly override it. Deep hierarchies do not affect the performance of the logging system because the loggers cache the priorities and update their children when they are changed.

A *filter* is a specialized `LogTarget`, which is used to filter out `LogEvents` between a logger and a destination `LogTarget`. It can also be used to modify the `LogEvent` for use by another `LogTarget`. For example, a `PriorityFilter` can be used to filter out messages of a particular priority before forwarding it to the destination.

An *asyncLogTarget* is another specialized `LogTarget` that allows `LogEvents` produced by a logger to be saved in a queue and be consumed by another thread, which will send the event to the destination. This is used when operations to a `LogTarget` are very slow and need to be done asynchronously.

A *formatter* is a way to serialize a `LogEvent` before writing to a destination unstructured store such as a file system or a remote network `LogTarget`. The `Formatter` interface defines a method format (`LogEvent` event) that returns a string representation of the `LogEvent`.

It is often necessary to save application-specific information such as the network parameters, method name, thread information, etc. The LogKit provides a *ContextMap* for use by the developer. A ContextMap is created and parameters are saved in it as name-value pairs using the `set(key, value)` method. The context object is bound to a particular thread and can be inherited by other threads. For securing the context, the method `makeReadOnly()` can be invoked, which prevents subsequent modification of the context object by other threads.

Phoenix

The Phoenix kernel is designed and implemented to run on the Avalon framework. This project defines the application programming interface (API) to be used by developers to create software systems. It is also the reference implementation that provides the infrastructure for managing other applications. It defines the facilities for management of the logging functions, loading of classes, thread management, and security. Part of the design goals are to provide features such as central server management and server pools, which have not been implemented at present but should be seen soon. There is a standard specified for designing and building a server using the server components available in the system.

Cornerstone

This subproject supports the Phoenix Project. It defines a set of services to be used by the Phoenix server. These services are called blocks, which plug into the Phoenix kernel. A partial list of the services follows:

ConnectionManager This service provides the mechanism to listen for incoming socket connections.

SocketManager This service provides a mechanism to look up a server that provides client sockets.

TimeScheduler This service provides a way to schedule actions at fixed time intervals.

SAXParserFactory This service provides a way to access the SAX Parser configured in the system.

ThreadManager This service provides access to the ThreadPool.

Store This service provides the mechanism to store objects and streams without knowing specifics of how they will be stored.

Testlet

This subproject created an infrastructure for testing of software modules within the Avalon framework. However, the Avalon development team has ceased further development on this project and has chosen to adopt JUnit as the testing framework. Any additional work on Testlet will include specific tests generated in JUnit for the Avalon framework.

The Document Object Model (DOM)

There are two APIs for parsing XML documents. DOM was the original API and is a Worldwide Web Consortium (W3C) recommendation. There are several enhancements to the DOM specification that are still in the draft stage and will become recommendations when they are finalized. It is a tree-based API and is platform and language independent. The second API is discussed in the section "Simple API for XML (SAX)."

The DOM specification defines the following:

- A standard set of objects to model the content of an XML document
- A standard set of rules for combining the objects
- A standard interface to access and manipulate the objects

The DOM API is the mechanism used by application programs to dynamically manipulate the content and structure of an XML document. The interface shields the application program from the internal representation of the objects and datastructures, which might be proprietary or vendor specific. Having a standardized interface to work with XML documents guarantees interoperability across platforms and languages.

XML Namespaces

XML namespaces are a simple mechanism used in XML documents to qualify elements and attributes and associate them with a particular application domain. Namespaces are implemented using named URI resources, which must be unique for a particular application domain. The actual resource pointed to by the URI does not need to exist and it is only the name that should be unique.

XML namespaces are implemented in a document using the attribute `xmlsns:` as highlighted in the definition of the following XSL namespace:

```
xmlns:xsl="http://www.w3.org/1999/XSL/Transform"
```

The namespace can then be used to qualify the elements and attributes that belong in that application domain. A simple example of the XSL domain is highlighted in the following code. Details of XSL elements are discussed in other sections of this chapter.

```
<xsl:template match="vcard/city">
     <xsl:value-of select="text()"/>,
</xsl:template>
```

The Three Levels of DOM

There are three levels to the DOM specification—DOM Level 1, DOM Level 2, and DOM Level 3. All the low-level interfaces for modeling a general unstructured document are defined in the Core DOM Level 1 specification. The rest of the specification defines extended interfaces for modeling structured XML documents and HTML documents. A specific implementation of the DOM must implement all the core interfaces and all the higher-level interfaces that pertain to its function. For example, an implementation that exclusively accesses XML documents implements all core and higher-level XML interfaces but need not implement the HTML interfaces.

The DOM Level 2 specification builds on the Level 1 specification and defines 14 modules, each dealing with a specific area to which a DOM implementation can conform. The module that is most relevant to this section is the XML module. An implementation conforms to DOM Level 2 if it implements the Core module. If the implementation supports all the interfaces and specifications contained in the XML module, then the implementation conforms to the DOM Level 2 XML module. For a complete list of the modules and the specification, please refer to the section "Additional Resources for Content Technologies."

The DOM Level 3 specification builds on the Level 2 specification and defines the Abstract Schemas Object Model, which is an optional feature. The specification also defines the API for loading and saving an XML document, which is independent of any specific definitions in any language.

Using the DOM API

The DOM parser traverses the XML document and creates a tree of nodes in memory. If the programming language is Java, the nodes are Java objects maintained in the virtual machine memory. The hierarchy of nodes is preserved and the virtual tree in memory matches the hierarchy in the XML document. The DOM API provides the application access to this tree in memory.

A node in the tree represents one (and only one) element in the XML document. The root of the tree is the document node and all other nodes are contained in hierarchies below the root node. The application first accesses this node and then walks down specific paths from the root node.

A node in the DOM tree is defined by a type, tag-name, and value. The DOM API defines methods for returning the details of a node. The tag-name is the name of the element in the XML document. The value is the data contained in the XML element and can be null.

Besides values, a node can have child nodes. The DOM API has methods that return a collection of child nodes of a node and this list can be used to traverse the tree in memory. In general, the leaf nodes contain only values and no child nodes, with the exception of the node that represents an empty element from the document. Leaf nodes indicate the end of a particular hierarchy or walk down the tree.

DOM Parsers

There are several DOM parsers available for most languages and each implements the DOM specification. As part of the Java XML Pack, Sun Microsystems has released the Java API for XML Processing (JAXP). This API supports the processing of SAX, DOM, and XSLT. This is available as a plug-in package to the production release of the Java Development Kit (JDK 1.3) and is included as part of the standard distribution in JDK 1.4.

The Apache Project has developed the Xerces parser, which is a validating parser and implements the Core interfaces in the DOM Level 1 and Level 2 interfaces as well as the XML interfaces defined in the W3C specification. Cocoon 1.0 used the DOM API of the Xerces parser.

There are two Xerces parsers available for Java that support both the DOM and SAX specification. This section highlights the DOM features.

Xerces Java 1 supports the following standards:

- XML 1.0 recommendation
- XML Schema recommendation version 1.0
- DOM Level 2 version 1.0
- DOM Level 1

Xerces Java 2 supports the following standards or features:

- Xerces Native Interface (XNI)
- Fully conforming XML Schema processor
- Partial implementation of DOM Level 3 specification

Drawbacks of DOM

A DOM parser processes an XML document and creates a tree of nodes in memory. The memory required for maintaining the tree in memory is a significant issue for larger XML documents. All processing actions are carried out on the objects in memory and speed becomes an issue. After processing, the objects must be serialized back out to a document. Thus speed and computing resources are the two major factors to consider when deciding to use a DOM parser. Some applications force the choice of a DOM parser, in which case a proper design for the application is critical. Additionally, choosing a good DOM parser and good choices of computing resources result in improved performance of the application.

The section "Additional Resources for Content Technologies" provides additional details on the DOM specification, DOM API, and specific DOM parsers.

Simple API for XML (SAX)

SAX is the second major type of XML API and is based on processing of events. It is an interface that can be used for event-based parsing of XML documents. An event-based API generates events and reports these events to the application using callbacks. It should be noted that these events are not the same as events used in Java AWT and JavaBeans applications. The parser does not create event objects like in Java client applications, but calls specific methods for processing the elements in the XML document. The callback methods for a start element are highlighted in the following code:

```
public void startElement(String uri,
                         String name,
                         String qname,
                         Attributes attrs)
{
  //application code to consume the data and attributes
}
```

This API is very convenient for applications that need to store elements in data structures that do not resemble trees. Without the SAX API, these applications would have to read in the data from an XML document using a DOM parser and then extract the data from the tree, save the data in the application data structure, and then discard the tree, which is a wasteful and inefficient process.

The tree-based DOM API is a W3C recommendation but the SAX API came out of a team effort on the XML-DEV mailing list. SAX is now a *de facto* standard and the number of languages supported is growing. SAX is now managed under a more formal process and is part of the SourceForge Project. There are two versions of the SAX API: SAX 1.0 and SAX 2.0, and some of the parsers support both versions. The following section provides an overview and salient features of both the APIs.

SAX 1.0

SAX 1.0 was the original API and it was exclusively for use by Java. It contained 11 core classes and interfaces, three optional helper classes, and five classes to demonstrate the functions of the parser. All these items can be grouped into the following five convenient categories:

- The interfaces for developing a parser
- The interfaces for developing an application
- The core SAX classes
- The classes specific for use by Java
- The Java demonstration classes

The first four categories are relevant to Cocoon, and the following highlights some of the specifics.

The Interfaces for Developing a Parser

There are only three interfaces that need to be implemented in this category. Some of the parsers implement all of them in a single class called the SAXDriver. The names and descriptions of these interfaces are as follows:

`Parser` This is the main interface that every SAX parser must implement. It is used for starting the parser operation, registering callback handles, and error reporting.

`AttributeList` This interface defines the methods for iterating through the attribute list of an element in the document.

`Locator` This interface is used to locate the current position within the document being parsed.

The Interfaces for Developing an Application

The following are the interfaces needed for application developers. These interfaces are optional, but can be implemented in a single class.

`DocumentHandler` This interface needs to be implemented to handle basic document callback events.

`ErrorHandler` This interface allows an application to handle special error conditions.

`DTDHandler` This interface allows an application to handle NOTATION and ENTITY declarations.

`EntityResolver` This interface allows the redirection to URIs contained in the document.

The Core SAX Classes

These are the classes that are used by both the developers of the applications and the developers of the parsers.

`InputSource` This class describes how the application will access the XML entity. It is created in the application and passed to the parser.

`SAXException` This is a general SAX exception.

`SAXParseException` This is an exception at a specific place in the XML document.

`HandlerBase` This class provides a default implementation for all the handlers and the resolver interfaces just described.

The Classes Specific for Java

These classes are not part of the core SAX package and cannot be implemented in other languages.

`ParserFactory` This class has static methods to let an application load SAX parsers dynamically using the Java class name.

`AttributeListImpl` This class has service methods to create a persistent instance of the `AttributeList` interface.

`LocatorImpl` This class has service methods to create a persistent instance of the `Locator` interface.

SAX 2.0

SAX 2.0 supports namespaces, filter chains, handling of queries, and setting of properties in the parser. An extension package called SAX2-ext includes handlers for parsing lexical items like CDATA sections and comments. It can also handle additional DTD declarations. SAX2 drivers are needed to utilize the features of the SAX2-ext package.

A SAX driver implements the SAX2 XMLReader interface. A driver can be used to parse XML directly or it can be invoked from other SAX interfaces in the API.

The following classes and interfaces have been deprecated in the SAX 2.0 API and will be removed from subsequent revisions of the standard:

- `Parser`
- `DocumentHandler`
- `AttributeList`
- `HandlerBase`
- `ParserFactory`
- `AttributeListImpl`

The following are the interfaces and classes that take their place in SAX 2.0:

`XMLReader` (replaces `Parser`) This is the interface that allows the application to read in an XML document using callbacks.

`XMLReaderFactory` (replaces `ParserFactory`) This is the factory for creating an XML Reader.

`ContentHandler` (replaces `DocumentHandler`) This is the main interface that receives basic document-related SAX events (for example, the start and end of elements) as well as character data.

`Attributes` (replaces `AttributeList`) This interface provides access to the attributes of elements.

`AttributesImpl` (replaces `AttributeListImpl`) This is the default implementation of the attributes interface.

`DefaultHandler` (replaces `HandlerBase`) This is the default base class for all SAX2 handlers and provides default implementations for all of the callbacks.

The following are the new interfaces and classes in SAX 2.0:

`XMLFilter` These interfaces are like `XMLReaders` except they take their input from another `XMLReader` and not from a native source. They modify the events before passing them on to the destination.

`SAXNotSupportedException` This exception indicates that the `XMLReader` has recognized the input but cannot process it.

`SAXNotRecognizedException` This exception indicates the `XMLReader` cannot recognize the input.

`NamespaceSupport` This class incorporates support for namespaces in the application and parser.

`XMLFilterImpl` This is the base class for creating instances of the `XMLFilter` interface.

`ParserAdapter` This class emulates `XMLReader` functionality by wrapping a SAX1 parser.

`XMLReaderAdapter` This class emulates SAX1 parser functionality in an application by wrapping an `XMLReader`.

Using the SAX API

This event-based API is the second major type of XML API. The tree-based API discussed in the previous section on DOM is the other type of API. Event-based parsers do not create a tree representation of the document in memory. They generate events as they parse the XML document. The callback event handlers in these parsers can be used to process elements and even create new parse trees in memory. The event-based API can also be used to traverse a prebuilt tree in memory.

SAX Parsers

There are several SAX parsers available for many different languages. Cocoon 2 components are developed in Java so we will limit our focus on the XML parsing support for Java. We will provide an abbreviated list of the parsers that have drivers for both SAX 1.0 and SAX 2.0.

Parsers with drivers for SAX 1.0 and SAX 2.0:

JAXP—Java API for XML Processing This is the newest XML parser from Sun Microsystems.

XML4J This is a 100 percent pure Java validating parser from IBM.

XDK for Java This is the XML Developer's Kit from Oracle.

Xerces Java 1 This is the parser developed by the Apache Project that supports the W3C XML 1.0 recommendation.

Xerces Java 2 (The Apache Project) This is the next generation parser developed by the Apache Project that is fully compliant with XML parsing recommendations.

Additional Resources for Content Technologies

The Avalon Project documentation can be found at `http://jakarta.apache.org` and is part of the Apache umbrella project. JUnit, the Unit testing framework for Java, can be found at `www.junit.org`. Additional information on the DOM can be found at `www.w3.org/DOM`.

SAX parsing and the associated technologies can be found at the following addresses:

```
www.saxproject.org
www.xml.org/xml/resources_focus_sax.shtml
```

The XML-DEV mailing list can be found at `www.xml.org/xml/xmldev.shtml`.

For more information about SAX, see *Mastering XML, Premium Edition,* by White, Quin, and Burman (Sybex, 2001).

Developing Logic

There are two distinct technologies used in Cocoon that can be utilized to create web applications that enforce the separation of business logic from data content. We will first describe the XSLT language and then provide an overview of XSP.

XSL Transformations (XSLT)

The XSL working draft has a section that addresses the issue of transforming XML documents into other XML documents. The XSLT language was defined as part of the XSL specification to be used for such transformations. XSLT is not a general-purpose language for the transformation of XML documents but is used in conjunction with XSL, the stylesheet language described in the previous section.

This section provides an overview of the subset of XSL that addresses the issues related to transforming XML documents. The section dealing with presentation technologies discusses XSL for styling.

An XSLT sheet is a document that defines the transformation rules that are applied to another XML document. The XSLT processor takes the input XML document and applies the rules in the sheet and produces the output document marked up according to the rules in the XSLT sheet.

Figure 3.1 shows how an XSLT processor works to transform an input document using an XSLT sheet with rules for the transformation.

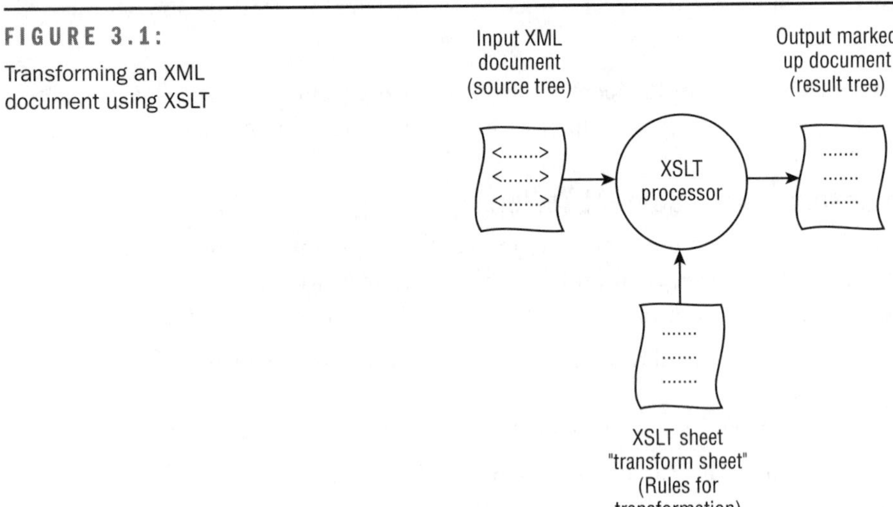

FIGURE 3.1: Transforming an XML document using XSLT

Listing 3.2 shows a sample XML document, `vcard.xml`. We will create an XSLT stylesheet to transform this document into an XHTML document.

Listing 3.2 A Sample XML Business Card, *vcard.xml*

```
<?xml version="1.0"?>
<?xml:stylesheet type="text/xsl" href="vcard_xslt.xsl"?>
<vcard>
  <name>
    John Doe
  </name>
  <company>
    Acme Supplies, Inc.
  </company>
  <address>
    101 Acme Blvd.
  </address>
  <city>Smallsville</city>
  <state>Ohio </state>
  <zip>43532</zip>
</vcard>
```

This XML file is a very simple document with markup elements describing the data contained within. The only line of code that needs to be highlighted is the one that defines the stylesheet declaration.

```
<?xml:stylesheet type="text/xsl" href="vcard_xslt.xsl"?>
```

This line associates the stylesheet `vcard_xslt.xsl` to this XML file `vcard.xml`. Any invocation to `vcard.xml` will result in the application of the stylesheet `vcard.xsl` and the output will be styled according to the rules contained in the stylesheet.

Listing 3.3 shows the XSLT sheet `vcard_xslt.xsl`, which contains all the rules to be applied when the elements in `vcard.xml` are being transformed.

Listing 3.3 A Sample XSLT Sheet to Transform the Document, *vcard_xslt.xsl*

```
<xsl:stylesheet xmlns:xsl="http://www.w3.org/1999/XSL/Transform" version="1.0"
   xmlns="http://www.w3.org/1999/xhtml">

<xsl:template match="vcard">
  <html xmlns="http://www.w3.org/1999/xhtml">
    <head>
      <title>Business Card</title>
    </head>
    <body>
      <xsl:apply-templates select="name"/>
      <xsl:apply-templates select="company"/>
      <xsl:apply-templates select="address"/>
      <xsl:apply-templates select="city"/>
      <xsl:apply-templates select="state"/>
      <xsl:apply-templates select="zip"/>
    </body>
  </html>
</xsl:template>

<xsl:template match="vcard/name">
  <h2><xsl:value-of select="text()"/></h2>
  <p />
</xsl:template>

<xsl:template match="vcard/company">
  <xsl:value-of select="text()"/>
  <p />
</xsl:template>

<xsl:template match="vcard/address">
  <xsl:value-of select="text()"/>
  <p />
</xsl:template>

<xsl:template match="vcard/city">
     <xsl:value-of select="text()"/>,
```

```
</xsl:template>

<xsl:template match="vcard/state">
     <xsl:value-of select="text()"/>
</xsl:template>

<xsl:template match="vcard/zip">
     <xsl:value-of select="text()"/>
</xsl:template>
</xsl:stylesheet>
```

As shown in Listing 3.3, each element in the source file is matched to a template in the XSLT sheet. The template contains fragments of the output document suitably marked up in the target language. The first line of the code listing defines the `<stylesheet>` root element and is highlighted in the following:

```
<xsl:stylesheet xmlns:xsl="http://www.w3.org/1999/XSL/Transform" version="1.0"
   xmlns="http://www.w3.org/1999/xhtml">
```

There are two namespace attributes defined in this element. The first defines the `xmlns:xsl` attribute and establishes the `xsl` namespace for the entire document. The XSLT engine will react to and process those elements in the stylesheet that are tagged with the `xsl` namespace.

A second namespace is defined to establish the `XHTML` namespace; however, none of the elements have to be explicitly tagged. The XHTML elements are implicitly tagged when the namespace is used as an attribute in the element `<html>`, which is the root element of the output HTML code as highlighted here:

```
<html xmlns="http://www.w3.org/1999/xhtml">
```

The XSLT processor begins processing the input document at the root node. When it finds an element, it searches the XSLT sheet for a template rule that matches the element name. The template is applied, which creates some output, and the processing continues recursively until all elements in the source tree are processed.

Listing 3.4 shows the XHTML output of our transformation. The output fragments are concatenated in the order they are generated by the XSLT processor to produce the final output document or streams.

Listing 3.4 The Output after the Transformation

```
<html xmlns="http://www.w3.org/1999/xhtml">
  <head>
    <title>Business Card</title>
  </head>
  <body>
```

```
      <h2>John Doe</h2>
      <p />
      Acme Supplies, Inc.
      <p />
      101 Acme Blvd.
      <p />
      Smallsville, Ohio 43532
    </body>
  </html>
```

The XSLT sheet is the key piece for transforming an XML document into another markup language. The section on presentation technologies outlines the second part of the XSL standard that deals with formatting of the output after the transformation. This concludes the overview of the XSLT language.

Extensible Server Pages (XSP)

XSP is a core technology available in Cocoon to support the separation of logic from content and presentation. XSP pages are XML documents that draw on concepts from Java Server Pages (JSP) but are not limited to the functionalities of JSP. They have additional features to support the separation of concerns and fit into the overall architecture of Cocoon.

A good understanding of this technology is essential to designing powerful Cocoon applications. We have dedicated two chapters in this book to XSP pages. Chapter 6 introduces the fundamentals and provides several examples of using XSP pages. Chapter 7 deals specifically with the XSP logicsheets that come with Cocoon 2.0; it also details how to create custom logicsheets for specific applications.

Additional Resources for Logic Technologies

For thorough coverage of XSLT, see Chuck White's *Mastering XSLT* (Sybex, 2002). The W3C website `www.w3c.org` is the repository for XSLT recommendations and drafts. For a detailed discussion of XSP, please refer to Chapters 6 and 7.

Developing Presentation

Cocoon supports a strong separation of concerns. Mutually exclusive teams can work in parallel on the different aspects of a web application with ease. The team working on the presentation aspects of the application can do so without affecting or being affected by the content and logic teams. This section covers the technologies that are used by the presentation teams to format the output responses for specific uses in the client browser. We also cover CSS and XSL, and discuss XHTML and how it comes into play when presenting XML documents.

Cascading Style Sheets (CSS)

CSS is a simple mechanism that can be used to control the style and presentation of web documents. CSS is a W3C recommendation and is currently at Level 2 (CSS2) of the specification. CSS can be used to apply precise formats to web documents by controlling the font, color, margins, spacing, and other parameters of the final output in the client browser. Cascading Style Sheets act like templates and are analogous to templates seen in other tools used to create and maintain documents. There are several different ways CSS rules can be used to style HTML documents, but the overview of CSS in this section is limited to the styling of XML documents.

The basic steps for creating a stylesheet is to create a CSS document, which contains rules built using the CSS attributes. This CSS document is invoked from within the data document. The content and structure of the data document is unaffected by the application of the stylesheet. The stylesheet is used as a template to control the placement of data on a web page.

Because CSS uses standard terminologies, even novice designers can come up to speed very quickly and create powerful stylesheets. Several stylesheets can be created to customize the format of the same content document. The separation of content and presentation supported by CSS makes it much easier to manage change in the web application.

The CSS document contains rules that follow a simple basic format as shown here:

```
<element-name> {attribute1; attribute2;}
```

Each rule begins with the name of the element to which it will be applied. The rules are contained within the curly braces after the element name. A semicolon separates attributes. Colors are specified either by name or a hexadecimal (RGB) value. Some of the most commonly used attributes are listed below, along with a brief description or an example usage:

- `font-family: Verdana` or `Monospace`
- `font-size: 10pt`
- `font-style: bold` or `italic`
- `text-align: center`
- `margin-left: 0.5in`
- `margin-right: 0.75in`
- `color: red or #F0F0F0`
- `display: block` (the element will be displayed on a new line)
- `display: inline` (the element will be displayed tied to the previous block)
- `display: none` (the element will be hidden and not displayed in the output)

We now give an example of how to use the CSS rules to style a simple XML document. Listing 3.5 shows an XML file that defines a business card document.

Listing 3.5 A sample XML Business Card, *vcard.xml*

```
<?xml version="1.0"?>
<?xml:stylesheet type="text/css" href="vcard.css"?>
<vcard>
  <name>
    John Doe
  </name>
  <company>
    Acme Supplies, Inc.
  </company>
  <address>
    101 Acme Blvd.
  </address>
  <city>Smallsville</city>
  <state>Ohio</state>
  <zip>43532</zip>
</vcard>
```

This XML file is a very simple document with markup elements describing the data contained within. The only line of code that needs to be highlighted is the one that defines the stylesheet declaration.

```
<?xml:stylesheet type="text/css" href="vcard.css"?>
```

This line associates the stylesheet `vcard.css` to this XML file `vcard.xml`. Any invocation to `vcard.xml` results in the application of the stylesheet `vcard.css` and the output will be styled according to the rules contained in the stylesheet.

We will now define the stylesheet that contains the rules for presenting the data. Listing 3.6 shows a CSS sheet with rules defined for formatting and presenting each element in the XML file.

Listing 3.6 A Sample Stylesheet to Format the Business Card, *vcard.css*

```
Vcard {
  color:green
}

name {
  display:block;
  font-family:verdana;
  font-size:24pt;
  font-weight:bold;
```

```
  color:maroon;
}

company {
  display:block;
  font-style:italic;
  font-size:20pt;
}

address {
  display:block;
  color:blue;
}

city {
  display:inline;
}

state {
  display:inline;
  color:black;
}

zip{
  display:inline;
}
```

The styling algorithm traverses the document (`vcard.xml`) and applies the rules for each of the elements that are defined in the stylesheet.

The final output of the styled document in a browser is shown in Figure 3.2.

The CSS rules can be placed in any order within the stylesheet and the algorithm chooses the rules that apply to a particular element in the XML document. The basic structure of the CSS is as shown in the preceding examples and advanced rules can be written to fit into the template.

FIGURE 3.2: The output of `vcard.xml`

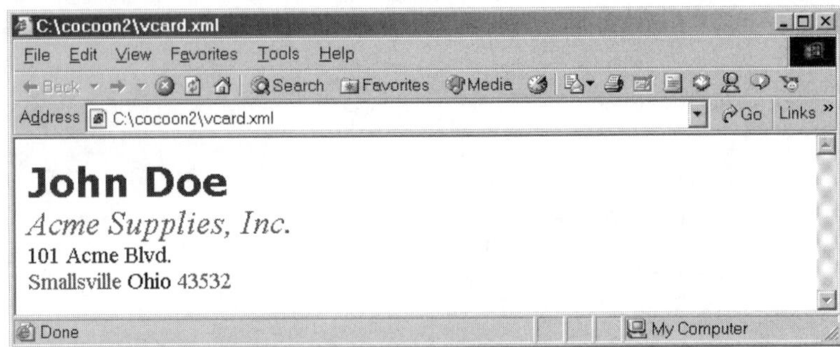

Extensible Stylesheet Language (XSL)

In 1999, the XSL Working Group of the W3C recommended the XSL working draft be split into two sections, one defining the formatting semantics using an XML vocabulary and the other defining a language for transforming XML documents. The section on Logic technologies introduced XSLT, one of the parts of the XSL specification. The second major part of XSL is the XSL Formatting Objects (XSL-FO) specification. XSLT was not designed as a general-purpose transformation language, although it fits well into that role, as shown earlier. XSLT was defined primarily for use with XSL-FO. The term *XSL* is used to define the sheets that are used for formatting XML documents.

XSL-FO is an XML language that specifies formatting and presentation rules at a very low level. This allows the application to have precise control of the output layout and format. This makes XSL-FO more powerful than CSS. There currently are no browsers that support XSL-FO, but web browsers and other display devices in the future will be able to process XSLT and XSL-FO.

We will present a small example of what an XSL-FO document looks like. Listing 3.7 shows a sample stylesheet with XSL-FO commands, `hello-fo.xsl`.

Listing 3.7 A Sample XSL-FO Stylesheet, *hello-fo.xsl*

```
<?xml version="1.0"?>
<fo:root xmlns:fo="http://www.w3.org/1999/XSL/Format">
  <fo:layout-master-set>
    <fo:simple-page-master master-name="hello-page">
      <fo:region-body margin="2in"/>
    </fo:simple-page-master>
  </fo:layout-master-set>

  <fo:page-sequence master-name="hello-page">
    <fo:flow flow-name="xsl-region-body">
      <fo:block font-family="Verdana" font-size="21pt">
        <fo:inline font-weight="bold">
          Hello</fo:inline>, Cocoon Users!
      </fo:block>
    </fo:flow>
  </fo:page-sequence>
</fo:root>
```

The following highlights some of the elements used in the preceding code:

- Layout Masters define the overall layout of a page.
- Page Sequences define how individual pages will be grouped.
- Flow Objects bind data in an element to specific regions.

- Blocks contain the actual data from the XML elements.
- Inline assigns properties to the output data.

The Apache XML Project has a Formatting Objects Processor (FOP) that can take an XSL file with XSL-FO commands and produce output in many different formats. The default output is the Adobe Portable Document Format (PDF). This FOP is used in Cocoon 2 and will be used in some of the examples we create in other chapters.

We will now show examples of how an XSL stylesheet can be used to style XML documents for display in a browser.

Listing 3.8 shows the same sample business card `vcard.xml` used in the last section. However, the stylesheet that will be used is going to change as we demonstrate formatting a single XML document content using different XSL stylesheets.

Listing 3.8 A Sample XML Business Card, *vcard.xml*

```
<?xml version="1.0"?>
<?xml:stylesheet type="text/xsl" href="vcard_one.xsl"?>
<vcard>
  <name>
    John Doe
  </name>
  <company>
    Acme Supplies, Inc.
  </company>
  <address>
    101 Acme Blvd.
  </address>
  <city>Smallsville</city>
  <state>Ohio</state>
  <zip>43532</zip>
</vcard>
```

We now create an XSL stylesheet that will format the data in `vcard.xml`. Listing 3.9 shows the code listing for the XSL file `vcard_one.xsl`.

Listing 3.9 The XSL File, *vcard_one.xsl*

```
<xsl:stylesheet xmlns:xsl="http://www.w3.org/1999/XSL/Transform" version="1.0"
   xmlns="http://www.w3.org/1999/xhtml">

<xsl:template match="vcard">
  <html xmlns="http://www.w3.org/1999/xhtml">
    <head>
```

```
      <title>Business Card</title>
    </head>
    <body>
     <center>
       <h1>My Business Card</h1>
    <p/>
       <table border="2" bgcolor="white">
         <tr>
           <th>Name</th>
        <th>Company</th>
           <th>Address</th>
        <th>State</th>
         </tr>
         <tr>
           <td><xsl:apply-templates select="name"/></td>
           <td><xsl:apply-templates select="company"/></td>
           <td><xsl:apply-templates select="address"/></td>
        <td><xsl:apply-templates select="state"/></td>
         </tr>
       </table>
     </center>
    </body>
  </html>
</xsl:template>

<xsl:template match="vcard/name">
    <h2><xsl:value-of select="text()"/></h2>
</xsl:template>

<xsl:template match="vcard/company">
  <xsl:value-of select="text()"/>
</xsl:template>

<xsl:template match="vcard/address">
  <xsl:value-of select="text()"/>
</xsl:template>

<xsl:template match="vcard/city">
     <xsl:value-of select="text()"/>,
</xsl:template>

<xsl:template match="vcard/state">
     <xsl:value-of select="text()"/>
</xsl:template>

<xsl:template match="vcard/zip">
     <xsl:value-of select="text()"/>
</xsl:template>
</xsl:stylesheet>
```

The output after applying this stylesheet is shown in Figure 3.3.

FIGURE 3.3: Output of `vcard.xml` styled with `vcard_one.xsl`

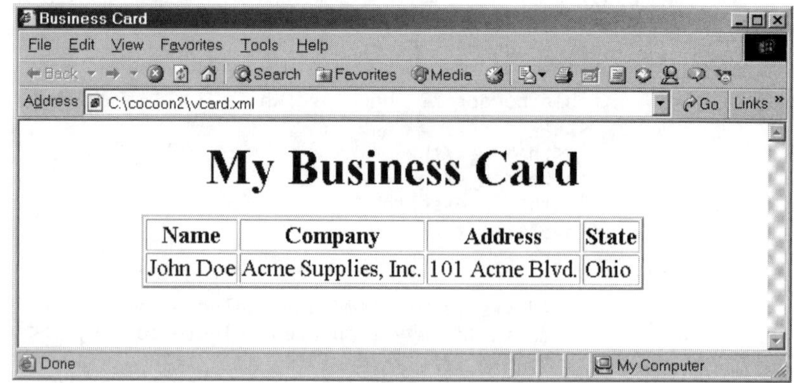

We will now use another stylesheet to present the same data contained in `vcard.xml` in another format.

There will be one line of code in `vcard.xml` that will be changed, and that is the stylesheet declaration. The code snippet below shows the new stylesheet invocation in `vcard.xml`:

```
<?xml:stylesheet type="text/xsl" href="vcard_two.xsl"?>
```

The stylesheet `vcard_two.xsl` will be used to format the data. Listing 3.10 shows the code for the stylesheet.

Listing 3.10 Another Stylesheet, *vcard_two.xsl*

```
<xsl:stylesheet xmlns:xsl="http://www.w3.org/1999/XSL/Transform" version="1.0"
   xmlns="http://www.w3.org/1999/xhtml">

<xsl:template match="vcard">
  <html>
    <body bgcolor="white">
      <center>
        <table border="5" bgcolor="pink">
       <h1><xsl:apply-templates select="name"/></h1>
          <br/>
       <h3><I><xsl:apply-templates select="company"/></I></h3>
       <br/>
       <xsl:apply-templates select="address"/>
       <br/>
       <xsl:apply-templates select="city"/>,
       <xsl:apply-templates select="state"/>
       <xsl:apply-templates select="zip"/>
       <br/>
        </table>
```

```
    </center>
     </body>
   </html>
</xsl:template>

<xsl:template match="vcard/name">
   <xsl:value-of select="text()"/>
</xsl:template>

<xsl:template match="vcard/company">
   <xsl:value-of select="text()"/>
</xsl:template>

<xsl:template match="vcard/address">
   <xsl:value-of select="text()"/>
</xsl:template>

<xsl:template match="vcard/city">
      <xsl:value-of select="text()"/>,
</xsl:template>

<xsl:template match="vcard/state">
      <xsl:value-of select="text()"/>
</xsl:template>

<xsl:template match="vcard/zip">
      <xsl:value-of select="text()"/>
</xsl:template>
</xsl:stylesheet>
```

The output after this stylesheet is applied is shown in Figure 3.4.

FIGURE 3.4: Output of `vcard.xml` styled with `vcard_two.xsl`

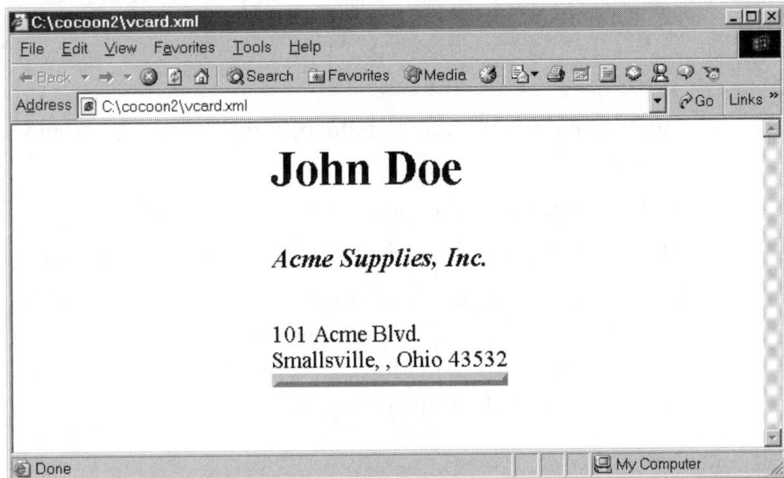

We have seen how one document with XML content can be presented in many different ways to the client browser using different stylesheets. Cocoon draws in these features of XSL to effectively separate content from presentation.

Extensible HTML (XHTML)

XHTML is not a new language and is a formal version of the existing HTML standard. It is a formal recommendation from the W3C. XHTML combines HTML and XML concepts. It came about as a solution to the problem of the number of bad HTML pages being created. XHTML uses all the tags formally defined in the HTML 4.01 specification and stipulates rules for their usage along the syntax of XML. XHTML is a markup language that contains data and can be used in existing browsers and other XML-enabled devices.

There are some differences between pages written exclusively to meet the HTML 4.01 standard and those written to be XHTML compliant. Some of these differences are as follows:

- XHTML elements must be properly nested.
- XHTML documents should be well formed.
- XHTML tags are all written in lowercase.
- XHTML elements should be explicitly closed with end tags.

Unlike pages written to the HTML 4.01 specification, XHTML pages, like XML documents, are case-sensitive. Additionally, all empty elements must be explicitly closed with an end tag. Empty elements can also use the shorthand notation used in XML documents—for example, `<some_element_name/>`. One important caveat is that empty elements in XHTML need an extra space between their name and the ending delimiter, as in `<some_element_name />`.

The following are some of the additional rules governing the use of XHTML:

- Attribute names are in lowercase.
- Attribute values are always quoted.
- Attribute minimization is forbidden, and all attributes should be written as name-value pairs.
- An `id` attribute is used in place of the `name` attribute.
- The XHTML Document Type Definition (DTD) defines the mandatory elements.

HTML 4.01 defined many minimized attributes and XHTML has rules to take care of those attributes. Table 3.1 gives a few examples of how minimized attributes should be represented when converting an HTML document to XHTML. It is not an exhaustive list and is provided just to highlight the technique.

TABLE 3.1: Converting HTML 4.01 Minimized Attributes to XHTML Attributes

HTML	XHTML
compact	compact="compact"
checked	checked="checked"
ismap	ismap="ismap"
nowrap	nowrap="nowrap"
noresize	noresize="noresize"

To be able to operate with older browsers, the XHTML elements should have both the `name` and the `id` attributes. There are several elements that are mandatory when developing XHTML pages. The XHTML document consists of the following three sections:

The DOCTYPE declaration Each XHTML document must begin with this declaration. It stipulates the version of HTML to which the document adheres.

The document Head This is the data contained within the `<head></head>` elements, such as the title, ownership, copyright, and keywords.

The document Body This is the data defined by the document and is between the `<body></body>` elements.

Every document must have a DOCTYPE declaration, which is not an XHTML element and does not have a closing tag. Within the main XHTML document, the HTML, Head, and Body tags are required and the title element should be present within the Head element.

XHTML 1.0

There are three variations of XHTML 1.0, as listed in this section. Each variation has its own DTD. The `<!DOCTYPE>` tag in the header of the XHTML document specifies which variant is being used, which is important for validating the document in the browser or toolkit.

XHTML 1.0 Strict This variant supports pages that have structural markup tags but are free of any layout tags. Web pages written in this variant use CSS for the presentation aspects of the document.

XHTML 1.0 Transitional This variant defines the rules for creation of web pages for use in older browsers that do not support stylesheets.

XHTML 1.0 Frameset This variant supports the use of HTML frames in web pages.

Listing 3.11 shows the DOCTYPE declaration for a web page, which contains only markup free of any presentation information. Formatting and styling of the content is achieved using CSS.

Listing 3.11 The DOCTYPE Declaration for XHTML 1.0 Strict

```
<!DOCTYPE htmlPUBLIC "-//W3C//DTD XHTML 1.0 Strict//EN"
  "http://www.w3.org/TR/xhtml1/DTD/xhtml1-strict.dtd">
```

Listing 3.12 shows the DOCTYPE declaration for a web page that needs to have presentation information together with data. This is very useful for defining general-purpose web pages to support older browsers that cannot take advantage of stylesheets.

Listing 3.12 The DOCTYPE Declaration for XHTML 1.0 Transitional

```
<!DOCTYPE html
PUBLIC "-//W3C//DTD XHTML 1.0 Transitional//EN"
"http://www.w3.org/TR/xhtml1/DTD/xhtml1-transitional.dtd">
```

Listing 3.13 shows the DOCTYPE declaration for web pages that utilize HTML frames for partitioning the browser display area into two or more frames.

Listing 3.13 The DOCTYPE Declaration for XHTML 1.0 Frameset

```
<!DOCTYPE html
PUBLIC "-//W3C//DTD XHTML 1.0 Frameset//EN"
"http://www.w3.org/TR/xhtml1/DTD/xhtml1-frameset.dtd">
```

Listing 3.14 shows the three sections of an XHTML document—the DOCTYPE tag, the Head, and the Body—as described in the previous section.

Listing 3.14 An XHTML Document

```
<!DOCTYPE html PUBLIC "-//W3C//DTD XHTML 1.0 Strict//EN"
    "http://www.w3.org/TR/xhtml1/DTD/xhtml1-strict.dtd">
<html>
  <head>
    <title>An Example XHTML Document</title>
  </head>
  <body>
    <h1>This is the body of the document</h1>
    <p/>

    <!-- document content goes here -->

  </body>
</html>
```

XHTML 1.1

A W3C recommendation in April 2001 defined the breakdown of the XHTML 1.0 standard into a standardized set of modules. These modules are abstract, but the specification also defines the DTDs to implement them. These definitions provide the guidelines to subset and extend the features of XHTML, which will help develop XHTML applications for various devices besides PC browsers.

XHTML modules support markup tags that will help the developer combine rich and diverse content such as vector graphics, multimedia, electronic commerce, and much more. It supports multiple platforms, such as mobile devices, and also defines rules for rendering content on the different platforms.

XHTML 1.1, also called module-based XHTML, is the formal recommendation of a DTD that implements the module-based framework per the modularization definition. XHTML 1.0 was constrained by the limitations of HTML 4. The XHTML 1.1 document provides the foundation for creating extended XHTML documents that do not have the same limitations of XHTML 1.0.

XHTML 1.1 is XHTML 1.0 Strict, redefined to include the modularization concepts. Support for frames is achieved by defining separate modules. Extended features can then be defined by creating new user-defined modules.

Additional Resources for Presentation Technologies

For thorough coverage of XHTML, see *Mastering XHTML, Premium Edition*, by Ed Tittel *et al.* (Sybex, 2002).

The W3C website at `www.w3.org` is the official repository of the documents on the CSS, XSL, and XHTML standards. Details of the FOP Project can be found at `http://xml.apache.org/fop/`. A compendium of links on XHTML and associated websites can be found at `www.xhtml.org`.

Summary

In this chapter we took a tour of all the essential technologies that give the Cocoon 2 architecture its strength and versatility. The chapter was subdivided along the lines of the functional areas of developing a web application in Cocoon. The section on developing content described the Avalon Project. Cocoon 2 does not attempt to reinvent the wheel but draws on the design strengths of this powerful Apache Project. The Avalon Project itself is made up of five subprojects:

- Framework
- Excalibur
- LogKit
- Phoenix
- Cornerstone
- Testlet

Several of the interfaces and classes from each of these five projects are used in the Cocoon Project. The most important ones from the Framework are the following:

- `ComponentManager`
- `Component`
- `Loggable`
- `AbstractLoggable`

The Poolable interface from the Excalibur subproject is implemented by many components, which facilitates their reuse by the framework.

The DOM API was the original specification for parsing XML documents. The parser converts the document into a treelike structure in memory, which can then be manipulated and modified into a result tree. The strength of the DOM API is that the document exists in memory in a tree structure and is available for reuse at a later point in the application. The drawback of the DOM API is the amount of resources needed for maintaining the tree in memory and the speed of processing the document.

The SAX API provides a mechanism for a more efficient and faster means of processing XML documents with much less demand on storage. The parser generates events for every stage of the processing of the document and these events are handled by callback methods in the application. The methods contain application code to consume the data and attributes contained in each element processed by the parser.

XML namespaces are used to qualify elements and attributes within an XML document and associate them with a particular application domain. Namespaces are implemented using named URI resources that are unique. There does not need to be any resource pointed to by the namespace.

The XSL working document is subdivided into the presentation aspects of XSL and XSLT, which define transforming XML documents. The section on Logic described how the XSLT language is used to transform documents from one XML language to another. The most common language for transformation is XHTML, which is used to format an XML document for display in a browser.

Cascading Style Sheets are a relatively simple way to add style and presentation to an XML document. The rules in the CSS control the display characteristics of the output data.

The second part of the XSL specification defines the formatting semantics using an XML vocabulary. The XSL Formatting Objects (XSL-FO) specification specifies low-level rules that allow applications to have precise control of output layout and format.

To round out the discussion on dynamic presentation and styles, we covered XHTML, which is a formal version of HTML 4.01 but follows an XML syntax. Some of the differences between HTML 4.01 and XHTML are as follows:

- XHTML elements must be properly nested.
- XHTML documents should be well formed.
- XHTML tags are all written in lowercase.
- XHTML elements should be explicitly closed with end tags.

XHTML documents must comply with the following rules:

- Attribute names are in lowercase.
- Attribute values are always quoted.
- Attribute minimization is forbidden, and all attributes should be written as name-value pairs.
- An `id` attribute is used in place of the `name` attribute.
- The XHTML Document Type Definition (DTD) defines the mandatory elements.

XHTML 1.0 was constrained by the limitations of HTML 4. The XHTML standard is continuously evolving and XHTML 1.1, also called module-based XHTML, is the formal recommendation of a DTD that implements the module-based framework per the modularization definition. The XHTML 1.1 document provides the foundation for creating extended XHTML documents that do not have the same limitations of XHTML 1.0.

Chapter 4

The Cocoon Serializers

- Simple Serializers
- More-Complex Serializers
- Output of MS Office Formats
- How to Build a Serializer
- Looking at Serializer Examples
- Internationalization

The Cocoon pipeline starts with generators and ends with serializers, so you might expect us to start explaining the details at the generator end. However, we think that the explanation of how Cocoon produces finished documents will make more sense if we look at the final step first.

In many ways, the serializer is the simplest part of the pipeline. Furthermore, the choice of serializer is generally directed by the kind of output you need, and doesn't involve a lot of decision making. Besides, this way we get to look at a lot of cool results first. Discussing the serializers also gives us a chance to further explain how Cocoon components make use of the Avalon Framework and other technologies discussed in Chapter 3, "A Review of the Essential Technologies."

Simple Serializers

It is a programming tradition to start with a simple "hello" example. The Cocoon distribution comes with variations on the "hello" example presented in several different formats. We are going to start with the HTML version. In a typical Tomcat installation, this example is accessed by the following URL:

```
http://localhost:8080/cocoon/hello.html
```

The following entry in the `sitemap.xmap` file defines the production pipeline:

```
<map:match pattern="hello.html">
  <map:generate src="docs/samples/hello-page.xml"/>
  <map:transform
    src="stylesheets/page/simple-page2html.xsl"/>
  <map:serialize type="html"/>
</map:match>
```

The source for the `generate` tag is the XML text shown in Listing 4.1. It has a built-in DTD and simple text content in a title and a paragraph. This page data will be used for all of the examples.

Listing 4.1 The Page Data

```
<?xml version="1.0"?>

<!DOCTYPE page [
 <!ELEMENT page (title?, content)>
 <!ELEMENT title (#PCDATA)>
 <!ELEMENT content (para+)>
 <!ELEMENT para (#PCDATA)>
]>
```

```
<page>
 <title>Hello</title>
 <content>
  <para>This is my first Cocoon page!</para>
 </content>
</page>
```

The source file is read by a SAX parser and turned into events that go to a transformation step. The source for the transform instructions is the XSL stylesheet shown in Listing 4.2. Note that some of the tags have been reformatted to fit this page.

Listing 4.2 **The *simple-page2html* Stylesheet**

```
<?xml version="1.0"?>

<xsl:stylesheet version="1.0"
   xmlns:xsl="http://www.w3.org/1999/XSL/Transform">
  <xsl:param name="view-source"/>
  <xsl:template match="page">
   <html>
    <head>
     <title>
      <xsl:value-of select="title"/>
     </title>
    </head>
    <body bgcolor="white" alink="red" link="blue"
       vlink="blue">
     <xsl:apply-templates/>
    </body>
   </html>
  </xsl:template>

  <xsl:template match="title">
   <h2 style="color: navy; text-align: center">
      <xsl:if test="not($view-source)">
         <xsl:apply-templates/>
      </xsl:if>
      <xsl:if test="$view-source">
      <A>
         <xsl:attribute name="HREF">
  ../view-source?filename=/<xsl:value-of select=
   "$view-source"/></xsl:attribute>
  <xsl:attribute name="TARGET">_blank</xsl:attribute>
         <xsl:apply-templates/>
      </A>
      </xsl:if>
   </h2>
  </xsl:template>
```

```
  <xsl:template match="para">
   <p align="left">
    <i><xsl:apply-templates/></i>
   </p>
  </xsl:template>
  <xsl:template match="@*|node()"
   priority="-2"><xsl:copy><xsl:apply-templates select="@*|node()"/></xsl:copy>
  </xsl:template>
  <xsl:template match="text()"
priority="-1"><xsl:value-of select="."/>
  </xsl:template>

</xsl:stylesheet>
```

The HTML Serializer

Passing over the details of operation of the `generate` and `transform` operations for the moment, we see that the map calls for "html" serialization. The text of the response returned to the browser is shown in Listing 4.3, with long lines reformatted to fit the page. Comparing the response text to the input XML file and the XSL stylesheet, we see that the serializer has added the `META` tag, while the stylesheet has added HTML tags with formatting information.

Listing 4.3 The HTML Response Text

```
<html>
<head>
<META http-equiv="Content-Type"
       content="text/html; charset=UTF-8">
<title>Hello</title>
</head>
<body vlink="blue" link="blue" alink="red"
      bgcolor="white">

<h2 style="color: navy; text-align: center">Hello</h2>

<content>

<p align="left">
<i>This is my first Cocoon page!</i>
</p>

</content>

</body>
</html>
```

This is, in fact, exactly the text we would get if we applied the `simple-page2html.xsl` stylesheet to the `hello-page.xml` data file in a command-line process. That is because the Xalan package contains a class specifically designed to output a character stream in HTML format. Cocoon also uses these built-in Xalan serializers for types "text" and "xml" indirectly through classes in the `org.apache.cocoon.serialization` package.

All of the serializers used in a Cocoon installation are defined in the sitemap file. Listing 4.4 shows the start of the `map:serializers` section and some of the `map:serializer` entries in the `sitemap.xmap` file. Note that the "html" type is declared as the default serializer and that the entry for this serializer names the `HTMLSerializer` class in the `org.apache.cocoon.serialization` package.

Listing 4.4 **Some Serializer Entries in the Sitemap**

```
<map:serializers default="html">
 <map:serializer name="links"
       logger="sitemap.serializer.links"
 src="org.apache.cocoon.serialization.LinkSerializer"/>

 <map:serializer name="xml"
   mime-type="text/xml"
  logger="sitemap.serializer.xml"
  src="org.apache.cocoon.serialization.XMLSerializer"
  pool-max="32" pool-min="16" pool-grow="4"/>

 <map:serializer name="html"
   mime-type="text/html"
   logger="sitemap.serializer.html"
 src="org.apache.cocoon.serialization.HTMLSerializer"/>
```

Although we have located `HTMLSerializer`, we are still far from the class that does the actual work. The parent class for `HTMLSerializer` is `AbstractTextSerializer`, which is also the parent for `XMLSerializer` and `TextSerializer`.

These three classes (HTML, XML, and Text-Serializer) make use of stock serialization capability built into the standard JAXP (Java API for XML Parsing) implementation of the XSLT specification. They simply create a SAX transformer instance that uses the stock "html" method to create the output stream.

Example Formatting for WML

One of the great attractions of the Cocoon approach is the possibility of using the same content for a variety of clients. These days there is a great deal of excitement about wireless applications such as cellular phones or PDAs that can access Internet content. One of the pioneering formats for this application is WML (Wireless Markup Language).

The same source XML as shown in Listing 4.1 can be served as a page formatted in WML by using different transformation and serialization steps. Here is the section of the `sitemap.xmap` file that defines the entry for `hello.wml`:

```
<map:match pattern="hello.wml">
  <map:generate src="docs/samples/hello-page.xml"/>
  <map:transform
     src="stylesheets/page/simple-page2wml.xsl"/>
  <map:serialize type="wml"/>
</map:match>
```

Listing 4.5 shows the stylesheet named in the `map:transform` tag. WML organizes content for the small displays characteristic of phones and PDAs in terms of "cards," and considerable embellishment of the input data is required.

Listing 4.5 The *simple-page2wml.xsl* Stylesheet for WML

```
<?xml version="1.0"?>
<xsl:stylesheet version="1.0"
  xmlns:xsl="http://www.w3.org/1999/XSL/Transform">
 <xsl:template match="page">
  <wml>
   <card id="index" title="{title}">
    <xsl:apply-templates select="content"/>
    <do type="accept" label="About">
     <go href="#about"/>
    </do>
   </card>

   <card id="about" title="About">
    <onevent type="ontimer">
     <prev/>
    </onevent>
    <timer value="25"/>
    <p align="center">
     <br/>
     <br/>
     <small>
      Copyright &#xA9; 2000<br/>
      Apache Software Foundation.<br/>
      All rights reserved.
     </small>
    </p>
   </card>
  </wml>
 </xsl:template>

 <xsl:template match="para">
  <p align="center">
```

```
    <xsl:apply-templates/>
   </p>
  </xsl:template>
 </xsl:stylesheet>
```

Because WML is completely compatible with XML standards, Cocoon can use the existing XMLSerializer class for this format. Here is the entry in the sitemap.xmap file for the "wml" serializer, with some lines reformatted to fit this page:

```
<map:serializer name="wml"
    mime-type="text/vnd.wap.wml"
    logger="sitemap.serializer.wml"
   src="org.apache.cocoon.serialization.XMLSerializer">
  <doctype-public>-//WAPFORUM//DTD WML 1.1//EN
  </doctype-public>
  <doctype-system>
    http://www.wapforum.org/DTD/wml_1.1.xml
  </doctype-system>
  <encoding>ASCII</encoding>
  <omit-xml-declaration>yes</omit-xml-declaration>
</map:serializer>
```

The XML elements inside the map:serializer element define parameters that are made available to the XMLSerializer object. Listing 4.6 shows the final output, with the long lines of the WML reformatted for easier understanding. Note that this final output is a mixture of elements from the original XML source, the stylesheet, and the serializer.

Listing 4.6 Output in WML Format

```
<!DOCTYPE wml PUBLIC "-//WAPFORUM//DTD WML 1.1//EN"
 "http://www.wapforum.org/DTD/wml_1.1.xml">
<wml>
<card title="Hello" id="index">
  <p align="center">This is my first Cocoon page!</p>
 <do label="About" type="accept">
 <go href="#about"/></do>
</card>
<card title="About"
  id="about">
 <onevent type="ontimer"><prev/>
 </onevent>
 <timer value="25"/><p align="center"><br/><br/><small>
      Copyright &#169; 2000<br/>
      Apache Software Foundation.<br/>
      All rights reserved.
     </small></p>
</card>
</wml>
```

Using the XMLSerializer

The `XMLSerializer` class is the simplest serializer because it outputs normal XML tags and text directly from the SAX events it receives from the pipeline. One use for the `XMLSerializer` is to assist with debugging other components because it outputs exactly the events that are sent to it. Simply change the `map:serialize` tag in the sitemap like this:

```
<map:serialize type="xml"/>
```

More-Complex Serializers

The serializers just discussed are able to work entirely in streaming fashion, because the order of output elements received from the transformation step is not changed by serialization. In contrast, some serializers are obliged to gather the entire document, or at least a substantial fraction of it, in memory before formatting the output.

The first example we look at creates documents in the Portable Document Format (PDF) created by Adobe Systems, Inc. The use of this format for documents accessed over the Internet is increasing because it gives better control of the final result than HTML. It is likely that you will find this output format extremely useful.

Creating a PDF Page Using FOP

FOP (Formatting Objects Processor) is an Apache organization project to create a rendering engine driven by XSL. The XSL-FO specifications outline how a stylesheet can create formatting objects that completely describe the desired appearance of a page.

NOTE The home websites for the Apache FOP project and the W3C specification are `http://xml.apache.org/fop/` and `www.w3.org/TR/2001/xsl`, respectively.

In its present state, the Apache FOP project version 0.20.3 is able to create output formats PDF, PCL, PS, SVG, XML (formatted as tree), Print, AWT, MIF, and TXT. This is not yet a complete implementation of the XSL-FO specification. The primary objective of the project is to deliver output complying with the March 1999 version 1.3 specification of the Portable Document Format as released by Adobe Systems.

In spite of the fact that FOP is very much a work in progress, the capabilities are good enough for use in the Cocoon system. Digging into the details of how FOP works is way beyond the scope of this book. The following entry from the `sitemap.xmap` file for the `hello.pdf` entry names the stylesheet and serializer to turn the now-familiar `hello-page.xml` source file into a PDF document.

```
<map:match pattern="hello.pdf">
  <map:generate src="docs/samples/hello-page.xml"/>
```

```
  <map:transform
        src="stylesheets/page/simple-page2fo.xsl"/>
  <map:serialize type="fo2pdf"/>
</map:match>
```

The `simple-page2fo.xsl` stylesheet, shown in Listing 4.7, inserts specialized `fo` tags into the basic document that describe the basic page layout in terms of page size and margins. In addition, it gives `fo` tags that are applied to the `title` and `para` elements in the `hello-page.xml` document.

Listing 4.7 The Stylesheet to Create an FOP-Compatible Document

```
<?xml version="1.0"?>
<xsl:stylesheet version="1.0"
  xmlns:xsl="http://www.w3.org/1999/XSL/Transform"
  xmlns:fo="http://www.w3.org/1999/XSL/Format">
 <xsl:template match="/">
  <fo:root
    xmlns:fo="http://www.w3.org/1999/XSL/Format">
   <fo:layout-master-set>
    <fo:simple-page-master master-name="page"
                  page-height="29.7cm"
                  page-width="21cm"
                  margin-top="1cm"
                  margin-bottom="2cm"
                  margin-left="2.5cm"
                  margin-right="2.5cm">
      <fo:region-before extent="3cm"/>
      <fo:region-body margin-top="3cm"/>
      <fo:region-after extent="1.5cm"/>
    </fo:simple-page-master>

   <fo:page-sequence-master master-name="all">
     <fo:repeatable-page-master-alternatives>
       <fo:conditional-page-master-reference
  master-reference="page" page-position="first"/>
     </fo:repeatable-page-master-alternatives>
   </fo:page-sequence-master>
   </fo:layout-master-set>

   <fo:page-sequence master-reference="all">
      <fo:static-content flow-name="xsl-region-after">
      <fo:block text-align="center"
          font-size="10pt"
          font-family="serif"
          line-height="14pt">page
        <fo:page-number/></fo:block>
      </fo:static-content>

     <fo:flow flow-name="xsl-region-body">
```

```
        <xsl:apply-templates/>
      </fo:flow>
    </fo:page-sequence>
  </fo:root>
</xsl:template>

<xsl:template match="title">
  <fo:block font-size="36pt"
     space-before.optimum="24pt"
     text-align="center">
    <xsl:apply-templates/>
  </fo:block>
</xsl:template>

<xsl:template match="para">
  <fo:block font-size="12pt"
     space-before.optimum="12pt"
     text-align="center">
    <xsl:apply-templates/></fo:block>
</xsl:template>
</xsl:stylesheet>
```

The following element from the `sitemap.xmap` file shows the serializer class that is used. Note that it includes the MIME type that will be sent with the resulting page.

```
<map:serializer name="fo2pdf"
  src="org.apache.cocoon.serialization.FOPSerializer"
  logger="sitemap.serializer.fo2pdf"
  mime-type="application/pdf"/>
```

Figure 4.1 shows the final product as served by Cocoon and viewed in an Adobe Acrobat Reader window.

FIGURE 4.1: The `hello-page` rendered as a PDF document

Output of PCL Format from FOP

PCL (Printer Control Language) is a pioneering effort by Hewlett-Packard to provide document formatting. It is supported by HP printers, and PCL-based printer drivers are available for many operating systems. In Cocoon 2.0.2, this is considered an optional serializer and is not well documented.

Output of RTF Format from FOP

Another possible output format from an FOP representation is Rich Text Format (RTF), a widely used alternative to Microsoft's proprietary DOC format that is usable with Microsoft Word and other word processors. As this is written, the capability for this output is not part of the standard Cocoon distribution but will be incorporated shortly.

NOTE Like many of the other Cocoon output formats, this development started independently but then found an obvious application in Cocoon. The original project website can be found at `www.jfor.org`.

Production of an RTF format document is very similar to production of the PDF format shown earlier in this chapter—it simply uses a different serializer for the final output. Here is the `sitemap.xmap` entry for creating a page in RTF format:

```
<map:match pattern="hello.rtf">
  <map:generate src="docs/samples/hello-page.xml"/>
  <map:transform
    src="stylesheets/page/simple-page2fo.xsl"/>
  <map:serialize type="fo2rtf"/>
</map:match>
```

The `fo2rtf` serializer is defined as using the `RTFSerializer` class in the `org.apache.cocoon.serialization` package.

Graphics Creation with SVG

SVG (Scalable Vector Graphics) is an XML-based markup language for creating two-dimensional graphics. The standard has been under development by a W3C working group since the first public draft in early 1999, and now has implementations in a variety of languages.

NOTE At present, SVG 1.0 is a W3C Recommendation, and work continues on version 1.1, which is nearing completion as of this writing. You can find the current documentation at `www.w3.org/TR/SVG`.

The SVG standard is based on three types of graphic objects: line paths, images, and text. These basic elements can be modified by a variety of special effects. However, SVG provides for much more than plain 2-D images and includes dynamic features, such as mouse events and animation.

The Cocoon example for SVG takes the same `hello-page.xml` source that our other examples have been drawn from and produces the image shown in Figure 4.2.

FIGURE 4.2: Presentation of the `hello-page` as an image

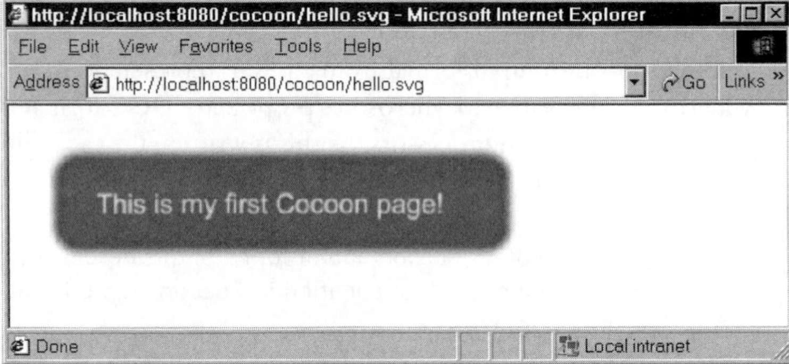

This amazing transformation is accomplished by the following sitemap entry:

```
<map:match pattern="hello.svg">
  <map:generate src="docs/samples/hello-page.xml"/>
  <map:transform
      src="stylesheets/page/simple-page2svg.xsl"/>
  <map:serialize type="svg2jpeg"/>
</map:match>
```

The stylesheet adds tags that define some SVG style information and tags that control the rendering of the title and para elements from `hello-page.xml`. Listing 4.8 shows the text of the stylesheet with some lines reformatted to fit the page.

Listing 4.8 The Stylesheet That Adds SVG Formatting to *hello-page.xml*

```
<?xml version="1.0"?>
<xsl:stylesheet version="1.0"
  xmlns:xsl="http://www.w3.org/1999/XSL/Transform">

 <xsl:template match="page">
  <svg width="450" height="160">
   <defs>
    <filter id="blur1">
      <feGaussianBlur stdDeviation="3"/></filter>
    <filter id="blur2">
      <feGaussianBlur stdDeviation="1"/></filter>
   </defs>
```

```
    <g title="this is a tooltip">
     <rect
       style="fill:#0086B3;stroke:#000000;
         stroke-width:4;filter:url(#blur1);"
       x="30" y="30" rx="20" ry="20"
       width="400" height="80"/>
     <xsl:apply-templates/>
    </g>
   </svg>
  </xsl:template>

  <xsl:template match="para">
   <text style="fill:#FFFFFF;font-size:24;
    font-family:TrebuchetMS-Bold;filter:url(#blur2);"
    x="65" y="80">
    <xsl:apply-templates/>
   </text>
  </xsl:template>
 </xsl:stylesheet>
```

The `svg2jpeg` serializer is defined as follows:

```
<map:serializer name="svg2jpeg"
  src="org.apache.cocoon.serialization.SVGSerializer"
  logger="sitemap.serializer.svg2jpeg"
  mime-type="image/jpeg"/>
```

The `SVGSerializer` class utilizes a rendering engine created by a project housed at the Apache organization known as Batik. The purpose of this project is to create a rendering engine capable of supporting all of the features of SVG 1.0—at present the static image creation works well and the dynamic features are under development.

NOTE For more information on the status of the Batik project, visit `http://xml.apache.org/batik`.

Output of MS Office Formats

The document formats used by Microsoft Office products are extremely widely used but are not easy to deal with in a Java program. Naturally the open-source community has responded to this challenge. Apache's Poor Obfuscation Implementation (POI) project seeks to provide pure Java tools for reading and writing MS Office data files, concentrating on the formats for documents and spreadsheets.

The POI project is undergoing rapid development so by the time this book sees print, there will undoubtedly be major improvements. The most advanced serializer from the POI project in Cocoon 2.0.2 is used for creating numeric documents in the Excel spreadsheet format. The POI project calls this the HSSF format for "Horrible Spread Sheet Format" and provides the `HSSFSerializer` class.

In the hypothetical sales example provided with Cocoon 2.0.2, the URL for the example is this:

```
http://localhost/cocoon202/samples/poi/hypothetical-sales.xls
```

The sitemap entry for the XLS serializer looks like this:

```
<map:serializer name="xls"
  src="org.apache.cocoon.serialization.HSSFSerializer"
  mime-type="application/vnd.ms-excel"/>
```

It is important to note that the MIME type controls the content-type header that the user's browser receives. If the browser recognizes that an application is available to display the format, the user will be presented with a dialog box giving a choice between opening the file immediately or saving the file. The pipeline to process this example looks like this:

```
<map:match pattern="*.xls">
   <map:generate src="content/static/{1}.xml"/>
   <map:serialize type="xls"/>
</map:match>
```

Because this is a static example, we can examine the XML used to generate the spreadsheet. The whole thing is too bulky to list, but the following excerpts are instructive. Entities such as the following determine the screen appearance and controls:

```
<gmr:Attributes>
  <gmr:Attribute>
     <gmr:name>WorkbookView::show_horizontal_scrollbar</gmr:name>
     <gmr:type>4</gmr:type>
     <gmr:value>TRUE</gmr:value>
  </gmr:Attribute>
```

Entries such as the following set the values contained in the spreadsheet cells:

```
<gmr:Cell Col="1" Row="0" ValueType="60">
   <gmr:Content>DOS</gmr:Content>
</gmr:Cell>
<gmr:Cell Col="2" Row="0" ValueType="60">
   <gmr:Content>Linux</gmr:Content>
</gmr:Cell>
<gmr:Cell Col="3" Row="0" ValueType="60">
   <gmr:Content>SCO</gmr:Content>
</gmr:Cell>
<gmr:Cell Col="0" Row="1" ValueType="60">
   <gmr:Content>January</gmr:Content>
</gmr:Cell>
```

```
<gmr:Cell Col="1" Row="1" ValueType="30">
   <gmr:Content>1000</gmr:Content>
</gmr:Cell>
```

The HSSFSerializer understands this notation and formats the binary data representation used by the Excel program. The result is a data stream correctly formatted for reading by Excel. The result as viewed in Excel is shown in Figure 4.3.

As this is written, the POI project is about to release version 1.5, which is expected to include more of Cocoon serializer documentation. If you want to keep up with the state of the POI project, visit the following website:

```
http://jakarta.apache.org/poi/index.html
```

FIGURE 4.3: Rendering of the spreadsheet example

File Edit View Insert Format Tools Data Window Help

B2 1000

	A	B	C	D	E
1		DOS	Linux	SCO	
2	January	1000	900	500	
3	February	900	2500	300	
4	March	800	4100	100	
5	April	700	5700	-100	
6	May	600	7300	-300	
7	June	500	8900	-500	
8	July	400	10500	-700	
9	August	300	12100	-900	
10	September	200	13700	-1100	
11	October	100	15300	-1300	
12	November	0	16900	-1500	
13	December	-100	18500	-1700	
14					
15	Totals:				
16					

Sheet 0

How to Build a Serializer

Fortunately for anyone who might want to build a custom serializer, Cocoon is built on publicly available source code that you can study. Unfortunately, the code that comes in the Cocoon package is only a small part of the total upon which Cocoon depends.

The Cocoon serializers and other classes inherit from a complex hierarchy of abstract classes and interfaces in a very large number of packages. We introduced you to some of these technologies in Chapter 3. In the following section, we provide a quick survey of where these classes and interfaces are used in serializers. Hopefully this material will help you understand the functionality of the Cocoon serializers without having to chase down all of the scattered documentation.

The Avalon Project

In early 1999, programmers working on various Java applications under the Apache organization recognized that certain design patterns they were using were suitable for abstraction into a framework that could be reused for server applications in general. The project to organize these support classes is called Avalon Apache Server Framework. As discussed in Chapter 3, the home website for this project is this:

`http://jakarta.apache.org/avalon/`

The Avalon project attempts to bring together a number of best practice design patterns for use in other Apache Java server projects such as Cocoon. The largest and most mature subproject is known as the Avalon Framework.

The Avalon Framework

The Framework project documentation uses the term *component* to describe the parts of an application. This is not to be confused with other uses of *component* in other Java APIs. The capabilities of a component are defined by the interfaces it implements.

The Framework consists mostly of abstract classes and interfaces in the `org.apache.avalon` package and sub-packages. Here are some that you are likely to run into:

`Component` This interface is used to tag classes that can be managed in the Avalon Framework.

`Composable` A class implementing this interface can connect to components using a component manager and the idea of component "roles."

`AbstractLoggable` An abstract utility class supporting the construction of logging components that use the `org.apache.log` package. Cocoon serializers all are based on `AbstractLoggable`.

`Loggable` This interface provides a method to accept a logger.

`Configuration` This interface provides support for arbitrary configuration data that can be expressed as a single XML node. Support for XML namespaces is provided.

`Configurable` This interface provides the `configure` method used to pass a Configuration object to a component.

The Avalon Excalibur Project

The Excalibur project contains a number of components and utility classes mostly related to management of resources. A typical use would be management of a pool of JDBC connections.

`Pool` This interface gives two methods for the operation of a resource pool.

`Poolable` This interface labels a component as suitable for being held in a resource pool.

`Recyclable` This interface provides the `recycle` method, which allows a component to be reused by reinitializing internal variables. The purpose of pooling and recycling is to improve execution speed by reducing the number of objects created.

NOTE A number of utilities are under development as part of the Excalibur project. You can find the current code and documentation at this site: `http://jakarta.apache.org/avalon/excalibur/`.

The SAX Interface Hierarchy

You will recall from Chapter 3 that the `org.xml.sax.ContentHandler` interface defines all of the core methods that receive notification of SAX events. In addition to this interface, the `LexicalHandler` interface in the `org.xml.sax.ext` package defines events that are not required by the SAX2 standard but are made use of by Cocoon to obtain information about an XML document. Both of these interfaces are combined in the `XMLConsumer` interface described in the following section.

`ContentHandler` This interface provides the core SAX event handling methods such as `startDocument`, `startElement`, and `characters`.

`LexicalHandler` This interface provides additional XML document information event handling methods such as `startCDATA` and `comment`.

The *org.apache.cocoon.xml* Package

In the `org.apache.cocoon.xml` package we find the following interfaces and classes. The `XMLConsumer` interface is the one used in serializers.

`XMLConsumer` This interface combines the `ContentHandler` and `LexicalHandler` interfaces from the `org.xml.sax` and `org.xml.sax.ext` packages, respectively. It exists to simplify declaration of further classes. All serializers implement this interface, either directly or indirectly, so that they can receive SAX events.

`XMLProducer` The interface is basically used as a tag to indicate a class that produces XML events. It defines the `setConsumer` method that is used to attach an `XMLConsumer` to receive the events.

XMLPipe This interface combines XMLConsumer and XMLProducer interfaces. Any object implementing XMLPipe will be able to receive and pass on SAX parsing events.

AbstractXMLProducer This is an abstract class that provides default implementations for the XMLProducer methods.

AbstractXMLPipe This is an abstract class that extends AbstractXMLProducer. It implements a number of interfaces including XMLPipe.

The *org.apache.cocoon.serialization* Package

Here we find the stock serializer classes provided with Cocoon.

AbstractSerializer This is an abstract class that extends the basic AbstractXMLPipe class (in the org.apache.cocoon.xml package) and implements the Serializer interface.

AbstractTextSerializer This abstract class is the immediate parent of the HTMLSerializer, TextSerializer, and XMLSerializer classes used in the Cocoon samples we looked at earlier.

FOPSerializer This is the class used in the PDF and SVG examples to create an FOP object.

Looking at Serializer Examples

Now let's look at the code for one of the Cocoon serializers in the light of the interfaces and classes just discussed. The full source is way too bulky to reproduce here, but is provided with the Cocoon distribution. The class we will look at is HTMLSerializer in the org.apache.cocoon.serialization package.

HTMLSerializer extends the AbstractTextSerializer abstract class and by virtue of inheritance, implements all of the following interfaces:

Cacheable Permits Cocoon to cache instances of the object. This interface provides for a method to generate a unique key that serves as a signature for the instance.

Component Labels the class as manageable by the Avalon Framework.

Configurable Means that an instance can be configured by XML data.

ContentHandler Provides the methods for getting SAX events.

LexicalHandler Provides the methods for getting document events.

Loggable Provides a method for accepting a logger.

Poolable This interface indicates that instances may be managed by a resource pool.

`Recyclable` Provides the `recycle` method that permits reuse of the object.

`Serializer` Labels the component as implementing `XMLConsumer` and `SitemapOutputComponent`.

`SitemapOutputComponent` Provides methods for setting the output stream and MIME type.

`XMLConsumer` Contains the interfaces `ContentHandler` and `LexicalHandler`.

`XMLPipe` Labels the component as containing both `XMLConsumer` and `XMLProducer` interfaces. This is a capability not used in the `HTMLSerializer` class.

`XMLProducer` Labels the component as capable of producing SAX events and provides a method to attach an `XMLConsumer`. This is also a capability not used in the `HTMLSerializer` class.

Internationalization

Because both Java and XML were designed from the start to support Unicode, Cocoon is theoretically well positioned to create output in any Unicode language. Although support for internationalization is distributed throughout Cocoon components, not just serializers, this seems like a good place to bring up the major points.

Language Encoding in Java

Character-based files are read and written in Java with classes that extend the `java.io.Reader` and `java.io.Writer` classes, respectively. Some of these classes assume a default encoding based on the default locale and encoding of the user's operating system. Other classes provide for specifying an encoding when the reader or writer is constructed.

Java uses the `java.util.Locale` class to characterize the details of a particular language and region. Locales are constructed using standard encoding for languages and countries. Encoding is also important in the utility methods of the `java.text` package. For example, formatting of floating-point numbers in the `DecimalFormat` class can be set according to locale.

Defining Serializer Encoding

The encoding used by serializers that write characters can be controlled by the sitemap entry that defines a serializer, as in this example:

```
<map:serializer name="html"   mime-type="text/html"
       logger="sitemap.serializer.html"
       src="org.apache.cocoon.serialization.HTMLSerializer">
    <encoding>iso-8859-1</encoding>
</map:serializer>
```

Alternately, you can override that encoding with an encoding tag inside a pipeline entry, as in this example:

```
<map:serialize type="html">
  <encoding>ISO-8859-1</encoding>
</map:serialize>
```

Language Resource Support

Cocoon provides a rudimentary system for dynamic translation with classes in the `org.apache.cocoon.i18n` package. The I18nTransformer can be set up with a catalog of simple message substitutions, which are read from an XML formatted file.

This system can only translate documents that have XML elements formatted with a special `i18n` tag like this:

```
<i18n:text>one</i18n:text>
```

If the message dictionary contains an entry like this:

```
<message key="one">eins</message>
```

The i18nTransformer can perform the substitution.

Summary

Serializers are the final step in the production of output by a Cocoon pipeline. By separating final output from the generation and transformation steps, Cocoon achieves tremendous flexibility. This is particularly powerful when using the document description capabilities of the XSL-FO approach, in which a document encoded as formatting object XML can be rendered in several different formats.

Serialization to the PDF format is a common use of the XSL-FO approach, particularly for cases in which the author needs more control over presentation than is provided by HTML. The availability of free viewers for most operating systems has made this format very popular.

Serializers that can write the complex formats used by Microsoft Office applications such as the Excel spreadsheet make it possible for Cocoon applications to dynamically create documents in these common formats.

The simplest serialization tasks are writing plain text, HTML, WML, or XML where the output elements correspond closely to the SAX events produced by a pipeline. For these cases Cocoon relies on serializers built into the Xalan XSLT library.

Chapter 5

Logic Control: The Sitemap

- Sitemap Design Principles
- The Contents of a Sitemap
- Sitemap Variables
- Subsitemap Operation
- The Components in Detail
- Component Management
- Pipelines

Cocoon provides two main concepts for control: the sitemap and Extensible Server Pages (XSP). Sitemap actions have the advantage of completely separating logic from content, whereas XSP suffers from the same problem as JSP—mixing logic and content in the same package. This chapter discusses how a sitemap is used to structure and control a Cocoon 2 web-publishing system.

Sitemap Design Principles

One of the major changes between Cocoon 1 and Cocoon 2 is the introduction of the sitemap to control the components and the logic that connects them. The purpose of the sitemap is to allow nonprogrammers to create websites and web applications by merging XML documents with logic components.

It is interesting to look at the design principles adopted by the authors as described in the Cocoon documentation:

- The sitemap must provide for every possible URI mapping needed by a site.
- The format must be compact but expressive: The idea being that a sitemap should be easy to read but not excessively verbose.
- The architecture must be scalable from the smallest site to large and complex sites.
- Creating a sitemap must not require any special tools for authoring but the format must be adaptable to tool creation.
- The architecture must support both dynamic operation online and offline page generation in a batch mode.
- The sitemap must provide for basic web-serving functions such as redirection, error pages, and authorization.
- The format must be extensible.
- The architecture must be capable of incorporating information from request parameters, environment variables, Servlet parameters, and the application environment.
- The format must provide for "semantic resources" to support future development of the "semantic Web."

Obviously, choosing XML for the sitemap format automatically takes care of several of these design goals. Those of you who have wrestled with the arcane formats and multiple files required to create websites under earlier systems will particularly appreciate this.

The primary sitemap file for a Cocoon-based web application is typically named `sitemap.xmap` and is located in the Cocoon root directory by default. However, configuration options for Cocoon are defined in a file named `cocoon.xconf`, which is located in the `WEB-INF` directory and defines various resources and control parameters. These configuration options include a `<sitemap/>` element such as the following, which can be used to place the `sitemap.xml` file anywhere:

```
<sitemap file="sitemap.xmap"
  reload-method="asynchron"
  check-reload="yes"
  logger="sitemap"/>
```

The `reload-method` attribute can have the values `synchron` or `asynchron`. This attribute controls what happens when Cocoon detects that the sitemap file has changed. Cocoon checks the timestamp on the sitemap file only if `check-reload` has the value `yes` and a request is received. What happens when a change is detected depends on the `reload-method`, as follows:

`synchron` The sitemap is regenerated while the request is waiting so the request is served with the new sitemap.

`asynchron` A background thread is started to regenerate the sitemap and the incoming request is served with the old sitemap. When the background thread has created the new sitemap, it replaces the current one.

During development, you should use the `synchron` method so that changes to the sitemap will show up in the first request.

The Contents of a Sitemap

A sitemap must be valid XML but does not cite a DTD. Here is the bare skeleton of a sitemap file showing all possible first-level tags:

```
<?xml version="1.0"?>
 <map:sitemap xmlns:map="http://apache.org/cocoon/sitemap/1.0">
   <map:components/>
   <map:views/>
   <map:resources/>
   <map:action-sets/>
   <map:pipelines/>
 </map:sitemap>
```

Each of these first-level tags encloses sets of tags that define various parts of the total system. Much of this chapter will be devoted to these tags, which can be outlined as follows:

`<map:components/>` Here we find the definitions of pipeline components that will be managed by the Avalon framework. Tags within each definition provide configuration data for each component.

<map:views/> This tag contains components that can define different views of the same resource. Having a view for a particular processing sequence allows a shorthand notation.

<map:resources/> This tag contains `<map:resource/>` tags that define reusable sequences.

<map:action-sets/> An action set groups `<map:act/>` tags for convenience in specifying common actions.

<map:pipelines/> The real work of the sitemap is accomplished in pipelines. The elements here make use of the various objects defined in the other elements.

Sitemap Variables

During pipeline operation you have access to data from a variety of sources, including parameters set when components are defined, parameters from the servlet context, and parameters from the request being processed. Some components can modify the available data when they operate.

You have already seen examples of sitemap variables designated by `{}` (curly braces) in sitemap expressions such as the following:

```
<map:match pattern="myApplication/*.html">
  <map:generate src="myApplication/{1}.xml"/>
  <map:serialize type="html"/>
</map:match>
```

In this example, the matcher extracts a variable that you can later refer to using the `"{1}"` nomenclature. Nesting of pipeline elements modifies the way you refer to variables created by a match. For each level of nesting, you must use `"../"` to refer to a variable of a previous level. For example:

```
<map:match pattern="myApplication/*.html">
  <map:generate type="sometype">
    <parameter name="filename" value="{../1}"/>
  </map:generate>
  <map:serialize type="html"/>
</map:match>
```

You can think of the nesting of elements as creating a *stack* of variables. For each level you want to go down in a stack, you apply the `"../"` nomenclature. In the preceding example, the `map:generate` element is nested inside the `map:match` element so the `"{../1}"` value will be the text that matches the `"*"` in the `map:match` element.

Subsitemap Operation

A subdirectory of the Cocoon application root can have its own sitemap file. This file will be compiled (or interpreted) as an extension of the main sitemap, but in order to transfer control to pipelines in the subsitemap, a pipeline in the main sitemap must use the `<map:mount/>` element. (See the "Pipeline Elements" section later in this chapter for a discussion of the operation of this tag.)

All component definitions are inherited in subsitemaps.

Compiled Versus Interpreted Sitemaps

A sitemap can either be compiled or interpreted. In the initial releases of Cocoon 2, all sitemap files were translated into a Java class and then compiled and executed to handle requests. The source file is named `sitemap_xmap.java` and makes interesting reading. You can find the source code under the `work` directory.

The primary sitemap class is placed in the `org.apache.cocoon.www` package and subsitemaps are distinguished by adding to the package name so that it reflects the sitemap's location.

Even the simplest sitemap creates several hundred lines of Java code. Although creating and compiling is relatively fast, it does introduce a delay whenever the sitemap is changed. Furthermore, because there is a fundamental limitation on the size of a single Java method, it is possible for you to create a sitemap that could not be compiled.

As of this writing, Cocoon developers are working on an interpreted alternative to the compiled sitemap. This would work from a DOM in memory and would have several advantages. Response to changes in the sitemap structure could be practically instantaneous, the sitemap size limitations would be removed, and content management applications could work directly with the DOM.

The Components in Detail

Components are entities that can be created beforehand and applied to a request as required by a pipeline. Components are managed by the Avalon framework, which provides logging and caching services. There are a lot of details to cover here, so let's get started.

Here are the elements that can be found inside the `<map:components/>` tag of a sitemap:

`<map:actions/>` Actions provide for the manipulation of runtime parameters and are typically used for forms processing and dynamic navigation.

`<map:generators/>` A generator creates a series of SAX events to be processed by the pipeline. In the simplest case, this can be done by reading and parsing an XML document file.

`<map:readers/>` A reader can be used when serving content is read or generated outside Cocoon. It improves response by providing for caching and not going through SAX event processing.

<map:serializers/> A serializer receives SAX events from the pipeline and produces an output stream.

<map:transformers/> A transformer receives SAX events and does a transformation (for example, by applying an XSLT stylesheet).

<map:matchers/> A matcher examines the environment of a request for a match to a specified pattern, typically a URI. As the first element in a pipeline, it is used to determine if that pipeline responds to a particular request. Strings extracted by a matcher are available later in the pipeline using the `"{n}"` notation.

<map:selectors/> A selector is similar to a matcher but is more flexible. Where a matcher just decides whether or not a pipeline is executed, a selector can apply more complex control.

Component Management

Before looking at actual components, we need to point out the important distinction between the configuration data a component object gets when it is created, and the data it gets when it participates in a pipeline when a request is handled. Because some of the names of parameters are very similar, distinguishing between creation time and request handling time can get tricky. Also, in some cases, a parameter set at creation time can be replaced by one added during request handling.

The entry a component has in the `<map:components/>` area of a sitemap controls the configuration data it gets when the object is created. All components get certain required attributes in the defining tag, and some take additional elements.

Required attributes are `name` and `src`, where the `name` attribute defines how the component will be referred to in the sitemap and `src` designates the Java class to be used. A `logger` attribute is frequently specified; this gives the name to be used in log messages from this component.

Additional parameters can be provided in elements contained in the definition tag. For example, in the following, parameters named `driver` and `base` are defined.

```
<map:generator name="xmldb"
  src="org.apache.cocoon.generation.XMLDBGenerator"
  logger="sitemap.generator.xmldb">
  <driver>org.dbxml.client.xmldb.DatabaseImpl</driver>
  <base>xmldb:dbxml:///db/</base>
</map:generator>
```

In a pipeline, the component known as `"xmldb"` will be activated in a `<map:generate/>` tag that has an attribute named `src` as shown in the following. Note this `src` attribute provides pipeline-specific information and has an entirely different function from the `src` attribute in the `<map:generator/>` tag.

```
<map:match pattern="xmldb-generator/db/**">
  <map:generate type="xmldb" src="/{1}"/>
  <map:serialize type="xml"/>
</map:match>
```

Now that you are sufficiently confused about that, let's look at the members of `<map:components/>` in detail.

Actions

The standard action classes are defined in the `org.apache.cocoon.acting` package. This package includes the `Action` interface, which must be implemented by an action component. This interface defines the `act` method, which manipulates data from pipeline environment parameters and creates a `Map` object as a return value. The `act` method is defined as follows:

```
java.util.Map act(
 org.apache.cocoon.environment.Redirector redirector,
 org.apache.cocoon.environment.SourceResolver resolver,
 java.util.Map objectModel,
 java.lang.String source,
 org.apache.avalon.framework.parameters.Parameters par
)
```

When a `<map:act/>` is encountered in a pipeline during request handling, the calling parameters are used as follows:

`redirector` A `Redirector` provides for redirecting a request to another page if necessary.

`resolver` A `SourceResolver` provides the `resolve` method, which returns a `Source` object from which data can be read. The `Source` class is one of the general-purpose helper classes defined in the `org.apache.cocooon.environment` package. Typically this is used to read from a file or URL, but it can also address a pipeline.

`objectModel` This is a standard `Map` from the `java.util` package that is used to provide access to a variety of parameters associated with a particular request. For example, in the `RequestParamAction` action, the `objectModel` carries a reference to a request object that in turn provides access to the request parameters as located by the Servlet container.

`source` Arbitrary text data.

`par` `Parameters` is a class provided in the Avalon framework. It provides parameters from `<map:parameter/>` tags inside a `<map:act/>` tag in a pipeline.

For example, the RequestParamAction class can return a Map with all of the request parameters. Recall that java.util.Map is an interface in the Java Collections API, defining methods that let you save and retrieve an arbitrary object by name.

Configuration of Actions

Actions are defined in the <map:actions/> section of the <map:components/> tag. Actions are executed when a pipeline is set up to handle a response and execute arbitrarily complex code which can modify the request environment. Each action is set up by a <map:action/> tag, which is defined entirely by the attributes name, logger, and src, where src gives the name of the class that executes the action. Here is an example from the Cocoon sitemap:

```
<map:action name="request"
 logger="sitemap.action.request"
 src="org.apache.cocoon.acting.RequestParamAction"/>
```

During pipeline processing, actions are called by name in a <map:act/> tag. An action has a limited ability to control pipeline flow. If the act method returns a *null* value, all tags inside a <map:act>...</map:act> element are not executed. In the following example, the <map:parameter/> tag tells the action to extract all of the request parameters to the returned Map.

```
<map:act type="request" src="some text" >
  <map:parameter name="parameters" value="true"/>
  <map:generate src="some.xml" />
</map:act>
```

You can get an idea about the kinds of things actions are used for from the names of the classes in the org.apache.cocoon.acting package. Here is a small sample: DatabaseAddAction, DatabaseAuthenticationAction, DatabaseDeleteAction, FormValidatorAction, ResourceExistsAction, ScriptAction, ServerPagesAction, SessionIsValidAction, and SessionStateAction.

Generators

Generators are responsible for creating the SAX events that start the pipeline process. Standard Cocoon generators are in the org.apache.cocoon.generation package. Essential to understanding generator operation are the interfaces implemented by generators—XMLProducer, Generator, Loggable, Recyclable, and Composable.

The XMLProducer interface in the org.apache.cocoon.xml package defines the setConsumer method, which is used to attach the object that performs the next step in the pipeline.

```
void setConsumer(XMLConsumer consumer)
```

The `Generator` interface in the `org.apache.cocoon.generation` package defines the `generate` method as follows:

```
void generate()
 throws IOException, SAXException, ProcessingException
```

The `org.apache.avalon.framework.logger` package provides the `Loggable` interface that defines the `setLogger` method to attach a Logger to the generator.

```
void setLogger(org.apache.log.Logger logger)
```

The `org.apache.avalon.excalibur.pool` package provides the `Recyclable` interface, which defines the `recycle` method. A call to recycle causes an object to release all variables related to a particular response so that the object may be reused.

```
public void recycle()
```

The `org.apache.avalon.framework.component` package provides the `Composable` interface. A class implementing `Composable` can locate and use `Component` (in the Avalon framework sense) objects according to the role a component fills. The `compose` method required by `Composable` attaches a `ComponentManager` that can perform this locating function.

```
void compose(ComponentManager componentManager)
```

Generator Attributes

A `<map:generator/>` tag has the following required attributes:

name Used in the sitemap to refer to this generator.

logger The name of a class implementing the `Logger` interface to be used for logging messages from the generator.

src The name of the class for this generator.

Optional attributes include:

label Use of this attribute is deprecated.

pool-max, pool-min, pool-grow These parameters affect object pooling.

Here is the sitemap code that sets up the file generator, usually the default and the most common generator:

```
<map:generator name="file"
  logger="sitemap.generator.file"
  label="content,data"
  src="org.apache.cocoon.generation.FileGenerator"
  pool-max="32" pool-min="16" pool-grow="4"/>
```

Additional configuration data can be supplied in a generator definition by included elements, as shown in this example:

```
<map:generator name="xmldb"
  src="org.apache.cocoon.generation.XMLDBGenerator"
  logger="sitemap.generator.xmldb">
    <driver>org.dbxml.client.xmldb.DatabaseImpl
    </driver>
    <base>xmldb:dbxml:///db/</base>
</map:generator>
```

Some Example Generators

Table 5.1 shows some of the generators used in a typical sitemap. These are all classes in the `org.apache.cocoon.generation` package. This is not a complete listing because developers create new generators all the time.

TABLE 5.1: Typical Generator Names and Classes

Name	Class Name	Function
`directory`	`DirectoryGenerator`	Generates the SAX event sequence to encode a directory hierarchy. The depth of the hierarchy and date formatting in the output can be configured.
`file`	`FileGenerator`	Reads from an XML formatted file or a URI. This is typically the default generator.
`html`	`HTMLGenerator`	Reads an HTML document, converting tags to XHTML using the `jtidy` utility.
`imagedirectory`	`ImageDirectoryGenerator`	Similar to `DirectoryGenerator` except it adds image size information.
`jsp`	`JspGenerator`	Executes a JSP, passing the request and converting the output to SAX events.
`request`	`RequestGenerator`	Converts the header and parameter data in a request to SAX events.
`script`	`ScriptGenerator`	Provides for executing arbitrary scripting languages using IBM's BSF framework.
`status`	`StatusGenerator`	Generates the SAX event sequence to represent the current state of the Cocoon engine.
`stream`	`StreamGenerator`	Handles an HTTP POST request, parsing the content of the request as an `InputStream`.
`velocity`	`VelocityGenerator`	Generates SAX events from a Velocity template.
`xmldb`	`XMLDBGenerator`	Generates SAX events from an XML:DB-compliant database such as Xindice.
`xmldbcollection`	`XMLDBCollectionGenerator`	Generates SAX events to show the structure of a collection of XML:DB databases.

Generating the Generators

It is interesting to note where some of these generators originated. A number of open-source projects, both those by the Apache organization and others, have found that their technology is easily integrated with Cocoon, thus creating an easy road to web publishing. Two examples are Velocity and Xindice.

Velocity is a general-purpose Java-based template engine suitable for generating a variety of formats, but it is frequently used as an alternative to JSP. See the following website for details:

```
http://jakarta.apache.org/velocity/index.html
```

Xindice is the continuation of the project that used to be called the dbXML Core. This implements a proposed standard referred to as XML:DB. The dbXML source code was donated to the Apache Software Foundation in December 2001. Find details on Xindice at the following URL:

```
http://xml.apache.org/xindice
```

The XML:DB initiative has a website at this URL:

```
www.xmldb.org
```

Readers

Readers exist to efficiently produce output streams from resources that do not need complex processing. A `<map:reader/>` tag has the attributes `name`, `logger`, and `src`, where `src` points to a class, as in this example:

```
<map:reader name="resource"
   logger="sitemap.reader.resource"
    src="org.apache.cocoon.reading.ResourceReader"/>
<map:reader name="jsp"
   logger="sitemap.reader.jsp"
   src="org.apache.cocoon.reading.JSPReader"/>
```

When used in a pipeline, the `resource` reader is activated by a `<map:read/>` tag, which uses attributes giving a string description to locate a source and a mime-type to be used in the response headers. Here is an example of a reader being used to serve image files, as used in Cocoon's root sitemap pipeline:

```
<map:match pattern="sites/images/*.gif">
  <map:read
    src="resources/images/{1}.gif"
    mime-type="image/gif"/>
</map:match>
```

Another reader provided in the Cocoon distribution is the JSPReader. When activated in the pipeline, this reader calls a JSP designated by the src attribute, passing the request and echoing the response. By using this reader, an application previously using JSP can be ported to work under the Cocoon environment using a pipeline element like this:

```
<map:match pattern="*.jsp">
  <map:read
      type="jsp"
      src="{1}.jsp"
      mime-type="text/html" />
</map:match>
```

Note the distinction between this reader and the JspGenerator. The generator creates SAX events that can be modified by further pipeline processing, whereas the JSPReader simply transmits the JSP output stream.

Serializers

Serializers are typically the final step in the pipeline process. In online operation of Cocoon, they produce the final output that is sent to a user's browser. In offline operation, they produce the output that goes to a file.

A serializer is defined in a <map:serializer/> element inside the <map:serializers/> section of the <map:components/> in a sitemap. A serializer always has a name, logger, and src attributes, and may specify a mime-type attribute. The mime-type attribute is used to ensure that the response headers are compatible with the data type. Typically the default serializer is named html and is defined like this:

```
<map:serializer name="html"
   mime-type="text/html"
   logger="sitemap.serializer.html"
   src="org.apache.cocoon.serialization.HTMLSerializer"
/>
```

Table 5.2 shows some of the characteristics of the commonly used serializers, including the default html serializer.

TABLE 5.2: Commonly Used Serializers

Name	Class	mime-type
html	HTMLSerializer	text/html
text	TextSerializer	text/text
wml	XMLSerializer	text/vnd.wap.wml
xml	XMLSerializer	text/xml

Continued on next page

TABLE 5.2 CONTINUED: Commonly Used Serializers

Name	Class	mime-type
svg2jpeg	SVGSerializer	image/jpeg
svg2png	SVGSerializer	image/png
svgxml	XMLSerializer	image/svg-xml
fo2pdf	FOPSerializer	application/pdf
fo2ps	FOPSerializer	application/postscript
fo2pcl	FOPSerializer	application/vnd.hp-PCL
vrml	XMLSerializer	model/vrml

When called in a pipeline, the `html` serializer can be passed a status code that is used in the HTML headers. You can see this in operation in the discussion of pipeline error handling later in the chapter.

Transformers

As the middle component of a pipeline, transformers receive SAX events, perform some transformation, and then pass events to the next stage. The standard transformer classes are found in the `org.apache.cocoon.transformation` package. The essential interface implemented by a transformer is `Transformer` in that package. This interface combines `XMLPipe` and `SitemapModelComponent` interfaces.

The `XMLPipe` interface provides the methods for attaching a SAX event producer and a consumer to the transformer. The `SitemapModelComponent` interface makes a transformer manageable by the Avalon framework. Table 5.3 summarizes the main transformers supplied with Cocoon.

TABLE 5.3: Summary of Transformer Components

Name	Class	Function
cinclude	CincludeTransformer	Includes XML from a separate source.
extractor	FragmentExtractorTransformer	Replaces selected content with a link; typically used to remove SVG specifications from a stylesheet and replace with a link.
filter	FilterTransformer	Restricts the elements it passes according to parameters.
i18n	I18nTransformer	Provides for replaceable text controlled by the request locale. Text is drawn from a message catalog.

Continued on next page

TABLE 5.3 CONTINUED: Summary of Transformer Components

Name	Class	Function
`Log`	`LogTransformer`	Logs all events to a specified log file and passes them on. Used only in debugging.
`readDOMsession`	`ReadDOMSessionTransformer`	Locates a DOM node in a session and inserts the data into the pipeline.
`sql`	`SQLTransformer`	Executes a query into a database and converts the results to a stream of SAX events.
`writeDOMsession`	`WriteDOMSessionTransformer`	Grabs a specified element from the pipeline and creates a DOM that is stored in the session.
`xinclude`	`XIncludeTransformer`	Follows the `Xinclude` specification to include all or part of a source in the event stream.
`xslt`	`TraxTransformer`	Carries out transformation using the default class for this JVM.
`xt`	`XTTransformer`	Carries out transformation using the XT transformer package.

The following sections describe in detail three of the principal transformers.

The *xslt* Transformer

Here is the sitemap declaration of the `xslt` transformer, typically the default transformer because it is widely used:

```
<map:transformer
 name="xslt"
 logger="sitemap.transformer.xslt"
 src="org.apache.cocoon.transformation.TraxTransformer"
 pool-max="32" pool-min="16" pool-grow="4">
 <use-request-parameters>false
 </use-request-parameters>
 <use-browser-capabilities-db>false
 </use-browser-capabilities-db>
 <use-cookies>false</use-cookies>
 <use-deli>false</use-deli>
</map:transformer>
```

Because it is expensive in CPU time to create an `xslt` transformer, Cocoon provides for caching instances in a pool. The pool characteristics are controlled by attributes such as pool-max as shown in the preceding code. In determining whether or not a pooled instance can be reused, the pool manager depends on a hash code key created from all of the transformer parameters.

If the <use-request-parameters/> element has the value *true*, the parameters submitted with the request is made available to the transformer. If the <use-browser-capabilities/> element has the value *true*, the transformer will have access to browser capabilities as determined by the User-Agent header in the request. Similarly, if the <use-cookies/> element has the value *true*, all of the request cookies are made available to the transformer. Generally speaking, don't set these parameters *true* unless you have to, because these extra parameters make it less likely that a pooled instance will be usable.

When used in a pipeline, the xslt transformer is configured with an src attribute pointing to a stylesheet:

```
<map:transform
   src="stylesheets/page/simple-page2html.xsl"/>
```

LogTransformer

This transformer is one of the few components that Cocoon supplies to aid in debugging. It writes a log file entry for every SAX event, including much of the event parameters. Here is an example of how a LogTransformer is described in the <map:transformers/> section of a sitemap:

```
<map:transformer name="log"
  logger="sitemap.transformer.log"
  src="org.apache.cocoon.transformation.LogTransformer"
/>
```

Note that the logger referred to is used to record execution problems, not the log of events. In the pipeline section of the sitemap, a log transformer for the particular pipeline segment is set up with the parameters name and append. The name parameter sets the file name. A value for the append parameter of *no* means the log file is rewritten every time the pipeline is used, and a value of *yes* causes new event messages to be appended.

```
<map:transform type="log">
  <map:parameter name="logfile"
    value="c:/Tomcat401/logs/debuglog.txt" />
  <map:parameter name="append" value="yes" />
</map:transform>
```

Needless to say, the log can grow rather rapidly with large documents. Listing 5.1 shows a fraction of the SAX events recorded by a log transformer when rendering a simple page.

Listing 5.1 Part of a Log of SAX Events

```
[startDocument]
[startDTD] name=page,publicId=null,systemId=null
[endDTD]
[startPrefixMapping] prefix=xi,uri=http://www.w3.org/2001/XInclude
[startElement] uri=,local=page,raw=page
[ignorableWhitespace]
[startElement] uri=,local=title,raw=title
[characters] Entry Page
[endElement] uri=,local=title,qname=title
[ignorableWhitespace]
[startElement] uri=,local=content,raw=content
[ignorableWhitespace]
[startElement] uri=,local=para,raw=para
[characters] Experimenting with simple stylesheets on
  this page!
[endElement] uri=,local=para,qname=para
```

Xinclude Transformer

The `xinclude` tag is similar to `cinclude` but is more powerful and follows the W3C Xinclude and Xpointer specifications, recommendations currently under consideration. You can find the full specifications at these sites:

```
www.w3.org/TR/xinclude
www.w3.org/TR/xptr
```

A typical use of `xinclude` would be to add a standard element such as a copyright notice to every page on a website. Let us suppose that your copyright notice is in a file named `footer.xml`. The following shows the tag to configure the `xinclude` transformer in the sitemap `<map:transformers/>` section (with long lines wrapped):

```
<map:transformer name="xinclude"
   logger="sitemap.transformer.xinclude"
   src="org.apache.cocoon.transformation
XIncludeTransformer"/>
```

In a pipeline, a reference to the `xinclude` transformer would be inserted before the `xslt transform` tag, like this:

```
<map:match pattern="index">
  <map:generate
      src="index.xml" />
  <map:transform type="xinclude" />
  <map:transform type="xslt"
      src="stylesheets/page2html.xsl" />
  <map:serialize/>
</map:match>
```

In a document being processed, you would have to include a declaration of the namespace for `xinclude` tags, like this:

```
<page
 xmlns:xi="http://www.w3.org/2001/XInclude" >
```

Subsequently in the source document, you can have a `<xi:include/>` tag that refers to a source file like this:

```
<xi:include href="footer.xml"/>
```

When the `xinclude` transformer hits this tag, events from the included file will be injected into the pipeline. Obviously, this is potentially very useful for including standardized elements such as copyright notices in web pages.

Additional flexibility is provided by the ability to select only parts of the included file according to a particular tag, and the capability of including plain text. For example, suppose `footer.xml` contains both a `copy` element and `webmaster` element and you only want the `copy` element on a particular page. This can be done by using `Xpointer` syntax in the `href` attribute of the tag as follows:

```
<xi:include
  href="/stockitems/footer.xml#xpointer(/footer/copy)"
  />
```

The operation of `<xi:include/>` parses the content from the `href` as XML by default, but you can specify that it be parsed as text by using the `parse` attribute as shown in the following:

```
<xi:include parse="text" href="/stockitems/sometext.txt" />
```

Matchers

Matchers are an essential part of a Cocoon pipeline. A matcher associates a particular URI specification or other value in the pipeline environment with a set of pipeline instructions. Matcher code is executed when a pipeline is being set up to handle a particular request.

Classes used as matchers are found in the `org.apache.cocoon.matching` package and implement the `Matcher` interface. This interface specifies one method, as follows:

```
Map match( String pattern,
     Map objectModel,
     Parameters parameters) throws PatternException;
```

Note that this `match` method is similar to the `act` method in the `Action` interface but is simpler. As with the `act` method, these parameters are used:

`pattern` Text data that specifies a matching pattern. Some matchers use a matching pattern in the *wildcard* style while others use a *regular expression.*

objectModel This is a standard Map from the java.util package that is used to provide access to a variety of parameters associated with a particular request. For example, in the RequestParamAction action, the objectModel carries a reference to a Request object that in turn provides access to the request parameters as located by the Servlet container.

parameters A class provided in the Avalon framework. It provides parameters from <map:parameter/> tags inside a <map:match/> tag in a pipeline.

As with the action components, a successful match causes creation of a Map collection of values that are made available to subsequent pipeline steps. A match failure causes a return of *null* and the pipeline section defined by the match tag is not executed.

The standard Cocoon matcher package provides a large number of classes, but many applications can be created with only a few. Table 5.4 shows the matchers used in the root sitemap as of this writing. Note that some of these can be configured when the sitemap is compiled to use specific variables found in the runtime environment.

TABLE 5.4: Standard Matchers

Name	Class	Configure by Values in	Function
wildcard	WildcardURIMatcher	-	x
regexp	RegexpURIMatcher	-	x
request-parameter	RequestParameterMatcher	request	Looks for named request parameter
sessionstate	WildcardSessionAttributeMatcher	session	Does a wildcard match in a named session attribute
next-page	WildcardRequestParameterMatcher	request	Does a wildcard match in a named request parameter value
referer-match	WildcardHeaderMatcher	header	Does a wildcard match in a named header value

Sitemap Compilation-Time Configuration of Matchers

Some matchers gain extra flexibility from configuration parameters added when the matcher is defined in the <map:matchers/> tag. For example, the following configures a matcher to be named referer-match, which uses an instance of the general-purpose WildcardHeader-Matcher class configured to look at the referer header:

```
<map:matcher name="referer-match"
     logger="sitemap.matcher.referer-match"
```

```
src="org.apache.cocoon.matching.WildcardHeaderMatcher">
    <header-name>referer</header-name>
</map:matcher>
```

It is important to note that matchers are executed in the order they appear in the sitemap; therefore, the most specific matchers must appear before the general ones.

Wildcard Syntax

Because regular expression syntax can become quite complex, Cocoon provides a *wildcard* syntax for matching that is much simpler.

Single * A single asterisk matches zero or more characters up to the point where the next / character occurs or the string ends. In other words, the resulting parameter does not include the / character.

Double ** A double asterisk matches zero or more characters including the / (slash) character or the end of the string. The resulting variable includes any terminating / character.

The order in which wildcards are encountered determines the way the resulting parameter can be used, with the first one being referred to as `{1}`, the second as `{2}`, etc.

Regular Expression Syntax

Regular expression syntax provides advanced capability for recognizing patterns in strings. Explaining the conventions used is beyond the scope of this book. Cocoon uses a regular expression library in Java that was created by Jonathan Locke and donated to the Apache Software Foundation. You can find details at this site:

`http://jakarta.apache.org/regexp/`

Selectors

Selectors are similar in function to matchers and actions. The standard Cocoon selectors are found in the `org.apache.cocoon.selection` package, and implement the `Selector` interface. This interface defines the `select` method as follows:

```
boolean select(java.lang.String expression,
  java.util.Map objectModel,
  org.apache.avalon.framework.parameters.Parameters parameters)
```

Note that `select` uses the same parameters as `match`, but returns a Boolean value instead of a collection. The typical application of a selector, and the default in the Cocoon distribution, is called browser. A selector provides for more powerful logical control in a pipeline because it can use a structure like the example use of browser from the Cocoon sitemap shown in Listing 5.2.

Listing 5.2 Use of the Browser Selector

```
<map:select type="browser" >
   <map:when test="wap">
     <map:transform
      src="stylesheets/simple-samples2html.xsl"/>
   </map:when>
   <map:when test="netscape">
     <map:transform
       src="stylesheets/simple-samples2html.xsl"/>
   </map:when>
   <map:otherwise>
     <map:transform
       src="stylesheets/simple-samples2html.xsl"/>
   </map:otherwise>
</map:select>
```

The tags inside `<map:select/>` act like a series of `if - else if - else if` logic test structures in Java. Each `<map:when/>` specifies a value that is passed to the `select` method of the browser selector. When `select` returns *`true`*, the tags enclosed in the `<map:when/>` are executed and then control passes out of the `<map:select/>` block.

Standard Selectors

Table 5.5 shows some of the selectors typically used in a Cocoon installation. All of the classes are in the `org.apache.cocoon.selection` package.

TABLE 5.5: Typical Cocoon Selectors

Name	Class	Selects on Parameter
`browser`	`BrowserSelector`	Partial match to User-Agent in request header
`header`	`HeaderSelector`	Exact match in named request header
`host`	`HostSelector`	Partial match in Host request header
`parameter`	`ParameterSelector`	Exact match to a sitemap environment parameter, possibly set by an action
`request-attribute`	`RequestAttributeSelector`	Exact match to a request attribute
`request-parameter`	`RequestParameterSelector`	Exact match to a request parameter
`session-attribute`	`SessionAttributeSelector`	Exact match to a session attribute

Note the distinction between partial matches and exact matches. Certain selectors look for an exact match of the environment parameter to the test string. In other words, a string `equals` test. Others, such as `browser` and `host`, return *`true`* if the test string can be found in the environment parameter.

About Attributes and Parameters

The request and session objects used in the selectors are wrappers for the standard HttpServletRequest and HttpSession classes in the javax.servlet package. These wrapper classes are HttpRequest and HttpSession in the org.apache.cocoon.environment.http package. In addition to the "real" request, the HttpRequest wrapper class carries some additional Cocoon environment-related information.

Recall that an HttpServletRequest holds two sets of items retrievable by name, attributes, and parameters. Parameters are String values that originate in a query string or posted form, and attributes are objects attached to the request during processing. In Cocoon, actions can be used to attach attributes to a request.

Configuring the Browser Selector

Listing 5.3 shows the entry for the browser selector in the <map:components/> section of the standard Cocoon distribution sitemap. Each <browser/> tag relates the name that is used internally to the text that appears in the User-Agent header of an HTTP request.

Listing 5.3 Configuring the Browser Selector

```
<map:selector name="browser"
  logger="sitemap.selector.browser"
  src="org.apache.cocoon.selection.BrowserSelector">
  <browser name="explorer" useragent="MSIE"/>
  <browser name="pocketexplorer" useragent="MSPIE"/>
  <browser name="handweb" useragent="HandHTTP"/>
  <browser name="avantgo" useragent="AvantGo"/>
  <browser name="imode" useragent="DoCoMo"/>
  <browser name="opera" useragent="Opera"/>
  <browser name="lynx" useragent="Lynx"/>
  <browser name="java" useragent="Java"/>
  <browser name="wap" useragent="Nokia"/>
  <browser name="wap" useragent="UP"/>
  <browser name="wap" useragent="Wapalizer"/>
  <browser name="mozilla5" useragent="Mozilla/5"/>
  <browser name="mozilla5" useragent="Netscape6/"/>
  <browser name="netscape" useragent="Mozilla"/>
</map:selector>
```

Each <browser/> tag contains attributes for a name and a useragent. When the browser selector is executed in a pipeline, as in Listing 5.2, the name is what appears in the <map:select/> tag, but the selection lookup is for the matching useragent. This approach allows one name, such as wap in Listing 5.3, to match any of several useragent values.

The order of <browser/> elements in the <map:selector/> tag is significant because more than one of the text chunks may appear in a real User-Agent header. In the following example, a set of request headers is transmitted when Microsoft Internet Explorer attempts to address the URL `http://localhost/` (with long lines wrapped). The order of `<browser/>` elements ensures that the match will be to `MSIE` instead of `Mozilla`.

```
GET /index HTTP/1.1
Accept: image/gif, image/x-xbitmap, image/jpeg,
  image/pjpeg, application/msword,
  application/vnd.ms-excel,
  application/vnd.ms-powerpoint, */*
Accept-Language: en-us
Accept-Encoding: gzip, deflate
User-Agent: Mozilla/4.0 (compatible; MSIE 6.0;
   Windows NT 5.1; Q312461)
Host: localhost:8080
Connection: Keep-Alive
```

The Resources Element

The `<map:resources/>` element of a sitemap holds one or more `<map:resource/>` elements. A `<map:resource/>` element provides a convenient way to hold pipeline segments that are used in several places in a sitemap. The Cocoon sitemap provides the example of the definition of a resource shown in Listing 5.4.

Listing 5.4 Defining a Resource

```
<map:resource name="slides">
   <map:generate
     src="docs/samples/slides/slides.xml"/>
  <map:transform
    src="stylesheets/slides/slides-navigation.xsl">
    <map:parameter name="use-request-parameters"
       value="true"/>
    <map:parameter name="use-browser-capabilities-db"
       value="true"/>
  </map:transform>
  <map:transform
      src="stylesheets/slides/slides-apachecon.xsl"/>
  <map:serialize/>
</map:resource>
```

Note that the example in Listing 5.4 terminates with a serializer, thus completing the operation of the pipeline. Here is an example of the `slides` resource in use:

```
<map:match pattern="slides/slides">
  <map:call resource="slides"/>
</map:match>
```

When a resource is called in a pipeline with tags, such as in the previous code, it is really more like a goto than a call, because any tag after the <map:call/> has no effect. Therefore, the main usefulness of a resource is in representing commonly used transformation and serialization steps.

WARNING Unfortunately, the name *resource* is also used with the reader that is typically named resource and is created by the ResourceReader class in the org.apache.cocoon.reading package. This is another opportunity for name confusion, so watch out.

The Views Element

The <map:views/> element encloses one or more <map:view/> elements that define named views. Views are defined with a final serialization step so a view lets you define a standard set of processes to finish up a pipeline. The intent of the views concept is to permit selection of a view of a resource by a parameter in a URL, as in this hypothetical example:

```
http://localhost/cocoon/documents/index.html?cocoon-view=content
```

Jumping to a view is controlled by an attribute named label in a pipeline component or by a <map:label/> element in the pipeline. As an indicator of the kind of labels that might be used, here is the entire views section from the default Cocoon sitemap:

```
<map:views>
  <map:view name="content" from-label="content">
   <map:serialize type="xml"/>
  </map:view>

  <map:view name="pretty-content" from-label="data">
    <map:transform src="stylesheets/simple-xml2html.xsl"/>
    <map:serialize type="html"/>
  </map:view>

  <map:view name="links" from-position="last">
   <map:serialize type="links"/>
  </map:view>

 </map:views>
```

In the present edition of Cocoon, it is clear that views are experimental and might not survive in this form in the next edition, so we are not devoting any more space to them.

The *Action-Sets* Element

Another convenient item similar to resources is the action-set. If you thought multiple uses of the same name were confusing before, now we are getting into some really confusing territory. The tags involved are <map:action-sets/>, <map:action-set/>, <map:action/>, and <map:act/>.

In the `<map:components/>` area, you can have a `<map:actions/>` element containing one or more `<map:action/>` elements that define and configure action components, as discussed in the "Actions" section earlier in this chapter. An action shows up in a pipeline as a `<map:act/>` tag.

The sitemap may contain a first-order `<map:action-sets/>` element that contains one or more `<map:action-set/>` elements. A `<map:action-set/>` is a convenience item for representing common groups of actions with a single name. A `<map:action-set/>` has a single name attribute and contains one or more `<map:act/>` tags. Here is an example from the Cocoon sitemap:

```
<map:action-sets>
  <map:action-set name="employee">
   <map:act type="add-employee" action="Add"/>
   <map:act type="del-employee" action="Delete"/>
   <map:act type="upd-employee" action="Update"/>
  </map:action-set>
 </map:action-sets>
```

The complete set of `<map:act/>` tags will now be executed in a pipeline where the following tag appears:

```
<map:act set="employee">
```

Pipelines

Now that we have covered all of the things that can go into a pipeline, let's look at how these parts are built into a working pipeline. All pipelines are contained within the first-level `<map:pipelines/>` element. At the first level of elements inside a `<map:pipeline/>` we can have only `<map:match/>` or `<map:handle-errors/>` elements.

As you have seen in the examples, the basic idea is simple: If a `<map:match/>` succeeds, the contained pipeline elements are executed. Listing 5.5 shows some common pipeline configurations.

Listing 5.5 A Small Set of Pipelines

```
<map:pipelines>
   <map:pipeline>

   <map:match pattern="">
      <map:redirect-to uri="index" />
   </map:match>

    <map:match pattern="index">
      <map:generate src="index.xml" />
      <map:transform type="xinclude" />
```

```
      <map:transform src="stylesheets/page2html.xsl" />
      <map:serialize/>
    </map:match>
  </map:pipeline>

  <map:pipeline>
    <map:match pattern="*.jpg">
      <map:read src="{1}.jpg" mime-type="image/jpg"/>
    </map:match>

    <map:match pattern="**/dir">
      <map:generate type="directory" src="{1}"/>
      <map:serialize type="xml"/>
    </map:match>

  </map:pipeline>

</map:pipelines>
```

When trying to find a pipeline segment to handle a request, the order of `<map:match/>` elements within a pipeline and the order of `<map:pipeline/>` elements within the `<map:pipelines/>` element of the sitemap are strictly observed.

Pipeline Error Handlers

Exceptions thrown during processing are trapped and the exception data is made available to a special pipeline sequence contained in a `<map:handle-errors/>` element. Here is an example definition of `<map:handle-errors/>` from the Cocoon distribution sitemap:

```
<map:handle-errors>
  <map:transform
      src="stylesheets/system/error2html.xsl"/>
  <map:serialize status-code="500"/>
</map:handle-errors>
```

As you can see, it provides for execution of a specific stylesheet and for sending a status code when the page is serialized to HTML. The resulting page includes the full stack trace of the exception. This approach has an annoying drawback, because a number of SAX events may have been processed and serialized to the output before the exception is thrown. The user might see a mixture of the original page followed by the error page.

Pipeline Elements

Table 5.6 summarizes the elements that might appear as first-level child elements within a `<map:match/>` or `<map:handle-errors/>` element in a pipeline. Note that some of these are defined by components that we have already discussed.

TABLE 5.6: First Order Elements under a Match within a Pipeline

Element	Component Definition is in	Function
map:act	map:action, map:action-set	Computation based on pipeline environment variables and control
map:aggregate	--	Combines <map:part> elements into a single stream of events
map:call	--	Executes a named resource (does not return)
map:generate	map:generator	Creates a SAX event stream
map:match	map:matcher	Control based on matching a pattern in a URI
map:mount	--	Establishes a subsitemap as responsible for URIs starting with a given prefix
map:read	map:reader	Direct output of a resource, bypassing SAX event processing
map:redirect-to	--	Sends a redirect message as the only response
map:serialize	map:serializer	Converts XML to an output stream; always the last element of a pipeline
map:transform	map:transformer	Computation based on the pipeline environment and a SAX event stream

The *map:aggregate* Function

The <map:aggregate/> element is used like a generator at the start of a pipeline. It is widely used in the creation of pages that combine multiple sources of information.

The operation is carried out by the ContentAggregator class in the org.apache.cocoon.sitemap package. It generates a single stream of SAX events from multiple pipelines that are defined by <map:part/> tags. The aggregated document has a root element defined by the element attribute in the <map:aggregate/> tag.

Listing 5.6 shows an example from the Cocoon base sitemap. This pipeline combines news items from three different sources into a new document with a root element of <page/>.

Listing 5.6 A Pipeline Using the *Aggregate* Function

```
<map:match pattern="news/aggregate.xml">
    <map:aggregate
    element="page"
    ns="http://foo.bar.com/myspace">
  <map:part
    src="cocoon:/slashdot/slashdot.xml"
    element="slashdot"
    ns="http://foo.bar.com/slashdot"/>
  <map:part
    src="cocoon:/moreover/moreover.xml"
```

```
      element="moreover"
      ns="http://foo.bar.com/moreover"/>
  </map:aggregate>
  <map:transform src="stylesheets/news/news.xsl"/>
  <map:serialize/>
</map:match>
```

Each `<map:part/>` element uses three attributes. The `element` and `ns` attributes give the name and namespace that will be used as the enclosing tag created by the aggregator for the contents of a particular source. The `src` attribute designates the source from which that XML content will be taken. An optional attribute not shown in the example is called `strip-root`. If your `<map:part/>` tag includes `strip-root="yes"`, then the root element of the document will not be included.

You really have to try this to appreciate it. Assuming you have Cocoon installed on a Servlet engine running as localhost on port 80, and that your Internet connection is live, enter the following URL on your browser:

```
http://localhost/cocoon/news/aggregate.xml
```

If all goes well, you will get a page with current headlines from both slashdot and moreover. As expected, the order on the page reflects the order of the `<map:part/>` elements.

The `"cocoon:"` nomenclature in Listing 5.6 is what Cocoon calls a *pseudo protocol*. These protocols are defined in the `<url-factory/>` element of the `cocoon.xconf` file in the Cocoon installation directory. The pseudo protocols defined in Cocoon 2.0.1 follow:

cocoon:/ Refers to a pipeline from the current sitemap

cocoon:// Refers to a pipeline from the root sitemap

context:// Refers to a resource using the Servlet context

resource:// Refers to a resource from the context classloader

Now we can see that the `src` value of `"cocoon:/slashdot/slashdot.xml"` will connect to a pipeline named `"slashdot/slashdot.xml"` in the current sitemap. This pipeline is defined as follows:

```
<map:match pattern="slashdot/slashdot.xml">
  <map:generate
    src="http://slashdot.org/slashdot.xml"/>
  <map:transform src="stylesheets/news/slashdot.xsl"/>
  <map:serialize/>
</map:match>
```

So the sequence of pipeline processing events is that the aggregator sends events corresponding to the start of a new document with a `<page/>` root. It then calls the first pipeline, which goes to the slashdot site for the current news feed (in XML). Those events are modified by the `xslt` transformer using `slashdot.xsl`, and are serialized as HTML (because `html` is the default serializer). A similar sequence adds the moreover news, also as HTML. This HTML is transformed again by a transformer using `news.xsl` and finally recast into HTML by the final serializer. Quite a *tour de force* of XSL processing!

Pipeline Control

Let's review the components used for the control of flow within pipelines:

Matcher Matchers examine variables within a request such as the request URI or request parameters, using a pattern. When a match occurs the pipeline segment enclosed in the `<map:match/>` element will be executed. If matching used wildcards or regular expressions, the matched tokens will be available as sitemap variables. Matcher control is essentially *yes* or *no*, like a Java `if` statement.

Selector Selectors provide more control by looking for one or more exact matches, or in certain selectors, partial matches. When a match occurs, a specific pipeline segment is executed. The control is effectively the equivalent of a Java `switch` statement.

Action Actions can perform complex calculation in support of decision-making. An action can manipulate runtime variables and insert any Java object into named parameters. However, the control is essentially *yes* or *no* because if an action fails, the associated pipeline is not executed.

Once execution of a pipeline has started, Cocoon provides components for generating, transforming, and finally outputting the formatted result, using parameters drawn from the entire Cocoon environment.

Summary

The use of the sitemap concept to control web publishing offers many advantages to all of those involved. For the administrator, the sitemap puts the entire structure into a consistent form that can be understood by designers, authors, and programmers. Furthermore, it is a form than can easily handle future growth and enhancement.

For designers, the sitemap promotes the use of unifying design patterns and consistent style. For content authors and managers, the industry-wide trend to the use of XML for data description and interchange is a welcome relief from proprietary formats. The widespread use of SOAP for transport of XML-formatted data means that a site can easily use data in a well understood format from a variety of sources.

For programmers, the well defined yet flexible interfaces for the various pipeline components make it easy to provide new functionality. The programmer can draw on many open-source projects without "reinventing the wheel" or upsetting existing applications.

Chapter 6

Introducing XSP Usage

- A Minimal XSP Page
- How XSP Works
- Creating Dynamic Pages
- Managing User Sessions
- A SQL Example

For logical control and building dynamic content, Cocoon uses two core technologies: the sitemap, described in Chapter 5, "Logic Control: The Sitemap," and Extensible Server Pages (XSP). An XSP page is a dynamic XML document containing logic and content. Logical control is implemented using language constructs such as Java Server Pages (JSP), and content is marked up with a descriptive language such as XML.

Remember that XSP is only a pillar of the Cocoon architecture. It allows the mixture of content with logic. Conversely, to guarantee separation of concerns and for simplified maintenance, we could build a Cocoon pipeline of content separated from logic. Using XSLT, we can transform from content sans logic to the XSP DTD. This puts the logic and style on the transformation layer of the Cocoon architecture, again supporting the separation of concerns.

XSP is classified as a *middleware programming language*. Other examples of this class of languages include Java Server Pages (JSP), ColdFusion Markup Language (CFML), Active Server Pages (ASP), and the PHP Hypertext Processor (PHP). XSP provides dynamic content-generation capabilities to authors without requiring them to be programmers. Logicsheets in conjunction with XSP provide technology supporting the separation of logic control from content and presentation. (Chapter 7, "XSP Logicsheets," presents logicsheets in more detail.)

In an XSP page, content and logical controls are combined to create a dynamic XML document based on external data or input. XSP has a syntax allowing the amalgam of programming logic and static content. A major characteristic of XSP is that this mix is independent of the logical control (programming language) and the binary executable (that is, the `.class` file) generated from the source XSP page.

XSP is very similar to JSP. As with JSP, XSP documents are transformed into Java source code and then compiled into Java classes. When executed, the classes read inputs and produce an output. Instead of producing an HTML page as JSP does, the output from XSP is simply XML. The output might be viewed in an XHTML-compliant web browser (which is an application of XML) or plumbed into other XML processing facilities.

In this chapter, the examples were developed on a PC running Linux RedHat 7.1. Therefore, specific installation instructions for the examples should be based on your specific Cocoon 2 installation.

This chapter documents typical XSP usage, including:

- Generating dynamic content
- Using session management
- Accessing a SQL database

A Minimal XSP Page

An XSP page must contain a minimum set of Cocoon and XSP directives. Therefore, a minimal XSP page is an XML document that conforms to the following requirements:

- The XSP page must contain a Cocoon directive launching the XSP processor `<?cocoon-process type="xsp"?>` (see `http://xml.apache.org/cocoon1/xsp.html`).
- The XSP page must contain the document root element `<xsp:page>`.
- The XSP page must contain any logicsheet and/or language declarations attributes in the `<xsp:page>` directive. For example:

  ```
  <xsp:page language="java" xmlns:xsp="http://www.apache.org/1999/XSP/Core">
  ```

- Finally, a minimal XSP page must contain at least some XSP logic controls (for example, a `<xsp:expr>` directive and/or a `<xsp:logic>` directive).

Listing 6.1 produces a string representing the current date and time (see Figure 6.1).

Listing 6.1 Example of a Minimal XSP Page, *chap6-getToday.xsp*

```
<?xml version="1.0"?>
<?cocoon-process type="xsp"?>
<?cocoon-process type="xslt"?>
<!-- This XSL stylesheet is consuming XML and producing HTML -->
<?xml-stylesheet href="stylesheets/dynamic-page2html.xsl" type="text/xsl"?>

<xsp:page
          language="java"
          xmlns:xsp="http://apache.org/xsp">

<!-- A simple logic element. Determine current date and time -->
<xsp:logic>
static private Date today;

private synchronized Date getToday() {
  today = new Date();
  return today;
}
</xsp:logic>

<!-- Start the XSP page element -->
<page>
<title>Get Today</title>
<p>The current date and time is
<strong><xsp:expr>getToday()</xsp:expr></strong></p>
</page>
</xsp:page>
```

FIGURE 6.1: chap6-getToday

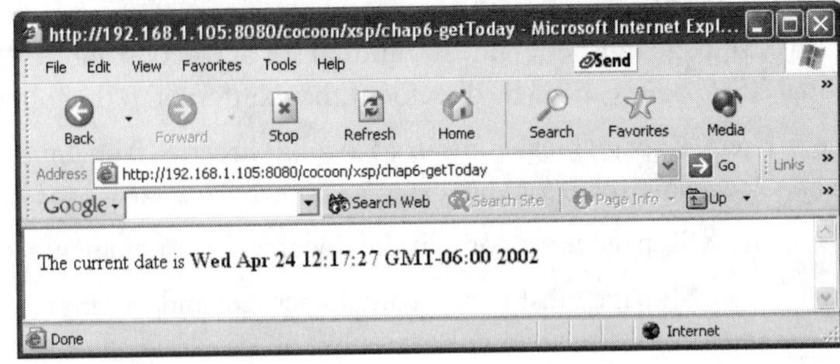

Our example XSP page output is an HTML document. The `xml-stylesheet` directive references the XSL stylesheet `dynamic-page2html.xsl`. We could have easily produced another format, such as XHTML or Portable Document Format (PDF), by specifying an alternative stylesheet. This is yet another powerful facet of Cocoon—one source, many output formats. Remember, Cocoon processes documents in pipeline fashion: Cocoon processes the entire XSP page, then generates a result document, which is in turn passed to the next Cocoon processor (in our example, an XSL stylesheet).

Listing 6.2 shows the resulting HTML document.

Listing 6.2 Resulting HTML from Processing *chap6-getToday.xsp*

```
<html>
<head>
<META http-equiv="Content-Type" content="text/html; charset=UTF-8">
<title>Get Today</title>
</head>
<body vlink="blue" link="blue" alink="red" bgcolor="white">

<p xmlns:xsp="http://apache.org/xsp">The current date is <strong>Thu Apr 11
22:18:37 GMT-06:00 2002</strong>
</p>

</body>
</html>
```

How XSP Works

An XSP page is a live, dynamic XML document. But how does XSP work within the Cocoon framework? The following list depicts a sequential set of events within the Cocoon framework when an XSP page is created, deployed, and referenced.

1. With your favorite editor, create an XSP page and save it. For example, `getToday.xsp`.

2. Because our output format is HTML, reference the XSP page with a web browser. As a result, the Cocoon framework transforms the XSP page into source code. For example, `chap6-getToday_xsp.java`.
3. Then, the Cocoon framework compiles the source code into a binary file. For example, `chap6-getToday_xsp.class`.
4. Finally, the binary file is executed at runtime in the Tomcat servlet environment. The binary file remains executable within the Tomcat servlet environment until the XSP page is edited and re-referenced; then we start all over again at step 1.

Creating Dynamic Pages

There are several ways to create dynamic content using XSP. Each has its own set of pros and cons and level of complexity. This chapter presents a mixture of XSP logic and content using some helpful examples. Chapter 7 discusses dynamic content generation using logicsheets and XSP.

Mixed Content and Logic

XSP allows you to mix content with logic. This is typical of most web middleware application languages. You can augment some static content with dynamically created content. The dynamic content can come from many external sources, such as a database, a file, or a web browser form. Using XSP in this manner is not highly recommended because this method is difficult to maintain. But, used for trivial XSP examples, it is noteworthy.

This section explores an example showing a mixture of logic with content using XSP. The XSP page is named `chap6-simple.xsp`. You can save it into the Cocoon directory (Unix) `$CATALINA_HOME/cocoon/docs/samples/xsp/`. It can be viewed by pointing your browser here:

```
http://localhost:8080/cocoon/xsp/chap6-simple
```

So, let's start looking at `chap6-simple.xsp`. The first section of code includes familiar parts that we presented in the "A Minimal XSP Page" section. Notice that we include the Request logicsheet called xsp-request (see `http://xml.apache.org/cocoon/userdocs/xsp/request.html`). It wraps XML around HTTP requests, providing an XML interface to associated methods of the HttpServletRequest object specified in the Java Servlet Specification 2.2 (see `http://java.sun.com/products/servlet/2.2/javadoc/index.html`). Listing 6.3 uses the method `get-remote-address` to determine the IP address of the Cocoon server.

Listing 6.3 Mixed Content and Logic XSP Example, *chap6-simple.xsp*

```
<?xml version="1.0"?>

<!-- start chap6-simple.xsp -->

<!-- Cocoon processing directives -->
<?cocoon-process type="xsp"?>
<?cocoon-process type="xslt"?>

<!-- transform XSP page and resulting XML to HTML -->
<?xml-stylesheet href="stylesheets/dynamic-page2html.xsl" type="text/xsl"?>

<!-- start an XSP page. Include the xsp logicsheet and the xsp-request logic
sheet -->
<xsp:page
  language="java"
  xmlns:xsp="http://apache.org/xsp"
  xmlns:xsp-request="http://apache.org/xsp/request/2.0"
>

<xsp:logic>

// global variables;
static private Date today;

// calculate todays date and time string
private synchronized Date getToday() {
  today = new Date();
  return today;
}

</xsp:logic>

<!-- start the XSP page body -->

<page>

<title>Dynamic Example using Mixed Content and Logic</title>

<hr />

<div align="center">
```

For illustrative purposes only, the preceding example code shows the use of request object methods (`request.getServerPort` and `request.getServerName`) rather than using their corresponding Request logicsheet methods (`xsp-request:get-server-port` and `xsp-request:get-server-name`). XSP allows this. You can interchange the use of the Request logicsheet (`xsp-request`) with the request object because the request object is an instance of the HttpServletRequest class and the Request logicsheet uses the request object itself. We prefer to use the Request logicsheet approach, as shown in Listing 6.4. (Chapter 7 discusses why in more detail.)

Listing 6.4 The Request Logicsheet Approach, *chap6-simple.xsp*

```
<table cellspacing="2" cellpadding="2" border="1">

<tr bgcolor="cornsilk">
  <td>Current date and time</td>
  <td><xsp:expr>getToday()</xsp:expr></td>
</tr>

<!-- use the request object methods getServerName rather than the Request
logicsheet method -->
<tr bgcolor="#f0f0f0">
  <td>Current server name</td>
  <td><xsp:expr>request.getServerName()</xsp:expr></td>
</tr>

<!-- use the Request logicsheet get-remote-address method to get the IP address
of the Cocoon server -->
<tr bgcolor="cornsilk">
  <td>Current server IP address</td>
  <td><xsp-request:get-remote-address/></td>
</tr>

<!-- use the request object methods getServerPort rather than the Request
logicsheet method -->
<tr bgcolor="#f0f0f0">
  <td>Current server port</td>
  <td><xsp:expr>request.getServerPort()</xsp:expr></td>
</tr>

</table>

</div>

</page>
</xsp:page>
<!-- end of chap6-simple.xsp -->
```

Listing 6.5 shows the resulting HTML; Figure 6.2 shows a rendering of the resulting HTML document.

Listing 6.5 Resulting Dynamically Generated HTML

```
<html>
<head>
<META http-equiv="Content-Type" content="text/html; charset=UTF-8">
<title>Dynamic Example using Mixed Content and Logic</title>
</head>
<body vlink="blue" link="blue" alink="red" bgcolor="white">

<h2 style="color: navy; text-align: center">Dynamic Example using Mixed Content
and Logic</h2>

<hr xmlns:xsp="http://apache.org/xsp">

<div xmlns:xsp="http://apache.org/xsp" align="center">

<table cellspacing="2" cellpadding="2" border="1">
<tr bgcolor="cornsilk">
  <td>Current date and time</td>
  <td>Tue Apr 16 23:23:14 GMT-06:00 2002</td>
</tr>

<tr bgcolor="#f0f0f0">
  <td>Current server name</td>
  <td>192.168.1.99</td>
</tr>

<tr bgcolor="cornsilk">
  <td>Current server IP address</td>
  <td>192.168.1.162</td>
</tr>

<tr bgcolor="#f0f0f0">
  <td>Current server port</td>
  <td>8080</td>
</tr>

</table>

</div>

</body>
</html>
```

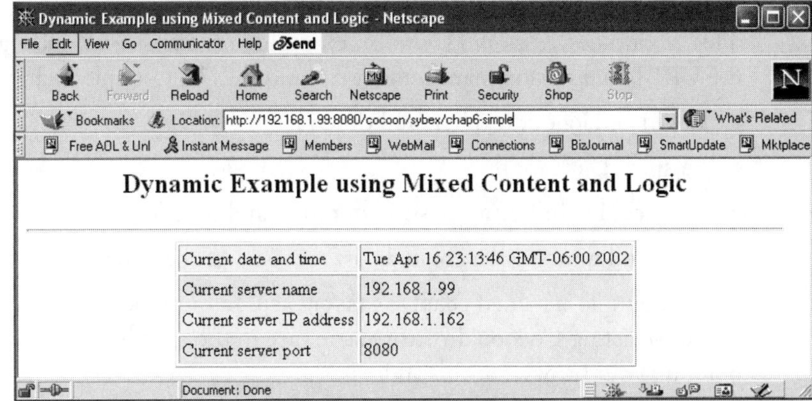

FIGURE 6.2: XSP example of mixing content and logic

Managing User Sessions

Historically, managing a user's session on your web server was difficult because HTTP was initially designed to be a stateless protocol. The reason was to keep the protocol simple. In hindsight, this made the Web a smash hit nearly overnight. But now, the Web has evolved, and managing state in a web server has become paramount. But how? There have been several attempts using client-side and server-side methods. Client-side methods include cookies, session IDs, and tokens appended to a URI. Server-side methods include application, session, and client variables.

The Cocoon framework is server-based. Therefore, session management data is stored on the Cocoon server. A user session consumes server resources such as disk space, CPU cycles, and memory. These resource taps could contribute to server performance problems and also reduce the scalability of a server-side session management solution. If performance and scalability are important facets of your project, you must be cognizant of server resources management (that is, removing stale session data, throttling user sessions, and so on).

The Cocoon framework offers you many ways to manage and track user sessions on the server side. The following is a list of methods from the Cocoon 2.0 documentation (see `http://xml.apache.org/cocoon/userdocs/xsp/sessions.html`):

- Creation of new session IDs
- Full session control by the underlying Java Servlet API 2.2 servlet engine
- Cookie and URI-based session management
- Automatic link rewrite (if you want your XSP pages to be URI-session-aware)

User Session Management Example

This section describes and shows an example of a user session management XSP page using the URI-based session management technique. The example includes the following:

- Login and logout (explicit and timeout)
- Session ID creation
- Progress bar indicating session duration and time left before it expires
- Date and time session created, last accessed, and expiration

The example is named `chap6-session.xsp`. In our Cocoon 2 Linux installation, we placed it in the existing Cocoon directory structure in the `session` directory. It can be referenced by pointing your browser at this address:

```
http://localhost:8080/cocoon/session/chap6-session.xsp
```

When you first access `chap6-session.xsp` in your browser, you will see a Login link. When you click that link, your session starts. Once the session is started, you are presented with a table containing session information such as the server-generated session ID; the calling URI; and the date and time the session was created, when it was last accessed, and when it expires. The display user name is a session parameter that is set in the XSP page.

Next, a progress meter bar is displayed, and it represents the status of the current session:

- If the meter bar is green, the session is currently active.

- If the bar is yellow, the session is about to expire (less than 25 percent of time is left).

- If the bar is red, either the session will expire very soon (less than 10 percent of time is left), or it has expired.

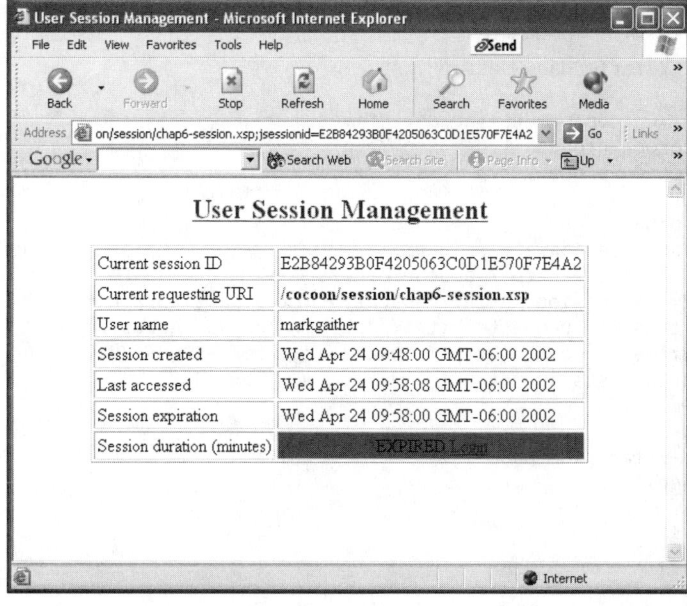

When the session expires, you will also be given a link to log in to a new session. With the link labeled Refresh, you can refresh the display to update the progress meter bar and the date and time the XSP page was last accessed. Lastly, you can Logout of the session. This invalidates the session, dumps all session parameters, and purges the session from the server.

One last note: If you want to have some fun, set the preference in your web browser to reject all cookies or set your Privacy settings to block all cookies. Then run this example. You'll notice that the session ID will be carried around on the URI throughout the example. If cookies are enabled, your browser will set a cookie and use it during the session rather than carrying forward the session ID on the URI. This is a browser's preferable mode of operation. Therefore, the URI-based session management is a good solution if you cannot guarantee that cookies are enabled on your client's web browser.

Let's start looking at the example code. The first section is required in a minimal XSP page. Notice the inclusion of a few important logicsheets:

`session` Manages user sessions.

`xsp-request` Retrieves important HTTP request information.

`response` Retrieves important HTTP response information.

Listing 6.6 includes the `create-session="true"` attribute of the `xsp:page` tag. This explicitly signals Cocoon to create a session.

Listing 6.6 User Session Management XSP Example Code, *chap6-session.xsp*

```
<?xml version="1.0" encoding="iso-8859-1"?>

<!-- start chap6-session.xsp -->

<!-- Cocoon processing directives -->
<?cocoon-process type="xsp"?>
<?cocoon-process type="xslt"?>

<xsp:page
  language="java"
  xmlns:xsp="http://apache.org/xsp"
  xmlns:session="http://apache.org/xsp/session/2.0"
  xmlns:xsp-request="http://apache.org/xsp/request/2.0"
  xmlns:response="http://apache.org/xsp/response/2.0"
  create-session="true"
>

<!-- start XSP page -->
<page>
```

```
<title>User Session Management</title>

<content>

<div align="center">
```

The next chunk of code initializes any global variables such as the maximum number of seconds a session is valid (`sessionMaxSeconds`) and the corresponding maximum number of minutes of a valid session (`sessionMaxMinutes`). We also set two date variables using methods from the Session logicsheet (see `http://xml.apache.org/cocoon/userdocs/xsp/session.html`). Each Session logicsheet method returns a long integer representing an epoch millisecond—the number of milliseconds since the epoch (January 1, 1970).

`get-creation-time` The date and timestamp when the current session was created in epoch milliseconds.

`get-last-accessed` The date and timestamp when the session data was last accessed by the client in epoch milliseconds.

The expiration date and timestamp are calculated by adding the maximum number of milliseconds (this is why we multiply `sessionMaxSeconds` by 1,000 in the following code) for a valid session (that is, 600 seconds) to the date and time of session creation.

We also check to see if any Request parameters were sent to the XSP page via the URI method (appended to the requesting URL) using the Request object method `request.getParameter()`. If the user has requested a logout action (actually, the only defined action of the XSP page), then the XSP logic will invalidate the current session using the Session logicsheet method `session:invalidate`. This purges the session and its data from the server. We use the `response:send-redirect` method of the Response logicsheet to redirect the browser to the specified URL.

Finally, in this chunk of code, we set a user-defined session parameter for tracking the user name using the Session logicsheet method `<session:set-attribute name="username">`. As shown in Listing 6.7, this variable's value is constant throughout the session and could be used more extensively.

Listing 6.7 User Session Management XSP Example Code, *chap6-session.xsp*

```
<xsp:logic>

// set the maximum number of seconds a session is valid
long sessionMaxSeconds = 600;
long sessionMaxMinutes = sessionMaxSeconds / 60;

// create a date representing the created date
Date createdDate = new Date(<session:get-creation-time/>);
```

```
// create a date representing the last accessed date
Date accessedDate = new Date(<session:get-last-accessed-time/>);

// create a date representing the exipration date
Date expireDate = new Date(<session:get-creation-time/> +
(sessionMaxSeconds*1000));

// get any URL parameters
if (request.getParameter("action") != null) {

   // purge session and its data from the server
   <session:invalidate/>

   // redirect to login page
   <response:send-redirect location="/cocoon/session/chap6-simple.xsp"/>
}

// determine the current duration of the session in minutes
long sessionDuration = (<session:get-last-accessed-time/> - <session:get-
creation-time/>) / 1000 / 60 + 1;

// set session parameter to track future visits
<session:set-attribute name="username">markgaither</session:set-attribute>

// if new session, provide login link
if (<session:is-new/>) {
  <session:encode-url href="chap6-session.xsp">Login</session:encode-url>
}
</xsp:logic>
```

In Listing 6.8, we begin the display of the information table including the progress meter bar and the Refresh and Logout links. In this section of code, we use methods from the Session and Request logicsheets. Notice the use of the `<xsp:content>` tag. It is used in the context of the `<xsp:logic>` tag. Using the `<xsp:content>` tag allows XSP to output chunks of HTML much like the line-oriented here-document syntax in Perl or the `<cfoutput>` tag in ColdFusion. Finally, the expiration date is calculated and displayed by calling the `expireDate.toString()` method.

Listing 6.8 User Session Management XSP Example Code, *chap6-session.xsp*

```
<table cellspacing="2" cellpadding="2" border="1">

<xsp:logic>
if (!<session:is-new/>) {

  <xsp:content>
    <tr>
```

```
        <td>Current session ID</td>
        <td><session:get-id as="xml"/></td>
      </tr>

      <tr>
        <td>Current requesting URI</td>
        <td><xsp-request:get-uri as="xml"/></td>
      </tr>
    </xsp:content>

    <!-- get the current user name, if any -->
    if (<session:get-attribute name="username"/> != null) {

      <xsp:content>

      <tr>
        <td>User name</td>
        <td><session:get-attribute name="username" default="n/a"/></td>
      </tr>

      </xsp:content>
    }

    <xsp:content>

      <tr>
        <td>Session created</td>
        <td><session:get-creation-time as="string"/></td>
      </tr>

      <tr>
        <td>Last accessed</td>
        <td><session:get-last-accessed-time as="string"/></td>
      </tr>

      <tr>
        <td>Session expiration</td>
        <td><xsp:expr>expireDate.toString()</xsp:expr></td>
      </tr>

    </xsp:content>
```

In the next code section, we check to see if the current session is still valid. There are two ways the session can expire:

- The user explicitly logs out.
- The current date and time exceeds the expiration date and timestamp initially set upon session creation.

If you refresh the page and the session has expired, you will see the expiration warning, as shown at the beginning of this section. If the session is still valid, then a progress meter bar is displayed.

Note the use of the tag `<![CDATA[ ... ]]>` in Listing 6.9. This is an old SGML construct. It tells the XML parser to treat anything in its context as pure character data and not to expand it to treat it in any way. Why use it? The "&&" and the "<=" in the Boolean expression throws the XML parser into a tailspin because the "&" and the "<" are reserved characters in XML. It's your job as the programmer to protect these sections of code from the XML parser. There isan alternative, which is to use the XML general entity replacements for "&" and "<". You can use "`&`" for the "&" and you can use "`<`" for the "<".

Listing 6.9 User Session Management XSP Example Code, *chap6-session.xsp*

```
if (!<session:is-new/>) {

  if (accessedDate.after(expireDate)) {

    <xsp:content>

     <tr>
       <td>Session duration (minutes)</td>
       <td bgcolor="red" align="center">EXPIRED <a href="chap6-
session.xsp?action=invalidate">Login</a></td>
     </tr>

    </xsp:content>

  }
  else {

    long sessionTimeleft = sessionMaxMinutes - sessionDuration;
    double widthUsed = ((double) sessionDuration/(double)
sessionMaxMinutes)*100.0;
    double widthLeft = 100.0 - widthUsed;

    String sessionColor = "lightgreen";

    <![CDATA[
    if (widthLeft <= 10) {
  sessionColor = "red";
    }
    else if (widthLeft > 10 && widthLeft <= 25) {
  sessionColor = "yellow";
    }
    ]]>
```

In Listing 6.10, we complete the information table. The highlight of this code section is how the progress meter bar is built using HTML table elements. We use the `xsp:attribute` tag to dynamically create attributes of the HTML element `<td>`; specifically, the `bgcolor` and `width` attributes of the `<td>` element. We also use `xsp:attribute` to dynamically set the `href` attribute of the <a> tag. Finally, we display a link to refresh the information table and a link to logout and purge the session. Listing 6.11 shows the resulting HTML.

Listing 6.10 User Session Management XSP Example Code, *chap6-session.xsp*

```
        <xsp:content>

        <tr>
          <td>Session duration (minutes)</td>
          <td>
            <table cellspacing="1" cellpadding="1" border="0" width="100%">
            <tr>
              <td align="left">0</td>
              <td align="right"><xsp:expr>sessionMaxMinutes</xsp:expr></td>
            </tr>
            <tr>
              <td height="20" align="center">
                <xsp:attribute
  name="width"><xsp:expr>widthUsed</xsp:expr></xsp:attribute>
                  <xsp:attribute
  name="bgcolor"><xsp:expr>sessionColor</xsp:expr></xsp:attribute> </td>
              <td height="20" align="center"><xsp:attribute
  name="width"><xsp:expr>widthLeft</xsp:expr></xsp:attribute>
                  <xsp:attribute name="bgcolor">cornsilk</xsp:attribute> </td>
            </tr>
            </table>
          </td>
        </tr>

        </xsp:content>

        <xsp:content>
        <tr>
          <td align="center" colspan="2">
            <a><xsp:attribute name="href"><xsp:expr>"chap6-
  session.xsp;jsessionid=" + <session:get-id
  as="string"/></xsp:expr></xsp:attribute>Refresh</a> |
            <a href="chap6-session.xsp?action=invalidate">Logout</a></td>
        </tr>

        </xsp:content>
      }
    }
  }
```

```
</xsp:logic>

</table>

</div>

</content>

</page>
</xsp:page>
```

Listing 6.11 Resulting HTML after Transformation of User Session Example

```
<html>
<head>
<META http-equiv="Content-Type" content="text/html; charset=UTF-8">
<title>User Session Management</title>
</head>
<body vlink="blue" link="blue" alink="red" bgcolor="white">

<h2 style="color: navy; text-align: center">
<a href="../view-source?filename=/docs/samples/session/chap6-session.xsp"
TARGET="_blank">User Session Management</a>
</h2>

<content xmlns:xsp="http://apache.org/xsp"
xmlns:session="http://apache.org/xsp/session/2.0" xmlns:xsp-
request="http://apache.org/xsp/request/2.0"
xmlns:response="http://apache.org/xsp/response/2.0">

<div align="center">

<table cellspacing="2" cellpadding="2" border="1">
<tr>
  <td>Current session ID</td>
  <td><session:id>74014053147274617638C7E5B2C83573</session:id></td>
</tr>

<tr>
  <td>Current requesting URI</td>
  <td><b>/cocoon/session/chap6-session.xsp</b></td>
</tr>

<tr>
  <td>User name</td>
  <td>markgaither</td>
</tr>
```

```
<tr>
  <td>Session created</td>
  <td>Tue Jul 09 23:02:56 GMT-06:00 2002</td>
</tr>

<tr>
  <td>Last accessed</td>
  <td>Tue Jul 09 23:02:56 GMT-06:00 2002</td>
</tr>

<tr>
  <td>Session expiration</td>
  <td>Tue Jul 09 23:12:56 GMT-06:00 2002</td>
</tr>

<tr>
  <td>Session duration (minutes)</td>
  <td>

    <table cellspacing="1" cellpadding="1" border="0" width="100%">
    <tr>
      <td align="left">0</td>
      <td align="right">10</td>
    </tr>

    <tr>
      <td height="20" align="center" width="10.0" bgcolor="lightgreen"></td>
      <td height="20" align="center" width="90.0" bgcolor="cornsilk"></td>
    </tr>
    </table>
  </td>
</tr>

<tr>
  <td align="center" colspan="2">
     <a href="chap6-
session.xsp;jsessionid=74014053147274617638C7E5B2C83573">Refresh</a> | <a
href="chap6-session.xsp?action=invalidate">Logout</a>
  </td>
</tr>
</table>

</div>

</content>

</body>
</html>
```

A SQL Example

This section describes and shows a SQL example using XSP and mySQL (see www.mysql.com). The example includes the following:

- Dynamically build a SQL query based on parameters
- URL parameter passing
- Session variable usage
- Sort elements in result set by a parameter

The example is named chap6-sql.xsp. It can be placed in the existing Cocoon directory structure in the $CATALINA_HOME/docs/samples/xsp/ directory. It can be referenced by pointing your browser at this address:

```
http://localhost:8080/cocoon/xsp/chap6-sql
```

Setting Up the SQL Example

To fully deploy this example on your Cocoon 2 server, you must do a few things. You must download and install mySQL (see www.mysql.com), modify your main sitemap, create a database named "sybex" and populate it, add the mySQL driver to the Cocoon Web.xml document, and add the datasource to your cocoon.xconf file. The database data is found in the chap6.sql file on this book's website.

1. Download and install mySQL from www.mysql.com.
2. Create a database named sybex and populate it.
3. On the command line type **mysqladmin create sybex**.
4. On the command line type **mysql sybex << chap6.sql**.
5. Add this chunk of XML to your main sitemap.xmap in the Dynamic section in the context of the map:match pattern="xsp/*" tag:

```
<map:transform type="sql">
  <map:parameter name="use-connection" value="sybex"/>
</map:transform>
```

6. Add this chunk of XML to your cocoon.xconf file in the context of the <datasources> tag:

```
<!-- mySQL -->
<jdbc name="sybex">
  <pool-controller min="5" max="10"/>
  <auto-commit>true</auto-commit>
  <dburl>jdbc:mysql://localhost.localdomain:3306/sybex</dburl>
  <user>root</user>
  <password></password>
</jdbc>
```

7. Add this piece of XML to your cocoon/WEB-INF/Web.xml file in the context of the <init-param> tag for the <param-name> of 'load-class':

```
<!-- mySQL driver -->
org.gjt.mm.mysql.Driver
```

8. Restart Cocoon by pointing your browser to this address:

```
http://localhost:8080/manager/reload?path=/cocoon
```

How the Example Works

When you first access chap6-sql.xsp in your browser, you will see a nicely formatted HTML table displaying data from the "sybex" database (see Figure 6.3). It lists the employee ID, employee name, and the employee's department. Initially, the data is sorted in ascending order on the employee name. You can click each column's header to sort the data on that column. The sort order will be the opposite of the last sort. The sort direction is a session variable and is toggled from ascending to descending on each sort request (see Figure 6.4). The field to sort on is passed via the URL. Its value is the actual table name and column name in the database. For instance, to sort on the employee ID, the sort on the variable's value is as follows:

employees.employee_id.

Notice the inclusion of the ESQL logicsheet in Listing 6.12. This provides many methods to query and manipulate the SQL database.

Listing 6.12 SQL XSP Example Code, *chap6-sql.xsp*

```
<?xml version="1.0"?>

<!-- start chap6-sql.xsp -->

<!-- Cocoon processing directives -->
<?cocoon-process type="xsp"?>
<?cocoon-process type="xslt"?>

<!-- stylesheet directive -->
<?xml-stylesheet href="stylesheets/dynamic-page2html.xsl" type="text/xsl"?>

<!-- include the esql logicsheet -->
<xsp:page
  language="java"
  xmlns:xsp="http://apache.org/xsp"
  xmlns:esql="http://apache.org/cocoon/SQL/v2"
  xmlns:session="http://apache.org/xsp/session/2.0"
>

<page>

<title>Golf Amigos Employees</title>

<content>
```

In Listing 6.13, we initialize the column to sort on and set some session variables; namely, the maximum inactive interval and direction in which to sort the initial query result set. If the user requests to sort on a column header by clicking its associated link, then the Request object method `request.getParameter()` is called. This also triggers the toggle of the sort direction. The session variable `sortdir` is updated before the SQL query is executed.

Listing 6.13 SQL XSP Example Code, *chap6-sql.xsp*

```
<!-- start a bit of logic -->
<xsp:logic>

<!-- initialize the column to sort on -->
String sorton = "employees.employee_name";

<!-- Use a session to track the sort direction -->
if (<session:is-new/>) {

  <!-- timeout the current session if inactive for 10 minutes -->
  <session:set-max-inactive-interval interval="600"/>

  <!-- initially set the sort direction session variable
       - default is ascending -->
  <session:set-attribute name="sortdir">asc</session:set-attribute>
}

<!-- determine table column to sort on - a URI parameter -->
if (request.getParameter("sorton") != null) {

  sorton = request.getParameter("sorton");

  <!-- every time the user follows a sort link, toggle the direction
       based on the last direction -->
  if (<session:get-attribute name="sortdir"/>.equals("asc")) {

    <!-- set session variable to sort descending -->
    <session:set-attribute name="sortdir">desc</session:set-attribute>
  }
  else {

    <!-- set session variable to sort ascending -->
    <session:set-attribute name="sortdir">asc</session:set-attribute>
  }
}

</xsp:logic>
```

In Listing 6.14, we set up the database connection and execute the SQL query. The query joins the employees table with the departments table using the department ID as the joining column. Notice how we build a dynamic SQL statement using the `xsp:expr` and `session:get-attribute` tags and their values.

Listing 6.14 SQL XSP Example Code, *chap6-sql.xsp*

```
<!-- create an esql connection and do some database querying and display
     the results in a nicely formatted HTML table -->

<esql:connection>

  <!-- establish a pool connection -->
  <esql:pool>sybex</esql:pool>

  <!-- do an SQL query -->
  <esql:execute-query>

    <!-- join the employees and departments table and
         sort on the URI parameter (if it exists) and
         sort in the direction determined by the
         session variable sortdir -->
    <esql:query>
       select employees.*, departments.*
       from employees, departments
       where departments.department_id = employees.department_id
       order by <xsp:expr>sorton</xsp:expr> <session:get-attribute
name="sortdir"/>
    </esql:query>


    <!-- display query results -->
    <esql:results>

      <div align="center">

      <!-- build an HTML table for nice presentation of query results -->
      <table cellspacing="2" cellpadding="2" width="500" border="1">
      <tr>
         <th><a href="chap6-sql?sorton=employees.employee_id">ID</a></th>
         <th><a href="chap6-
sql?sorton=employees.employee_name">Employee</a></th>
         <th><a href="chap6-
sql?sorton=departments.department_name">Department</a></th>
      </tr>
```

Listing 6.15 displays the SQL query results in a formatted HTML table. Notice how we alternate table row background colors using the modulus function and the `esql:get-row-position` method. You should notice it starts at 0 and its final value for the current record set will be one less than the number of records in the result set. Hence, we add one to its value. Finally, we use the ESQL logicsheet method `esql:get-string` to get and display a column's value. Listing 6.16 shows the resulting HTML.

Listing 6.15 SQL XSP Example Code, *chap6-sql.xsp*

```
<esql:row-results>

  <!-- alternate the background color of each table row -->
  <xsp:logic>

    <!-- default table row background color -->
    String trBgcolor = "cornsilk";

    <!-- get-row-position is the current row count of the result set -
         its value starts at 0 -->
    int rowCount = <esql:get-row-position/> + 1;
    if (rowCount%2 == 0) {

      <!-- change the background color for even rows -->
  trBgcolor = "#f0f0f0";
    }
  </xsp:logic>

  <!-- display the current row with data and correct background color -->
  <tr>
    <xsp:attribute
name="bgcolor"><xsp:expr>trBgcolor</xsp:expr></xsp:attribute>
    <td align="center"><esql:get-string column="employee_id"/></td>
    <td><esql:get-string column="employee_name"/></td>
    <td><esql:get-string column="department_name"/></td>
  </tr>
</esql:row-results>

</table>

</div>

</esql:results>

<!-- produce a warning message for no records found -->
<esql:no-results>
  <para><em>No records found.</em></para>
</esql:no-results>
```

```
    </esql:execute-query>

  </esql:connection>

</content>

</page>

</xsp:page>
```

Listing 6.16 Resulting HTML after Transformation

```
<html>
<head>
<META http-equiv="Content-Type" content="text/html; charset=UTF-8">
<title>Golf Amigos Employees</title>
</head>
<body vlink="blue" link="blue" alink="red" bgcolor="white">

<h2 style="color: navy; text-align: center">
<A HREF="../view-source?filename=/docs/samples/xsp/chap6-sql.xsp"
TARGET="_blank">Golf Amigos Employees</A>
</h2>

<content
  xmlns:xsp="http://apache.org/xsp"
  xmlns:xspdoc="http://apache.org/cocoon/XSPDoc/v1"
  xmlns:esql="http://apache.org/cocoon/SQL/v2"
  xmlns:session="http://apache.org/xsp/session/2.0">

<div align="center">

<table cellspacing="2" cellpadding="2" width="500" border="1">
<tr>
  <th><a href="chap6-sql?sorton=employees.employee_id">ID</a></th>
  <th><a href="chap6-sql?sorton=employees.employee_name">Employee</a></th>
  <th><a href="chap6-sql?sorton=departments.department_name">Department</a></th>
</tr>

<tr bgcolor="cornsilk">
  <td align="center">101</td>
  <td>Dusty Bottoms</td>
  <td>Sales</td>
</tr>

<tr bgcolor="#f0f0f0">
  <td align="center">104</td>
  <td>El Guapo</td>
  <td>Sales</td>
```

```
</tr>

<tr bgcolor="cornsilk">
  <td align="center">100</td>
  <td>Jefe</td>
  <td>Engineering</td>
</tr>

<tr bgcolor="#f0f0f0">
  <td align="center">103</td>
  <td>Lucky Day</td>
  <td>Marketing</td>
</tr>

<tr bgcolor="cornsilk">
  <td align="center">102</td>
  <td>Neddy Nederlander</td>
  <td>Marketing</td>
</tr>

</table>

</div>

</content>

</body>
</html>
```

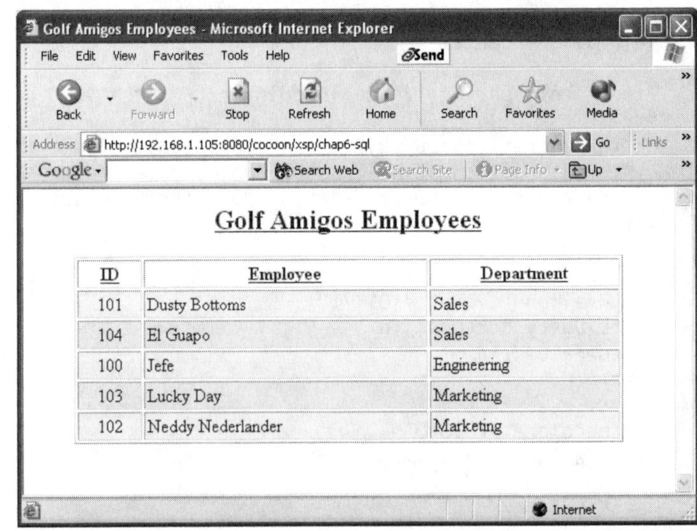

FIGURE 6.3: SQL example initial results. The data is sorted on the employee's name.

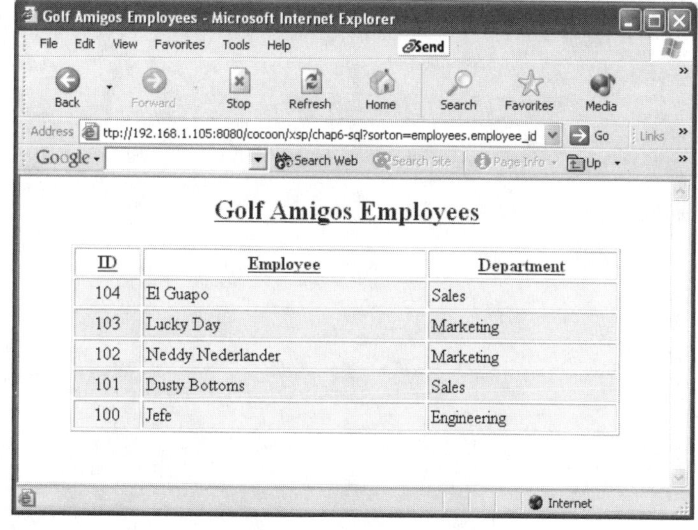

FIGURE 6.4: SQL example after clicking ID column header. It is sorted in descending order because the last sort was done in ascending order. (The initial query is shown in Figure 6.3.)

Summary

XSP is a powerful technology of the Cocoon 2 architecture. To use XSP effectively, a number of important concepts must be understood:

- What constitutes a minimal XSP
- How Cocoon 2 processes an XSP page
- How to use XSP elements to produce dynamic content

A minimal XSP page must contain Cocoon processing elements, an element designating the XSP document root element, any logicsheet or language declarations, and some logic controls. XSP is a way to automatically generate program code from a declarative description.

Cocoon 2 processes an XSP page by reading the XSP page and then transforms it into source code used by a Cocoon Generator. This is typically Java code from an XSP page. The XSP elements in the XSP page define the structure of the resulting source code whereas the other page elements tell the Generator how to display the resulting output from the executed source code. Finally, the resulting source code is compiled into a Java class and then executed in the Cocoon 2 environment.

Using XSP is similar to using declarative markup such as XML. Typically, `xsp:expr` and `xsp:logic` are the most used XSP elements. They provide logic controls in an XSP page. In conjunction with XSP, Cocoon 2 has built-in logicsheets providing dynamic content generation capabilities that separate logic from content and presentation. Logicsheets are covered in more depth in Chapter 7.

CHAPTER 7

XSP Logicsheets

- How a Logicsheet Works
- Built-in XSP Logicsheets
- Building a Custom Logicsheet

Cocoon 2 comes with a collection of built-in XSP capabilities known as *logicsheets*. According to the Cocoon 2 documentation (see `http://xml.apache.org/cocoon/userdocs/xsp/logicsheet-concepts.html`),"a logicsheet is an XML filter used to translate user-defined, dynamic markup into equivalent code embedding directives for a given markup language." In other words, a logicsheet provides additional dynamic content generation capabilities to XSP.

Logicsheets are another pillar of the Cocoon architecture, providing separation of logic from content and presentation. They provide a powerful abstraction mechanism by burying detailed programming code in a logicsheet while providing a simple parameterized XML tag to the nonprogramming author. This allows the author to concentrate on providing meaningful content rather than worrying about programming, something the content author might not know (or care) anything about. A logicsheet is implemented using XSL and XSLT transformations and is a collection of XML tags that are used in an XSP program to include externally defined blocks of code.

One key logicsheet feature is that it makes an XSP page more readable because the code has been replaced with logicsheet XML tags. Logicsheets also centralize the code and can be reused in multiple XSP pages; if you need to make a change to the code, you do it in one XSL stylesheet (stylesheets are the tools with which a logicsheet is developed and deployed) rather than having to modify the code in multiple places. Additionally, a logicsheet defines a specific namespace and XML elements within the namespace, which provides specific functionality to the logicsheet.

Logicsheets are programming-language dependent because the XSL stylesheet transforms XML tags into actual programming language code (Java code is inserted in an XSP page). For example, the following XML tag can be used to determine the current name of the Cocoon server:

```
<xsp-request:get-server-name/>
```

The preceding XML is transformed by the Request logicsheet into the following XSP code:

```
<xsp:expr>
     request.getServerName()
</xsp:expr>
```

Fortunately, a Cocoon helper class can alleviate this language dependency. Each built-in logicsheet has an associated helper class. Helper classes are normally used in creating more useful and readable logicsheets. For example, this next bit of XML code determines the current time and day using the Util logicsheet (it uses the `XSPUtil` Java helper class):

```
<util:time-of-day format="hh:mm:ss"/>
```

The preceding XML is transformed by the Util logicsheet into the following XSP code:

```
<xsp:expr>
  SimpleDateFormat.getInstance().format(new Date(), "hh:mm:ss")
</xsp:expr>
```

Each built-in logicsheet included in this chapter is based on Cocoon 2.0.1. New elements are continually added to the logicsheets because Cocoon is a framework that encourages innovation. Therefore, cataloging each built-in logicsheet includes many but not all of the elements and attributes known to the Cocoon community as of this writing. The definitive source for logicsheet elements and attributes can be found at `http://xml.apache.org/cocoon/`.

In this chapter, the examples were developed on a PC running Linux RedHat 7.1. Therefore, specific installation instructions for the examples should be based on your specific Cocoon 2 installation.

This chapter discusses the following:

- Exploring how a logicsheet works
- Cataloging all of the built-in logicsheets
- Building a customized logicsheet

How a Logicsheet Works

There are a couple of important features of a logicsheet that are vital to how a logicsheet works. First, it has an associated namespace and XML element set created to perform certain functions. Second, it is implemented by using XSLT transformations. Third, it is instrumental in the transformation of an XSP page into Java source code. This is where a logicsheet comes into play. It provides additional transformations before the final Java source code is created by Cocoon. For details on the XSP creation process, see `www6.software.ibm.com/developerworks/education/x-xsp/x-xsp-2-3.html`.

This is a powerful concept because sections of code can be abstracted out of the XSP page and kept in a centralized XSL stylesheet. The result is the replacement of the code in the XSP page with associated logicsheet XML elements, child elements, and attributes. As Cocoon processes the XSP page, it determines which logicsheet's namespaces are referenced in the XSP page and applies any logicsheet transformations specified in the XSP page. During this process, each logicsheet substitutes the code back into the original XSP page while preserving the integrity of the entire XSP page.

Here's the basic process:

1. Cocoon reads an XSP page and determines all declared namespaces.
2. Cocoon checks the `cocoon.xconf` file to see if the namespace has been configured and determines the correct XSL stylesheet to apply.
3. If the XSL stylesheet exists, then the transformations are executed.

4. Repeat steps 2 and 3 until all logicsheet transformations have been completed for all namespaces except for the XSP namespace. At this point, Cocoon executes the final transformation (for the XSP namespace) and generates the Java source code equivalent of the original XSP page.

Built-In XSP Logicsheets

Cocoon 2 comes with the following built-in logicsheets:

Action applies standard XML action operations.

Capture applies standard XML operations for capturing parts of the XSP-generated XML as XML fragments or DOM nodes.

Cookie applies standard XML cookie operations.

ESQL applies standard SQL queries and serializes the results as XML.

Formval applies a set browser form input validation operations.

Log applies standard XML log operations.

Request applies standard XML request operations (methods of the `HttpServerRequest` object).

Response applies standard XML response operations (methods of the `HttpServerResponse` object).

Sel applies the aggregation of multiple XSP pages into one.

Session applies standard XML session operations (methods of the `HttpSession` object).

SOAP applies standard Simple Object Access Protocol (SOAP) operations.

Util applies standard XML utility operations.

XScript supports the XML Scripting Language (XScript)

All of the built-in logicsheets are described in detail in the following sections.

Action Logicsheet

The Action logicsheet provides XML tags for handling action-related services, such as setting the action status, accessing the result map, and performing browser redirects.

The entry for the Action logicsheet in the `<target-language name="java">` section of `cocoon.xconf` looks like the following:

```
<builtin-logicsheet>
  <parameter name="prefix" value="action"/>
  <parameter name="uri" value="http://apache.org/cocoon/action/1.0"/>
  <parameter name="href" value="resource://org/apache/cocoon/components/
  language/markup/xsp/java/action.xsl"/>
</builtin-logicsheet>
```

Map the XSP namespace to the `action` prefix:

```
<xsp:page
  ...
  xmlns:action="http://apache.org/cocoon/action/1.0"
  ...
>
```

Table 7.1 lists the elements of the Action logicsheet. Table 7.2 lists the elements and attributes.

TABLE 7.1: Action Logicsheet Elements

Element	Description
redirect-to	Redirects the browser to a specified URL
set-result	Adds an entry in the Action result map, and set the action status to successful
get-result	Gets the value of an entry in the Action result map previously set
set-status	Sets the action to successful
set-failure	Sets the action to failure

TABLE 7.2: Action Logicsheet Elements and Attributes

Element	Attribute	Data Type	Required?	Default	Description
redirect-to	uri	String	Yes		Redirects the browser to a specified URI
redirect-to	session-mode	Boolean	No	true	Sets and keeps session mode alive across a redirect
set-result	name	String	Yes		Defines the entry name
set-result	value	String	Yes		Defines the entry value
get-result	name	String	Yes		Gets the value of an entry in the Action result map

Capture Logicsheet

The Capture logicsheet provides XML tags for capturing parts of the XSP-generated XML as XML fragments or DOM nodes. The content is captured and stored in an XMLFragment variable.

The entry for the Capture logicsheet in the <target-language name="java"> section of cocoon.xconf looks like the following:

```
<builtin-logicsheet>
  <parameter name="prefix" value="capture"/>
  <parameter name="uri" value="http://apache.org/cocoon/capture/1.0"/>
  <parameter name="href" value="resource://org/apache/cocoon/components/
  language/markup/xsp/java/capture.xsl"/>
</builtin-logicsheet>
```

Map the XSP namespace to the capture prefix:

```
<xsp:page
  ...
  xmlns:capture="http://apache.org/cocoon/capture/1.0"
  ...
>
```

Table 7.3 lists the elements of the Capture logicsheet. Table 7.4 lists the elements and attributes.

TABLE 7.3: Capture Logicsheet Elements

Element	Description
Fragment-variable	Captures the generated XML content and stores it as an XMLFragment variable
fragment-request-attr	Captures the generated XML content and stores it in an XMLFragment in a Request attribute
dom-variable	Captures the XML generated XML content and stores it as an org.w3c.dom.Node variable (which is actually a DocumentFragment variable)
dom-request-attr	Captures the XML generated XML content and stores it as a org.w3c.dom.Node in a request attribute

TABLE 7.4: Capture Logicsheet Elements and Attributes

Element	Attribute	Data Type	Required?	Default	Description
fragment-variable	name	String	Yes		Name of the generated variable holding the fragment

continued on next page

TABLE 7.4 CONTINUED: Capture Logicsheet Elements and Attributes

Element	Attribute	Data Type	Required?	Default	Description
`fragment-variable`	`id`	Cocoon ID			Cocoon generated ID
`fragment-request-attr`	`name`	String	Yes		The request attribute name
`fragment-request-attr`	`id`	Cocoon ID			Cocoon generated ID
`dom-variable`	`name`	String	Yes		Name of the generated variable holding the DOM node
`dom-variable`	`id`	Cocoon ID			Cocoon generated ID
`dom-request-attr`	`name`	String	Yes		The request attribute name
`dom-request-attr`	`id`	Cocoon ID			Cocoon generated ID

Cookie Logicsheet

The Cookie logicsheet provides XML tags for standard cookie operations. The entry for the Cookie logicsheet in the `<target-language name="java">` section of `cocoon.xconf` looks like the following:

```
<builtin-logicsheet>
   <parameter name="prefix" value="xsp-cookie"/>
   <parameter name="uri" value="http://apache.org/xsp/cookie/2.0"/>
   <parameter name="href" value="resource://org/apache/cocoon/components/
   language/markup/xsp/java/cookie.xsl"/>
</builtin-logicsheet>
```

Map the XSP namespace to the `xsp-cookie` prefix:

```
<xsp:page
  ...
  xmlns:xsp-cookie="http://apache.org/xsp/cookie/2.0"
  ...
>
```

Table 7.5 lists the elements of the Cookie logicsheet. Table 7.6 lists the elements and attributes.

TABLE 7.5: Cookie Logicsheet Elements

Element	Description
create-cookies[1]	Creates a set of cookies
cookie[2]	Creates an individual cookie
getCookies	Gets a set of cookies and their values as a Cookie object of XML
getCookie	Gets an individual cookie by either its name or index and returns either a Cookie object or as XML
getName	Gets the name of the cookie
getComment	Gets a comment associated with a cookie
getDomain	Gets the domain of the cookie
getMaxAge	Gets the maximum age of a cookie
getPath	Gets the path of the cookie
getSecure	Gets the value of the secure property of the cookie
getValue	Gets the current value of the cookie
getVersion	Gets the version of the cookie

1. `Create-cookies` is a wrapper XML tag that allows the multiple setting of cookies.
2. The elements and attributes of the `cookie` element are derived from the class definition: `org.apache.cocoon.components.language.markup.xsp.XSPCookieHelper.addCookie`

TABLE 7.6: Cookie Logicsheet Elements and Attributes

Element	Attribute	Data Type	Required?	Default	Description
cookie	name	String	Yes		Defines the name of the cookie
cookie	value	String	Yes		Defines the value of the cookie
cookie	setComment	String	Yes	""	Adds a comment for the cookie
cookie	setDomain	String	Yes	""	Sets the domain for the cookie
cookie	setMaxAge	Integer	Yes	0	Sets the maximum age of the cookie in seconds
cookie	setPath	String	Yes	""	Sets the path of the cookie
cookie	setSecure	String	Yes	""	Sets the security; indicates to the browser whether the cookie should only be sent using a secure protocol, such as HTTPS or SSL

continued on next page

TABLE 7.6 CONTINUED: Cookie Logicsheet Elements and Attributes

Element	Attribute	Data Type	Required?	Default	Description
cookie	setVersion	Integer	Yes	0	Sets the version of the cookie
getCookies	as	(cookie | xml)		cookie	Gets a set of cookies as a cookie object or as XML
getCookie	name	String	Yes[1]	null	Gets a cookie by its name
getCookie	index	Integer	Yes[1]	-1	Gets a cookie by its index
getCookie	as	(cookie | xml)		cookie	Gets a cookie and returns either a Cookie object or as XML
getName	name	String	Yes[1]	null	Gets the name of the cookie by its name
getName	index	Integer	Yes[1]	-1	Gets the name of the cookie by its index
getComment	name	String	Yes[1]	null	Gets a cookie's associated comment by its name
getComment	index	Integer	Yes[1]	-1	Gets a cookie's associated comment by its index
getDomain	name	String	Yes[1]	null	Gets a cookie's domain by its name
getDomain	index	Integer	Yes[1]	-1	Gets a cookie's domain comment by its index
getMaxAge	name	String	Yes[1]	null	Gets a cookie's maximum age by its name
getMaxAge	index	Integer	Yes[1]	-1	Gets a cookie's maximum age by its index
getPath	name	String	Yes[1]	null	Gets a cookie's path by its name
getPath	index	Integer	Yes[1]	-1	Gets a cookies' path by its index
getSecure	name	String	Yes[1]	null	Gets a cookie's security designation by its name
getSecure	index	Integer	Yes[1]	-1	Gets a cookie's security designation by its index
getValue	name	String	Yes[1]	null	Gets a cookie's value by its name
getValue	index	Integer	Yes[1]	-1	Gets a cookie's value by its index
getVersion	name	String	Yes[1]	null	Gets a cookie's version by its name
getVersion	index	Integer	Yes[1]	-1	Gets a cookie's version by its index

1. The element requires one attribute, either its name or its index. If called with the name, then the index attribute is not required. If called with the index, then the name attribute is not required.

ESQL Logicsheet

The ESQL logicsheet provides XML tags for standard SQL queries and serializes the results as XML. The entry for the ESQL logicsheet in the `<target-language name="java">` section of `cocoon.xconf` looks like the following:

```
<builtin-logicsheet>
   <parameter name="prefix" value="esql"/>
   <parameter name="uri" value="http://apache.org/cocoon/SQL/v2"/>
   <parameter name="href"
value="resource://org/apache/cocoon/components/language/markup/xsp/java/
esql.xsl"/>
</builtin-logicsheet>
```

Map the XSP namespace to the `esql` prefix:

```
<xsp:page
  ...
  xmlns:esql="http://apache.org/cocoon/SQL/v2"
  ...
>
```

Table 7.7 lists the elements of the ESQL logicsheet. Table 7.8 lists the connection elements.

TABLE 7.7: ESQL Logicsheet Elements

Element	Description
connection	Opens a new database connection

Table 7.8 lists elements of the `<esql:connection>` tag.

TABLE 7.8: ESQL Logicsheet Connection Elements

Element	Description
Driver	Sets the name of the database driver
Dburl	Sets the URL of the database
Username	Sets the username for authenticated database access
Password	Sets the password for the authenticated username for database access
Pool	Sets the name of the database pool
autocommit	Sets automatic commit to either true or false

continued on next page

TABLE 7.8 CONTINUED: ESQL Logicsheet Connection Elements

Element	Description
use-limit-clause[1]	Sets the database you are using so the correct LIMIT clause will be used select from (mysql | jdbc | postgresql | auto[2])
Property[3]	Sets a property of the connection element given an element name as a value of the name attribute
execute-query	Executes a SQL query on a database

1. Values derived from the class method: org.apache.cocoon.components.language.markup.xsp .EsqlConnection.setLimitMethod.
2. The 'auto' value directs Cocoon to try to discover the correct database using the dburl element.
3. This element can set the value of any element of the connection element. For example: <esql:property name="password">foo</esql:property> is the same as <esql:password>foo</esql:password>.

Table 7.9 lists elements of the <esql:execute-query> tag.

TABLE 7.9: ESQL Logicsheet Execute-Query Elements

Element	Description
Query	Defines the SQL query
max-rows	Sets the maximum number of rows in the result set
skip-rows	Sets the number of rows to skip before building the result set
results	Instantiates the resulting elements in the result tree for each row in the result set
error-results	Instantiates the results in the result tree if the query results in a database error
no-results	Query returns no results
update-results	Instantiates the query results in the result tree if the query returns a number of rows

Table 7.10 lists elements of the <esql:query> tag.

TABLE 7.10: ESQL Logicsheet Query Elements

Element	Description
parameter	Set a query parameter

Table 7.11 lists elements of the <esql:results> tag.

TABLE 7.11: ESQL Logicsheet Results Elements

Element	Description
`get-column-count`	Gets the number of rows returned
`get-metadata`	Returns the metadata associated with the results set
`get-resultset`	Returns the results set
`row-results`	Iterates over a result set and returns each row separately
`get-row-position`	Returns the position of the current row in the result set

As of this writing, row-count was implemented only for `<esql:use-limit-method>jdbc </esql:use-limit-method>.` For other use limit methods, row-count is not yet implemented.

Table 7.12 lists elements of the `<esql:error-results>` tag.

TABLE 7.12: ESQL Logicsheet Error-Results Elements

Element	Description
`get-message`	Returns the current exception message
`to-string`	Returns the current exception message as a string
`get-stackstrace`	Returns the stack trace of the current exception

Table 7.13 lists elements of the `<esql:row-results>` tag.

TABLE 7.13: ESQL Logicsheet Row-Results Elements

Element	Description
`get-columns`	Returns a set of records whose names are the column names and whose values are the column values represented as a string
`encoding`	Sets the Java encoding for a column
`get-array`	Returns the value of the given column as a `java.sql.Array`
`get-ascii`	Returns the value of the given column as a clob
`get-boolean`	Returns the value of the given column in the current row as a Boolean
`get-column-label`	Returns the label of the given column in the current row given the column number
`get-column-name`	Returns the name of the given column in the current row given the column number
`get-column-type`	Returns the type of the given column in the current row as an integer given the column number

continued on next page

TABLE 7.13 CONTINUED: ESQL Logicsheet Row-Results Elements

Element	Description
get-column-type-name	Returns the name of the type of the given column in the current row given the column number
get-date	Returns the value of the given column in the current row as a date
get-time	Returns the value of the given column in the current row as a time
get-timestamp	Returns the value of the given column in the current row as a timestamp
get-string	Returns the value of the given column in the current row as a string
get-double	Returns the value of the given column in the current row as a double
get-float	Returns the value of the given column in the current row as a float
get-int	Returns the value of the given column in the current row as an integer
get-long	Returns the value of the given column in the current row as a long integer
get-short	Returns the value of the given column in the current row as a short integer
get-xml	Parses the value of the given column in the current row as XML, then returns the XML
get-row-position	Returns the position of the current row in the result set
get-object	Returns the value of the given column in the current row as an object
get-struct	Returns the value of the given column in the current row as a struct
is-null	Allows null column testing. Returns true if column in the current row contains a null value

Table 7.14 lists elements of the `<esql:get-string>` tag.

TABLE 7.14: ESQL Logicsheet Get-String Elements

Element	Description
encoding	Sets the Java encoding for a column

Table 7.15 lists elements of the `<esql:get-columns>` tag.

TABLE 7.15: ESQL Logicsheet Get-Columns Elements

Element	Description
tagcase	Sets column name tag case to either lower or upper

Formval

The Formval logicsheet provides XML tags for standard browser form input validation operations.

The entry for the Formval logicsheet in the `<target-language name="java">` section of `cocoon.xconf` looks like the following:

```
<builtin-logicsheet>
   <parameter name="prefix" value="xsp-formval"/>
   <parameter name="uri" value="http://apache.org/xsp/form-validator/2.0"/>
   <parameter name="href" value="resource://org/apache/cocoon/components/
   language/markup/xsp/java/form-validator.xsl"/>
</builtin-logicsheet>
```

Map the XSP namespace to the `xsp-formval` prefix:

```
<xsp:page
  ...
  xmlns:xsp-formval="http://apache.org/xsp/form-validator/2.0"
  ...
>
```

Table 7.16 lists the elements of the Formval logicsheet. Table 7.17 lists the elements and attributes.

TABLE 7.16: Formval Logicsheet Elements

Element	Description
`descriptor`	Gets attributes from the descriptor file (not required if doing just form validation)
`results`	Returns a map containing all validation results
`is-ok`	Returns *true* if parameter successfully checked
`on-ok`	Returns the enclosed markup if the form element's validation is true
`is-error`	Returns *true* if some error occurred
`on-error`	Returns the enclosed markup if the form element's validation returned an error
`is-null`	Returns *true* if the form element is null but it is required
`on-null`	Returns the enclosed markup if the form element's validation returned a "is null" error
`is-toosmall`	Returns *true* if either the value or the string length is less than the specified size attribute
`on-toosmall`	Returns the enclosed markup if the form element's validation returned a "too small" error
`is-toolarge`	Returns *true* if either the value or the string length is greater than the specified `maxlength` attribute

continued on next page

TABLE 7.16 CONTINUED: Formval Logicsheet Elements

Element	Description
`on-toolarge`	Returns the enclosed markup if the form element's validation returned a "too large" error
`is-nomatch`	Returns *true* if a form element's string value does not match the specified regular expression
`on-nomatch`	Returns the enclosed markup if the form element's validation returned a "no match" error
`is-notpresent`	Returns *true* if a validation operation was requested but no such result was found in the request attribute
`on-notpresent`	Returns the enclosed markup if the form element's validation returned a "not present" error
`get-attribute`	Get an attribute from a form element's declaration in the descriptor file
`validate`	Provides a context for form validation and associated form elements

TABLE 7.17: Formval Logicsheet Elements and Attributes

Element	Attribute	Data Type	Required?	Default	Description
`descriptor`	`name`	String	Yes		Name of descriptor file[1]
`descriptor`	`constraint-set`	String	Yes		Name of current constraint set
`descriptor`	`reloadable`	Boolean	No	True	Reloads the descriptor file if it is modified
`validate`	`name`	String	Yes		Form element name
`is-ok`	`name`	String	Yes[2]	-1	Form element name
`on-ok`	`name`	String	Yes[2]	-1	Form element name
`is-toosmall`	`name`	String	Yes[2]	-1	Form element name
`on-toosmall`	`name`	String	Yes[2]	-1	Form element name
`is-error`	`name`	String	Yes[2]	-1	Form element name
`on-error`	`name`	String	Yes[2]	-1	Form element name
`is-toolarge`	`name`	String	Yes[2]	-1	Form element name
`on-toolarge`	`name`	String	Yes[2]	-1	Form element name
`is-nomatch`	`name`	String	Yes[2]	-1	Form element name
`on-nomatch`	`name`	String	Yes[2]	-1	Form element name
`is-null`	`name`	String	Yes[2]	-1	Form element name
`on-null`	`name`	String	Yes[2]	-1	Form element name
`is-notpresent`	`name`	String	Yes[2]	-1	Form element name

continued on next page

TABLE 7.17 CONTINUED: Formval Logicsheet Elements and Attributes

Element	Attribute	Data Type	Required?	Default	Description
`on-notpresent`	`name`	String	Yes[2]	-1	Form element name
`get-attribute`	`parameter`	String	No	-1	Parameter name
`get-attribute`	`name`	String	Yes		Form element name

1. A typical example is `name="context:///docs/samples/formval/descriptor.xml"`.
2. If the element is used within the an `xsp-formval:validate` context, the parameter is not required.

Log Logicsheet

The Log logicsheet provides XML tags for standard log operations. The entry for the Log logicsheet in the `<target-language name="java">` section of `cocoon.xconf` looks like the following:

```
<builtin-logicsheet>
   <parameter name="prefix" value="log"/>
   <parameter name="uri" value="http://apache.org/xsp/log/2.0"/>
   <parameter name="href" value="resource://org/apache/cocoon/components/
   language/markup/xsp/java/log.xsl"/>
</builtin-logicsheet>
```

Map the XSP namespace to the `log` prefix:

```
<xsp:page
  ...
  xmlns:log="http://apache.org/xsp/log/2.0"
  ...
>
```

Table 7.18 lists the elements of the Log logicsheet. Table7.19 lists the elements and attributes.

TABLE 7.18: Log Logicsheet Elements

Element	Description
`logger`	Sets the logging process
`debug`	Writes debug data to the log file (i.e., developer messages)
`info`	Writes information data to the log file (i.e., state changes, client connection, user login)
`warn`	Writes warning data to the log file (i.e., problem or conflict has occurred but it may be recoverable)
`error`	Writes error data to the log file (i.e., problem has occurred but it is not fatal but the system will still function)
`fatal-error`	Writes fatal error data to the log file (i.e., system failure and requires attention)

TABLE 7.19: Log Logicsheet Elements and Attributes

Element	Attribute	Data Type	Required?	Default	Description
logger	name	String	Yes		Name of the logging agent
logger	filename	String	Yes		Name of the log file
logger	level	String	No	DEBUG	Level of data to report; choose from (DEBUG | WARN | ERROR | FATAL_ERROR | INFO)

Request Logicsheet

The Request logicsheet provides XML tags for standard request operations (methods of the HttpServerRequest object). The entry for the Request logicsheet in the <target-language name="java"> section of cocoon.xconf looks like the following:

```
<builtin-logicsheet>
    <parameter name="prefix" value="xsp-request"/>
    <parameter name="uri" value="http://apache.org/xsp/request/2.0"/>
    <parameter name="href" value="resource://org/apache/cocoon/components/
    language/markup/xsp/java/request.xsl"/>
</builtin-logicsheet>
```

Map the XSP namespace to the xsp-request prefix:

```
<xsp:page
  ...
  xmlns:xsp-request="http://apache.org/xsp/request/2.0"
  ...
>
```

Table 7.20 lists the elements of the Request logicsheet. Table 7.21 lists the informational elements and attributes.

TABLE 7.20: Request Logicsheet Elements

Element	Description
get-uri	Gets the URL of the request
get-sitemap-uri	Gets the URL of the request with the sitemap applied
get-session-attribute	Gets an attribute of the request session
get-session-id	Gets the session ID contained in the request
get-parameter	Gets the value of the named request parameter
get-parameter-values	Gets all values for the named request parameter

continued on next page

TABLE 7.20 CONTINUED: Request Logicsheet Elements

Element	Description
`get-parameter-names`	Gets the names of all the request parameters as XML
`get-header`	Gets the value of the named request header
`get-header-names`	Gets the names of all the request header parameters as XML
`get-attribute`	Gets a named attribute either set by the Servlet or by an `xsp-request:set-attribute` operation
`get-attribute-names`	Gets the names of all request attributes as XML
`remove-attribute`	Removes the named attribute from the request
`get-requested-url`	Gets the part of the request URL from the protocol name up to the query string
`get-remote-address`	Gets the IP address of the requesting client
`get-remote-user`	Gets the login name of an authenticated user
`get-context-path`	Gets the context of the request from the requesting URI
`get-server-name`	Gets the name of the server receiving the request
`get-server-port`	Gets the server port on which the request was received
`get-method`	Gets the name of the request method (i.e., `GET`, `POST`, or `PUT`)
`get-query-string`	Gets the request query string for the `GET` method (i.e., `"?name=Mark&dept=Web"`)
`get-protocol`	Gets the name and version of the request protocol (i.e., HTTP/`1.1`)
`get-remote-host`	Gets the fully qualified name of the request client (i.e., set to IP address of the request client if the name cannot be resolved)
`name`	Sets the name of a request parameter
`default`	Sets the default value of a request parameter

TABLE 7.21: Request Logicsheet Informational Elements and Attributes

Element	Attribute/ Child Element	Data Type	Required?	Default	Description
`get-uri`	as	String		string	Returns element as value of attribute (`string | xml`)
`get-sitemap-uri`	as	String		string	Returns element as value of attribute (`string | xml`)
`get-session-attribute`	as	String	string		Returns element as value of attribute (`string | xml`)

continued on next page

TABLE 7.21 CONTINUED: Request Logicsheet Informational Elements and Attributes

Element	Attribute/ Child Element	Data Type	Required?	Default	Description
get-session-attribute	name	String	Yes[1]		Names of session attributes
get-session-attribute	default	String	No[2]	null	Sets default value of the element
get-session-id	as	String		string	Returns element as value of attribute (string | xml)
get-parameter	name	String	Yes[1]		Defines the name of request parameter
get-parameter	default	String	No[1]	null	Sets default value of the element
get-parameter	as	String		string	Returns element as value of attribute (string | xml)
get-parameter	form-encoding	String	No	ISO-8859-1[3]	Defines the encoding of the page that sent the form data
get-parameter	container-encoding	String	No	ISO-8859-1[3]	Defines the encoding of the Servlet container
get-parameter-values	name	String	Yes[1]		Defines the name of request parameter
get-parameter-values	as	String		xml	Returns element as value of attribute (xml | array)
get-parameter-values	form-encoding	String	No	ISO-8859-1[3]	The encoding of the page that sent the form data
get-parameter-values	container-encoding	String	No	ISO-8859-1[3]	Defines the encoding of the Servlet container
get-header	name	String	Yes[1]		Defines the name of request header parameter
get-header	as	String		string	Returns element as value of attribute (xml | string)
get-attribute	name	String	Yes[1]		Defines the name of request attribute
get-attribute	as	String		string	Returns element as value of attribute (xml | string | object)

continued on next page

TABLE 7.21 CONTINUED: Request Logicsheet Informational Elements and Attributes

Element	Attribute/ Child Element	Data Type	Required?	Default	Description
remove-attribute	name	String	Yes[1]		Defines the name of request attribute to remove
get-requested-url	as	String		string	Returns element as value of attribute (xml | string)
get-remote-address	as	String		string	Returns element as value of attribute (xml | string)
get-remote-user	as	String		string	Returns element as value of attribute (xml | string)
get-context-path	as	String		string	Returns element as value of attribute (xml | string)
get-server-name	as	String		string	Returns element as value of attribute (xml | string)
get-server-port	as	String		string	Returns element as value of attribute (xml | string)
get-method	as	String		string	Returns element as value of attribute (xml | string)
get-query-string	as	String		string	Returns element as value of attribute (xml | string)
get-protocol	as	String		string	Returns element as value of attribute (xml | string)
get-remote-host	as	String		string	Returns element as value of attribute (xml | string)

1. The element can have either a named attribute or the element can have a child element. For example, these two are equivalent for the get-parameter element and the name attribute/child element:

```
<xsp-request:get-parameter name="car"/>

<xsp-request:get-parameter>
  <xsp-request:name>car</xsp-request:name>
</xsp-request:get-parameter>
```

2. The element can have either a named attribute or the element can have a child element. For example, these two are equivalent for the get-parameter element and the default attribute/child element:

```
<xsp-request:get-parameter default="auto"/>

<xsp-request:get-parameter>
  <xsp-request:default>auto</xsp-request:default>
</xsp-request:get-parameter>
```

3. Standard Servlet configuration value for encoding.

Response Logicsheet

The Response logicsheet provides XML tags for standard response operations (methods of the `HttpServerResponse` object). The entry for the Response logicsheet in the `<target-language name="java">` section of `cocoon.xconf` looks like the following:

```
<builtin-logicsheet>
   <parameter name="prefix" value="xsp-response"/>
   <parameter name="uri" value="http://apache.org/xsp/response/2.0"/>
   <parameter name="href" value="resource://org/apache/cocoon/components/
   language/markup/xsp/java/response.xsl"/>
</builtin-logicsheet>
```

Map the XSP namespace to the `xsp-response` prefix:

```
<xsp:page
  ...
  xmlns:xsp-response="http://apache.org/xsp/response/2.0"
  ...
>
```

Table 7.22 lists the elements of the Response logicsheet. Table 7.23 lists the elements and attributes.

TABLE 7.22: Response Logicsheet Elements

Element	Description
`set-header`	Sets response header parameters

TABLE 7.23: Response Logicsheet Elements and Attributes

Element	Attribute	Data Type	Required?	Default	Description
`set-header`	Name	String	Yes[1]		Name of response parameter
`set-header`	`Value`	String	Yes[1]		Value of named response parameter

1. The element can have either a named attribute or the element can have a child element. For example, these three are equivalent for the `set-header` element and the `name` attribute/child element:

```
<xsp-response:set-header name="car" value="chevelle"/>

<xsp-response:set-header name="car">
  <xsp-response:value>chevelle</xsp-response:value>
</xsp-response:set-header>

<xsp-response:set-header>
  <xsp-response:name>car</xsp-response:name>
  <xsp-response:value>chevelle</xsp-response:value>
</xsp-response:set-header>
```

Sel Logicsheet

The Sel logicsheet provides XML tags for aggregation of multiple XSP pages into one. Sel is short for selector. The entry for the Sel logicsheet in the `<target-language name="java">` section of `cocoon.xconf` looks like the following:

```
<builtin-logicsheet>
   <parameter name="prefix" value="sel"/>
   <parameter name="uri" value="http://apache.org/xsp/sel/1.0"/>
   <parameter name="href" value="resource://org/apache/cocoon/components/
   language/markup/xsp/java/sel.xsl"/>
</builtin-logicsheet>
```

Map the XSP namespace to the `sel` prefix:

```
<xsp:page
  ...
  xmlns:sel="http://apache.org/xsp/sel/1.0"
  ...
>
```

Table 7.24 lists the elements of the Sel logicsheet. Table 7.25 lists the elements and attributes.

TABLE 7.24: Sel Logicsheet Elements

Element	Description
`subpage-set`	Selects the page set to display
`subpage`	Displays the named subpages
`default-subpage`	Displays the default page if no other subpages named

TABLE 7.25: Sel Logicsheet Elements and Attributes

Element	Attribute	Data Type	Required?	Default	Description
`subpage-set`	`type`	String	Yes		Type of page set (i.e., `type="sitemap"`)
`subpage-set`	`parameter`	String	Yes		Named parameter (i.e., `parameter="subpage"`)

Session Logicsheet

The Session logicsheet provides XML tags for standard session operations (methods of the `HttpSession` object). The entry for the Session logicsheet in the `<target-language name="java">` section of `cocoon.xconf` looks like the following:

```
<builtin-logicsheet>
   <parameter name="prefix" value="session"/>
   <parameter name="uri" value="http://apache.org/xsp/session/2.0"/>
   <parameter name="href" value="resource://org/apache/cocoon/components/
   language/markup/xsp/java/session.xsl"/>
</builtin-logicsheet>
```

Map the XSP namespace to the `session` prefix:

```
<xsp:page
  ...
  xmlns:session="http://apache.org/xsp/session/2.0"
  ...
>
```

Table 7.26 lists the elements of the Session logicsheet. Table 7.27 lists the elements and attributes.

TABLE 7.26: Session Logicsheet Elements

Element	Description
`get-attribute`	Gets the value of the named session attribute
`get-attribute-names`	Gets the names of all the session attributes
`get-creation-time`	Gets the creation time of the session in seconds
`get-id`	Gets the session ID (generated by the Servlet)
`get-last-accessed-time`	Gets the time of the last session access in seconds
`get-max-inactive-interval`	Gets the minimum time, in seconds, that the server will maintain the current session between client requests
`invalidate`	Invalidates the current session; any current session attributes are flushed
`is-new`	Indicates if this session is newly created
`remove-attribute`	Removes the named attribute from the current session
`set-attribute`	Sets the named session attribute
`set-max-inactive-interval`	Sets the minimum time, in seconds, that the server will maintain the current session between client requests
`encode-url`	Encodes an URL with the current session ID
`form-encode-url`	Encodes an URL with the current session ID as an HTML form
`name`	Sets the session attribute name

TABLE 7.27: Session Logicsheet Elements and Attributes

Element	Attribute/ Child Element	Data Type	Required?	Default	Description
get-attribute	name	String	Yes[1]		Provides the name of the attribute
get-attribute	as	String	No	object	Returns the value of the attribute (object | xml)
get-attribute	default	String	No		Used as the default value if the attribute is not defined
get-attribute-names	as	String	No	array	Returns the value of the attribute names (array | xml)
get-creation-time	as	String	No	long	Returns the value of creation time in seconds (long | xml | string)
get-id	as	String	No	string	Returns the value of session ID (string | xml)
get-last-accessed-time	as	String	No	long	Returns the value of last time accessed in seconds (long | xml | string)
get-max-inactive-interval	as	String	No	int	Returns the value of maximum inactive interval in seconds (int | xml | string)
is-new	as	String	No	Boolean	Returns the value of function (boolean | xml | string)
remove-attribute	name	String	Yes		Defines the name of session attribute to remove from current session
set-attribute	name	String	Yes		Defines the name of session attribute
set-max-inactive-interval	interval	String	Yes		Sets the maximum inactive interval in seconds
encode-url	href	String	Yes		Provides the URL to encode
form-encode-url	action	String	Yes		Defines a form action script reference
form-encode-url	method	String	Yes		Defines a form method (POST | PUT)
form-encode-url	onsubmit	String	Yes		Defines a script to run when the form is submitted

1. The element can have either a named attribute or the element can have a child element. For example, these two are equivalent for the get-attribute element and the name attribute/child element:

```
<xsp-session:get-attribute name="car"/>

<xsp-session:get-attribute>
  <xsp-session:name>car</xsp-session:name>
</xsp-session:get-attribute>
```

SOAP Logicsheet

The SOAP logicsheet provides XML tags for standard SOAP operations. The entry for the SOAP logicsheet in the `<target-language name="java">` section of `cocoon.xconf` looks like the following:

```
<builtin-logicsheet>
    <parameter name="prefix" value="soap"/>
    <parameter name="uri" value="http://apache.org/xsp/soap/3.0"/>
    <parameter name="href" value="resource://org/apache/cocoon/components/
    language/markup/xsp/java/soap.xsl"/>
</builtin-logicsheet>
```

Map the XSP namespace to the soap prefix:

```
<xsp:page
  ...
  xmlns:soap="http://apache.org/xsp/soap/3.0"
  ...
>
```

Table 7.28 lists the elements of the SOAP logicsheet. Table 7.29 lists the elements and attributes.

TABLE 7.28: SOAP Logicsheet Elements

Element	Description
`call`	Calls a SOAP method
`env`	Sets a SOAP envelope
`header`	Sets a SOAP header
`body`	Sets a SOAP body
`enc`	Sets encryption type

TABLE 7.29: Soap Logicsheet Elements and Attributes

Element	Attribute	Data Type	Required?	Default	Description
`call`	`url`	String	No	""	URL of call
`call`	`method`	String	No	""	Method of call
`call`	`scope`	String	No		Scope of call
`call`	`context`	String	No		Context of call
`call`	`creation-scope`	String	No		Scope of creation
`call`	`creation-context`	String	No		Context of creation

Util Logicsheet

The Util logicsheet provides XML tags for utility operations such as determining the current date and time. The entry for the Util logicsheet in the `<target-language name="java">` section of `cocoon.xconf` looks like the following:

```
<builtin-logicsheet>
   <parameter name="prefix" value="util"/>
   <parameter name="uri" value="http://apache.org/xsp/util/2.0"/>
   <parameter name="href" value="resource://org/apache/cocoon/components/
   language/markup/xsp/java/util.xsl"/>
</builtin-logicsheet>
```

Map the XSP namespace to the `util` prefix:

```
<xsp:page
  ...
  xmlns:util="http://apache.org/xsp/util/2.0"
  ...
>
```

Table 7.30 lists the elements of the Util logicsheet. Table 7.31 lists the elements and attributes.

TABLE 7.30: Util Logicsheet Elements

Element	Description
cacheable	Determines if the current page is cacheable
include-uri	Includes URL contents as SAX
include-file	Includes file contents as SAX
include-expr	Includes expression as SAX
get-file-contents	Includes file contents as text
counter	Displays a simple counter; if in session scope, displays a session counter
time	Gets current time and date

TABLE 7.31: Util Logicsheet Elements and Attributes

Element	Attribute	Data Type	Required?	Default	Description
include-uri	href	String	Yes		Include URL
include-file	name	String	Yes		Name of file
include-expr	expr	String	Yes		Expression
get-file-contents	name	String	Yes		Name of file
time	format	String	Yes[1]	""	Format the current date and time according to the Java Date class[2]

1. Minimal example that gets the current date and time:

```
<util:time format=""/>
```

2. Typical usages:

```
<util:time format="MM-dd-yyyy"/>
<util:time format="MM/dd/yyyy hh:mm:ss"/>
```

XScript Logicsheet

The XScript logicsheet provides XML tags for the XML Scripting Language (XScript). The entry for the XScript logicsheet in the `<target-language name="java">` section of `cocoon.xconf` looks like the following:

```
<builtin-logicsheet>
   <parameter name="prefix" value="xscript"/>
   <parameter name="uri" value="http://apache.org/xsp/xscript/1.0"/>
   <parameter name="href" value="resource://org/apache/cocoon/components/
   language/markup/xsp/java/xscript.xsl"/>
</builtin-logicsheet>
```

Map the XSP namespace to the `xscript` prefix:

```
<xsp:page
  ...
  xmlns:xscript="http://apache.org/xsp/xscript/1.0"
  ...
>
```

Table 7.32 lists the elements of the Xscript logicsheet. Table 7.33 lists the elements and attributes.

TABLE 7.32: XScript Logicsheet Elements

Element	Description
`variable`	Creates a new XScript variable
`get`	Gets the value of an XScript variable
`remove`	Undeclares an XScript variable
`transform`	Transforms an XScript object using an XSLT stylesheet

TABLE 7.33: XScript Logicsheet Elements and Attributes

Element	Attribute/ Child Element	Data Type	Required?	Default	Description
`variable`	`scope`	String	No	session	Scope of variable (`session | global | page`)
`variable`	`context`	String	No	session	Context of variable (`session | global | page`)
`variable`	`name`	String	Yes		Name of variable
`variable`	`href`	String	No		URL reference to XSLT stylesheet that transforms the content of the named variable

continued on next page

TABLE 7.33 CONTINUED: XScript Logicsheet Elements and Attributes

Element	Attribute/ Child Element	Data Type	Required?	Default	Description
get	scope	String	No	all-scopes	Scope of variable (all-scopes | global | page | session)
get	context	String	No[1]	all-scopes	Context of variable (all-scopes | global | page | session)
get	name	String	Yes		Name of variable
get	as	String	No[2]		Return value of variable (object)
remove	scope	String	No	all-scopes	Scope of variable (all-scopes | global | page | session)
remove	context	String	No[1]	all-scopes	Context of variable (all-scopes | global | page | session)
remove	name	String	Yes		Name of variable
transform	name	String	Yes		Name of variable
transform	scope	String	No	all-scopes	Scope of variable (all-scopes | global | page | session)
transform	context	String	No[1]	all-scopes	Context of variable (all-scopes | global | page | session)
transform	stylesheet	String	Yes		Name of XSLT stylesheet
transform	stylesheet-scope	String	No	all-scopes	Scope of XSLT stylesheet
transform	stylesheet-context	String	No	all-scopes	Context of XSLT stylesheet
transform	parameters	String	No		XSLT stylesheet parameters

1. If the scope parameter is omitted or when its value is all-scopes, an expression that contains both the session and the page scope is returned.
2. If the as parameter is omitted, then the content of the XScript variable in the SAX event stream is inserted in the resulting XML document.

Building a Custom Logicsheet

In this section, we build a custom logicsheet named myUtil, deploy it, and build an example to show its use. We also add an element and parameters to display a formatted "last modified" stamp that can be used in the footer section of a web page.

Building a custom logicsheet is straightforward. It involves creating an XSLT stylesheet used to process the transformations listed in the XSP page. It should be noted that a logicsheet is required to preserve any input that it doesn't recognize; such input should pass through untouched.

There are a few things to keep in mind when building a custom logicsheet: use a helper Java class, create logicsheet macros, consider who will use the logicsheet, and document its usage. For additional logicsheet development tips, go to `http://www6.software.ibm.com/developerworks/education/x-xsp/x-xsp-5-4.html`.

Use a Java helper class You need to place as much code as possible in a Java helper class. This reduces the amount of implemented code in the stylesheet. You can provide the bare bones element and its associated parameters in the stylesheet and yet again abstracting the code into the helper class. It also simplifies the development of large, complex sections of code because you can eliminate the Cocoon environment and use your Java development environment. The built-in logicsheets use this approach. For instance, the Request logicsheet has a helper class named `XSPRequestHelper` and the ESQL logicsheet has a helper class named `EsqlHelper`.

Create logicsheet macros You can reduce the XSP page complexity by creating a macro that represents a repeatable common function defined by a series of code expressions. The macro is a succinct and quick way to access the common functionality. For example, you might create a macro that produces a specific formatted date and timestamp used in the footer of each XSP page.

Consider the users of the logicsheet This is a commonsense but important detail of creating a custom logicsheet. First, you must name elements. This may seem mundane, but it is vital that you select a verb-noun (i.e., get-preference) or conversely the noun-verb (i.e., preference-get) paradigm and stay consistent with it. Second, you should consider the nomenclature or vernacular of the audience. If you are building a logicsheet to access and display paleontology data, you will need to use words and phrases from paleontology vernacular to name your elements. Finally, you must choose carefully an element's associated parameters. Further, you should identify which parameters can be dynamically set using the `xsp:expr` element.

Document the logicsheet's usage Simply put, you need to comment your logicsheet extensively so your users can apply it easily. You don't want your users to search through the XSLT code to figure out what parameters are required, what their default values are, and what and how any child elements are used.

myUtil Logicsheet

Our custom logicsheet provides functionality that calculates and displays a "last modified" timestamp. This is typically an integral part of a web page.

In the first section of code (see Listing 7.1), we set up and initialize our logicsheet by specifying the logicsheet's namespace (`xmlns:myUtil="http://k2/myUtil/2.0"`). Next, we import some nonstandard Java classes, most importantly, `org.apache.cocoon.components.language.markup.xsp.XSPUtil`. This is a built-in Java helper class. Remember, each built-in logicsheet has a corresponding built-in Java helper class.

Listing 7.1 myUtil Logicsheet Template, *myUtil.xsl*

```
<xsl:stylesheet
  version="1.0"
  xmlns:xsp="http://apache.org/xsp"
  xmlns:xsl="http://www.w3.org/1999/XSL/Transform"
  xmlns:myUtil="http://k2/myUtil/2.0"
>


<!--
Script: myUtil.xsl
Author: Mark Gaither (mark@markgaither.com)
Date: 29 May 2002 (about tea time)
-->

<xsl:template match="xsp:page">

   <xsp:page>

      <xsl:apply-templates select="@*"/>

      <!-- import non-standard Java packages -->
      <xsp:structure>
        <xsp:include>java.util.Date</xsp:include>
        <xsp:include>java.io.File</xsp:include>
        <xsp:include>java.text.SimpleDateFormat</xsp:include>

<xsp:include>org.apache.cocoon.components.language.markup.xsp.XSPUtil</xsp:
include>
      </xsp:structure>

      <!-- Add methods and variables within the logic element
      <xsp:logic></xsp:logic>
      -->

      <!-- process the rest of the XSP page -->
      <xsl:apply-templates/>

   </xsp:page>

</xsl:template>
```

In the next chunk of code, we specify the `myUtil:lastmodified` element of the logicsheet. This element will take an XSP page's absolute file path as its content and determines the last time the file was modified. It has one optional parameter named `dateformat`. It dictates the format of the date and time string according to the `java.util.Date` Java class. Its default value is `dow mon dd hh:mm:ss zzz yyyy`.

For example, we add the `myUtil:lastmodified` element to an XSP page with an absolute path of `/usr/cocoon/xsp/test.xsp`. Here's the XML:

```
<myUtil:lastmodified>/usr/cocoon/xsp/test.xsp</myUtil:lastmodified>
```

In another example, we add the `dateformat` parameter that controls how the date and time string is formatted:

```
<myUtil:lastmodified dateformat="MM/dd/yyyy">
  /usr/cocoon/xsp/test.xsp
</myUtil:lastmodified>
```

In Listing 7.2, note the use of the `XSPUtil` helper class; it is used to format the date and time string.

Listing 7.2 myUtil Logicsheet Template, *myUtil.xsl*

```
<!-- create last modified stamp to be included in the
footer of a web page.

Attribute: dateformat
Required?: no
Default: "dow mon dd hh:mm:ss zzz yyyy"
Description: Date format per Java Date class

Attribute/Child Element: author
Required?: yes
Description: Name of author

-->

<xsl:template match="myUtil:lastmodified">

    <xsl:variable name="dateformat">
      <xsl:choose>
        <xsl:when test="@dateformat">
          "<xsl:value-of select="@dateformat"/>"
        </xsl:when>
        <xsl:otherwise>
          "dow mon dd hh:mm:ss zzz yyyy"
        </xsl:otherwise>
      </xsl:choose>
    </xsl:variable>
```

```
    <xsp:logic>
        File f = new File("<xsl:value-of select="."/>");
        String datestr = "";
        if (f.isFile()) {
            datestr = XSPUtil.formatDate(
            new Date(f.lastModified()),
            String.valueOf(<xsl:copy-of select="$dateformat"/>).trim());
            datestr = "Last modified: " + datestr;
        }
    </xsp:logic>

    <xsp:expr>datestr</xsp:expr>

</xsl:template>
```

Finally, in the last section of code, we specify the `myUtil:author` element. It displays the author's name and is typically used in conjunction with the `myUtil:lastmodified` element of our logicsheet. Its content is the author's name or e-mail address.

For example, the following specifies the author's name:

```
<myUtil:author>Mark Gaither</myUtil:author>
```

Here's an example where the content is calculated from a previously set XSP variable:

```
<myUtil:author><xsp:expr>authorname</xsp:expr></myUtil:author>
```

Here's an example where the content is calculated from a Request object. It is the authenticated user's ID:

```
<myUtil:author>
  <xsp-request:get-remote-user/>
</myUtil:author>
```

Listing 7.3 details the `myUtil:author` element and the rule to pass through any XML that did not match any other elements.

Listing 7.3 myUtil Logicsheet Template, *myUtil.xsl*

```
<!-- Author name -->

<xsl:template match="myUtil:author">
  <xsl:apply-templates/>
</xsl:template>

<!-- passthrough all other XML data not matched here -->
<xsl:template match="node()|@*">

   <xsl:copy>
   <xsl:apply-templates select="@*"/>
```

```
      <xsl:apply-templates/>
      </xsl:copy>

   </xsl:template>

   </xsl:stylesheet>
```

Deploying the myUtil Logicsheet

Before you begin developing your own custom logicsheet, you need to map its namespace and the associated logicsheet in Cocoon 2. In our case, `myUtil.xsl` was stored in the Cocoon environment as follows:

```
$CATALINA_HOME/webapps/cocoon/WEB-INF/classes/sybex/logicsheets/myUtil.xsl
```

Now that it is in the Cocoon environment, we have to map the namespace to its associated logicsheet. The mapping is configured in the `cocoon.xconf` file. We added the following XML to our `cocoon.xconf` file:

```
<builtin-logicsheet>
   <parameter name="prefix" value="myUtil"/>
   <parameter name="uri" value="http://k2/myUtil/1.0"/>
   <parameter name="href" value="resource://sybex/logicsheets/myUtil.xsl"/>
</builtin-logicsheet>
```

Notice the value of the `uri` parameter. It references a hostname `k2`. This is our local Cocoon server. You will need to replace this string with your hostname if you plan to deploy this example logicsheet.

A built-in logicsheet is bundled into the `cocoon-2.0.1.jar` file. Our user-defined logicsheet is stored in the file system. Notice in the preceding configuration, we identify the logicsheet using `resource://sybex/logicsheets/myUtil.xsl`. The `resource` prefix means that the logicsheet is stored in the Cocoon `/WEB-INF/classes/` directory. We could have also specified the logicsheet's location with the `file` prefix. For example:

```
<parameter name="href" value="file:///usr/local/cocoon/WEB-INF/classes/sybex/
logicsheets/myUtil.xsl"/>
```

After making the additions to the `cocoon.xconf` file, you must restart Tomcat. As of this writing, if you make changes to the `myUtil.xsl` file, and you want to apply these changes to an XSP page, you must "touch" the XSP page in the file system. This means to update the date and time the XSP page was last modified. In Unix, you can do it with a `touch` command. In the Microsoft world, you will have to make an edit to the XSP page. For example, just add a spurious carriage return to the XSP page with an editor, then delete it, and then save the file. This guarantees to update the date and timestamp on the file. If you have multiple XSP pages depending on the transformation, we suggest:

1. Stop Tomcat.
2. Flush the cache. We do this by removing all directories and files for our hostname found at: /usr/local/tomcat/work/k2/.
3. Start Tomcat.

Now, the first time an XSP page that references that logicsheet is browsed, it is transformed using the new version of the logicsheet and the resulting document is stored in the Cocoon environment. In our case, the file created is chap7-lastmodified.html.

We have created a simple XSP page example called chap7-lastmodified.xsp (see Listing 7.4). It uses elements from the myUtil logicsheet. In the first section of code, we reference the myUtil namespace and set the prefix:

```
xmlns:myUtil="http://k2/myUtil/2.0"
```

Listing 7.4 ***Chap7-lastmodified.xsp***

```
<?xml version="1.0"?>

<!-- chap7-lastmodified.xsp -->

<!-- Cocoon processing directives -->
<?cocoon-process type="xsp"?>
<?cocoon-process type="xslt"?>

<!-- stylesheet directive -->
<?xml-stylesheet href="stylesheets/dynamic-page2html.xsl" type="text/xsl"?>

<!-- start an XSP page -->
<xsp:page
  language="java"
  xmlns:xsp="http://apache.org/xsp"
  xmlns:myUtil="http://k2/myUtil/2.0"
>
```

In Listing 7.5, we set an XSP variable named authorname. Finally, we add the myUtil:lastmodified element. It has listed the optional parameter dateformat. It directs the XSP page to display the date and timestamp as month/day/year rather than the default format. Its content is the absolute file path of the XSP page. We also insert the myUtil:author element in the page. Its content is calculated from a previously set XSP variable.

Listing 7.5 ***Chap7-lastmodified.xsp***

```
<!-- start the XSP page body -->
<page>

<!-- set the name of the author -->
<xsp:logic>
  String authorname = "mark@markgaither.com";
</xsp:logic>

<title>Chapter 7 Last Modified Example</title>

<hr />

<div align="center">

<myUtil:lastmodified dateformat="MM/dd/yyyy">
  /usr/local/cocoon/chap7-lastmodified.xsp
</myUtil:lastmodified>
(<myUtil:author><xsp:expr>authorname</xsp:expr></myUtil:author>)

</div>

</page>

</xsp:page>
```

Listing 7.6 provides details for transforming the XSP page results in the file `chap7-lastmodified.html` HTML document. Figure 7.1 shows how it is rendered.

Listing 7.6 ***chap7-lastmodified.html***

```
<html>
<head>
<META http-equiv="Content-Type" content="text/html; charset=UTF-8">
<title>Chapter 7 Last Modified Example</title>
</head>
<body vlink="blue" link="blue" alink="red" bgcolor="white">

<h2 style="color: navy; text-align: center">
<A HREF="../view-source?filename=/docs/samples/xsp/chap7-lastmodified.xsp"
TARGET="_blank">Chapter 7 Last Modified Example</A>
</h2>


<hr xmlns:xsp="http://apache.org/xsp" xmlns:myUtil="http://k2/myUtil/2.0">
```

```
<div xmlns:xsp="http://apache.org/xsp" xmlns:myUtil="http://k2/myUtil/2.0"
align="center">

Last modified: 05/30/2002
 (mark@markgaither.com)

</div>


</body>
</html>
```

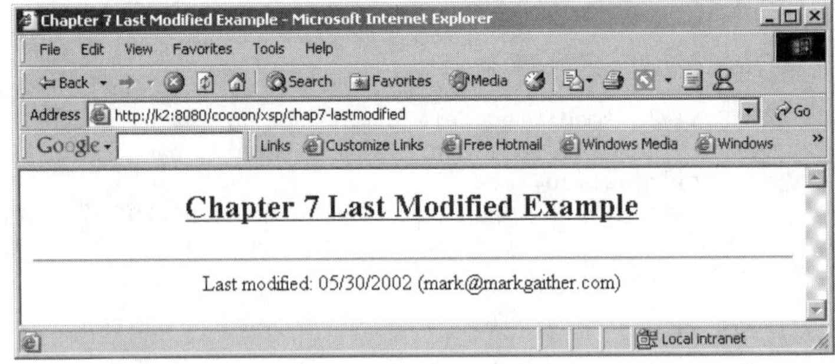

FIGURE 7.1: Browser rendering of chap7-lastmodified.html

Summary

Cocoon logicsheets provide custom elements that can be added to an XSP page. They are implemented using XSL and XSLT transformations providing yet another method to separate concerns in the Cocoon environment. Using logicsheet elements can make reading an XSP page easier because you can factor out code from the XSP page to the logicsheet. A logicsheet can also enhance reusability by placing code in a centralized logicsheet compared to in each individual XSP page. This also reduces duplicate code and increases maintainability of your XSP code.

How does a logicsheet work? First, Cocoon reads an XSP page evaluating all declared namespaces. Then, Cocoon checks the `cocoon.xconf` file to see if the namespace has been configured and determines the correct XSL stylesheet to apply. Next, if the XSL stylesheet exists, then the transformations are executed. Finally, the last two steps are repeated until all logicsheet transformations have been completed for all namespaces except for the XSP namespace. At this point, Cocoon executes the final transformation (for the XSP namespace) and generates the Java source code equivalent of the original XSP page.

Cocoon includes built-in logicsheets such as Session, Request, ESQL, and Util. Each included logicsheet provides general mechanisms for a specific function. For example, the Session logicsheet includes the element `get-creation-time` which displays the date and time the current session was created. As Cocoon evolves, more built-in logicsheets will be included.

If you are a developer skilled in Java and XSLT, you can create your own custom logicsheet or extend a built-in logicsheet When rolling your own logicsheet, you should consider using a Java helper class, creating logicsheet macros, determining who the users are, and documenting its usage.

Chapter 8

Content Generators

- Generators As Cocoon Components
- Creating a Custom Generator

Generators form the start of a typical Cocoon pipeline by creating SAX events from some input source. The most obvious generator simply reads an XML-formatted document, parsing out the tags and content, but you are not restricted to starting with XML. The Cocoon programmers have created a wide variety of other generators, which we explore in detail in this chapter.

The really cool thing about generators is that it is relatively easy to create your own generator to read data in just about any format and create SAX events that simulate parsing an XML document. This means that all that legacy data you have hanging around could be turned into useful Web documents. We will give a simple example later in the chapter.

You may also be able to make use of existing programs in a variety of scripting languages such as JavaScript or Python. Scripting languages can be ideal for rapid prototyping of a generator.

Generators As Cocoon Components

As discussed in Chapter 5, "Logic Control: The Sitemap," any generator used in a pipeline must be declared in the `<map:generators>` section of the `<map:components>` section of the `sitemap.xmap` file. This declaration must include attributes for `name`, `logger`, and `src`. A `label` attribute, as shown in this typical `<map:generator>` entry, is optional:

```
<map:generator name="directory"
    logger="sitemap.generator.directory"
    label="content,data"
    src="org.apache.cocoon.generation.DirectoryGenerator"/>
```

The Standard Generators

Before getting into the details, let's do a quick survey of the generators available in the standard Cocoon distribution.

`DirectoryGenerator` Formats file system directory information into a convenient representation for display as HTML.

`FileGenerator` Typically the default generator, it reads and parses an XML document from a file or URL.

`FragmentExtractorGenerator` A combination of transformer and generator, this removes selected nodes from a SAX stream and puts them in a separate pipeline. This is mainly used for offline generation to separate SVG image data from a document.

`HTMLGenerator` Reads an HTML-formatted document and converts it to XHTML compatibility using the JTidy package on the fly. This is necessary because typical HTML pages are not well formed by XML rules.

ImageDirectoryGenerator Similar to the DirectoryGenerator but adds image size data to directory listing.

JSPGenerator Directly executes the JSP engine with a specified JSP page and parses the output into SAX events for the pipeline. This is provided to make it easier to convert JSP-based Web applications to Cocoon. Note that your JSP must generate correct XML and not use shortcut markup.

MP3DirectoryGenerator Similar to ImageDirectoryGenerator but adds MP3 specific information such as recording mode, artist, etc.

ProfileGenerator The Cocoon Profiler interface is used in classes that can gather information on the time consumed in various parts of the pipeline. This generator can serialize the results from a Profiler for viewing. The profiler-related classes are in the com.apache.components.profiler package.

RequestGenerator This handy generator can extract much of the data in an HTML request into an XML format. In addition to the request parameters and headers, the configuration parameters are displayed, making this an ideal debugging tool for questions related to the actual content of a request.

ScriptGenerator This generator works with the Bean Scripting Framework (BSF) and a script interpreter to execute arbitrary scripting languages. The BSF library is included with Cocoon.

SearchGenerator This generator works with Cocoon's Lucene content-indexing system to control searches and report search results.

ServerPagesGenerator This is the generator that is used with XSP pages.

StatusGenerator This generator essentially dumps the current state of the Cocoon system as XML. Such parameters as total memory available to the JVM and current memory used can be very helpful in debugging.

StreamGenerator Reads and parses XML data from the HTTP request input stream. An XML-formatted input stream might come from a JavaScript method in an HTML page or an XML-RPC or SOAP Web service request.

VelocityGenerator Velocity is an open-source XML-based template engine housed at jakarta.apache.org. This generator provides for supplying request data, Cocoon sitemap context data, and a Velocity template to the template engine. The output of the template engine is then parsed into SAX events.

XMLDBCollectionGenerator Used to generate a listing of the contents of an XML:DB-compatible database. This class has been deprecated as of Cocoon 2.0.2, and it is suggested that the XML:DB pseudo-protocol should be used instead. See the discussion of `Source` in the section entitled "The *FileGenerator*," later in this chapter.

`XMLDBGenerator` This class generates events from data retrieved from an XML:DB-compatible database. It has also been deprecated.

Before we jump into disc ussion of the generators just listed, we look at a generator that is not on the list and that you can't get at directly. This is the generator that creates the data for a Cocoon error page.

The Generator for Error Handling

The following snippet from a typical Cocoon pipeline appears to have no generator of the events that the transformer uses:

```
<map:handle-errors>
   <map:transform src="stylesheets/system/error2html.xsl"/>
   <map:serialize status-code="500"/>
</map:handle-errors>
```

Actually, a complex series of events turns an exception or error generated during pipeline execution into an object that encapsulates the details. These details are then encoded as a series of SAX events. The interfaces and classes involved in this process are shown in Table 8.1. In the event of an `Exception` or `Error` being thrown during pipeline processing, the error-processing routine tries to dispose of any content already generated and rebuilds the pipeline to use the components defined in the `<map:handle-errors>` tag. A `Simple-NotifyingBean` containing the details is built and becomes the source of events that are turned into the error report.

TABLE 8.1: Interfaces and Classes Involved in Cocoon Error Reporting

Class	Package	Responsible for
`NotifyingBuilder`	`org.apache.cocoon.component.notification`	The interface for an object that can build a `Notifying` object. This interface defines the `ROLE` of a class that can build a `Notifying` object.
`DefaultNotifyingBuilder`	`org.apache.cocoon.components.notification`	The class implementing `NotifyingBuilder`. An object of this class can create a `SimpleNotifyingBean` incorporating the details from an `Exception` or `Error`. These details can include the stack trace.

Continued on next page

TABLE 8.1 CONTINUED: Interfaces and Classes Involved in Cocoon Error Reporting

Class	Package	Responsible for
`Notifying`	`org.apache.cocoon.components.notification`	Interface for objects that perform a notification.
`SimpleNotifyingBean`	`org.apache.cocoon.component.notification`	This class implements the `Notifying` interface and holds text data from an `Exception` or `Error`.
`Notifier`	`org.apache.cocoon.components.notification`	This class takes an object that implements `Notifying` and can create SAX events representing the data contained in a `Notifying` object, or write HTML formatted text to an output stream.

Due to the way the pipeline architecture for error reporting is constructed from the interfaces shown in Table 8.1, it would be relatively straightforward to build your own error-reporting system.

Using Scripting Languages with BSF

Many "scripting" languages have been created by programmers who needed quick methods for putting together functionality for utilities or for fast prototypes. Another impulse leading to scripting languages has been the desire to create dynamic documents that combine content with processing instructions as in JavaScript.

Scripting languages are generally weakly typed, don't provide for complex data structures, and are interpreted rather than compiled. Frequently, the intent of a scripting language is to provide easy access to more powerful components or programs. It is a remarkable fact that although all of these languages seem to have started for the purpose of writing small-scale utilities or functions, they frequently end up being used for projects involving many thousands of lines of code.

Several scripting language interpreters have been created in Java. To provide a unified approach to using these interpreters, the Bean Scripting Framework (BSF) was created. BSF is an open-source utility licensed under IBM's public license and is included in the Cocoon distribution. If you want to learn more about BSF, the main site for the current version follows:

```
http://oss.software.ibm.com/developerworks/projects/bsf
```

Cocoon uses the `ScriptGenerator` class to provide a system for executing scripts through the BSF. `ScriptGenerator` plus BSF provides a uniform system for supplying the interpreter of a scripting language with data from the Cocoon sitemap in terms that the scripting language understands. The other input needed is a script in that language. When the script is interpreted, the text that is generated, which must be valid XML, is parsed like any other XML source for further processing in the Cocoon pipeline.

Here is the Cocoon sitemap entry for the "script" generator:

```
<map:generator name="script"
   src="org.apache.cocoon.generation.ScriptGenerator"
   logger="sitemap.generator.script"
   label="content,data"/>
```

When the `ScriptGenerator` responds to a request, it creates a new `BSFManager` object, hands it references to various sitemap objects, and then executes the script. Because a new manager is created for every request, this approach is inherently thread-safe. The manager determines which script interpreter to use from the type part of the script file name. Here is a section of pipeline from the Cocoon distribution that associates the script generator with a specific directory pattern:

```
<map:match pattern="scripts/*">
  <map:generate type="script" src="docs/samples/scripts/{1}"/>
  <map:transform src="stylesheets/page/simple-page2html.xsl"/>
  <map:serialize type="html"/>
</map:match>
```

All output from the interpretation of the script is caught in a `StringBuffer`. When the interpretation is finished, the resulting string is parsed to create the SAX events that feed the pipeline. Obviously, because this approach keeps the entire output in memory, using the `ScriptGenerator` could cause memory problems with large scripts.

The BSF manager already knows about a number of scripting languages and Cocoon has a mechanism for adding more. Table 8.2 shows some information on the scripting languages supported by BSF version 2.2. The Dependencies column shows the extra Java or other language libraries required.

TABLE 8.2: Scripting Languages Supported by BSF Version 2.2

Language	Version	Dependencies
Mozilla Rhino (server-side JavaScript)	1.5 R2	rhino-1.5r2.jar is provided with Cocoon. For the most recent implementation and further information go to `www.mozilla.org/rhino`.
NetRexx	2.00	NetRexxC.jar available from `www2.hursley.ibm.com/netrexx`.
Jython (Java Python)	2.1	jython.jar available from `www.jython.org`.
Jacl	1.2.6	jacl.jar and tcljava.jar from `www.scriptics.com/java`.
Win32 ActiveScript langs: JScript, VBScript, PerlScript	x	MSVCP60.DLL from Microsoft, appropriate language DLLs from `http://msdn.microsoft.com/scripting`; ActivePerl from `www.activestate.com`.

The following sections give more details on these supported languages.

Mozilla Rhino

Rhino is an open-source implementation of JavaScript written entirely in Java. After starting life as Netscape's LiveScript and being renamed JavaScript to take advantage of the hype surrounding Java, the JavaScript language is now a standard—ECMA-262. It should now be known as ECMAScript, but everybody continues to call it JavaScript. Rhino 1.5 implements JavaScript 1.5, which conforms to Edition 3 of the ECMA standard.

Although most users will be familiar with JavaScript as a client-side manipulator of HTML elements in browsers, Rhino does not provide for HTML manipulation at all. You can get a bit of the flavor of programming in Rhino with BSF from Listing 8.1, which shows the JavaScript sample provided with Cocoon.

This sample shows how the sitemap data is made available to the script through the BSF manager object. The `output` object is a `StringBuffer` created in the `ScriptGenerator` `generate` method. Note that the output is entirely formatted as XML text.

Listing 8.1 The *hello.js* Sample JavaScript Provided with Cocoon

```
// Sample javascript script for use with ScriptGenerator
// Step 1 -- Retrieve helper "beans" from the BSF framework
out      = bsf.lookupBean( "output" )
logger   = bsf.lookupBean( "logger" )
resolver = bsf.lookupBean( "resolver" )
source   = bsf.lookupBean( "source" )
objModel = bsf.lookupBean( "objectModel" )
params   = bsf.lookupBean( "parameters" )

// Step 2 -- Generate xml using whatever means you desire

xml = " \
<page> \
  <title>Hello</title> \
  <content> \
    <para>This is my first Cocoon2 page!</para> \
    <para>With help from JavaScript!</para> \
  </content> \
</page>"

// note that you have access to the Cocoon logger
logger.debug( "Debug message from JavaScript" )

// Step 3 -- Append the generated xml to the output StringBuffer
out.append( xml )
```

When the `ScriptGenerator` gets the `StringBuffer` that is returned, the resulting `String` is parsed to create SAX events for the pipeline.

NetRexx

NetRexx is a language that attempts to be an alternative to Java that is simpler and faster to program. It is a Java implementation of the Rexx language, which was invented in 1979 at IBM for writing utilities.

NetRexx programs can be interpreted or compiled. Many primitive and object type conversions are handled automatically. The following sites have downloads, documentation, and FAQs for NetRexx and Rexx:

```
http://www2.hursley.ibm.com/netrexx
http://www2.hursley.ibm.com/rexx/
```

Jython

Python was created in 1991 by Guido van Rossum, and before you ask, yes it is named for the British comedy troupe, Monty Python. Jython is an implementation of Python in Java that implements most of the Python functions. You will also see references to the implementation in Java as "JPython;" the language was renamed when the project moved to Sourceforge in October of 2000.

Python is an object-oriented scripting language that fits well with the Java programming model. The Jython implementation provides easy access to Java classes and language constructs. We believe that unless you are very familiar with JavaScript or one of the other supported scripting languages, Jython is your best choice for experimenting with scripting languages in Cocoon.

A Jython Example

Let's look at a simple example Jython script, starting in Listing 8.2. This script is named `testrequest.py` and is included on this book's website. In this example, we will extract and display all of the headers sent in an `HttpRequest`. As with the JavaScript example in Listing 8.1, the first step is to recover references to the available objects from the BSF manager. Note that the lines beginning with "#" are comments in Python. A comment can occur anywhere in a line and continues to the end of the line.

Listing 8.2 Start of the *testrequest.py* Jython Script

```
# recover references from the BSFManager
out      = bsf.lookupBean( "output" )
# out is a java.lang.StringBuffer
logger   = bsf.lookupBean( "logger" )
# logger is a org.apache.log.Logger
```

```
resolver = bsf.lookupBean( "resolver" )
# resolver is a org.apache.cocoon.environment.SourceResolver
source   = bsf.lookupBean( "source" )
# source is a java.lang.String
objModel = bsf.lookupBean( "objectModel" )
#objModel is a java.util.Map
params   = bsf.lookupBean( "parameters" )
# params is a org.apache.avalon.framework.parameters.Parameters
```

The example continues in Listing 8.3 with the first addition to the output `StringBuffer`. The first `out.append` illustrates the use of Python's literal quoting method using triple quote characters. Everything between the triple quotes forms a literal string. This is one way of getting around Python's normal convention in which a statement ends with the end of a source code line.

Listing 8.3 Jython Script Continued

```
# start page generation using simple-page2html.xsl conventions
out.append( """
<page>
  <title>Test Request Dump</title>

    <para>Contents of objModel - Request headers first.</para>
    """ )
out.append("<table>")
request = objModel.get("request")
keys = request.getHeaderNames()
for x in keys:
  out.append("<header><param>" + x + "</param>" )
  out.append("<value>")
  out.append( request.getHeader( x ) )
  out.append("</value></header>")
out.append("</table>")
out.append("<para>Request method = "
     + request.getMethod()
     + "</para>")
sb = request.getRequestURI()
out.append("<para>Request URI = " + sb
     + "</para>")

out.append( """
    <para>Jython rules!</para>

</page>""" )

logger.debug( "Debug message from Python" )
```

Naturally there must be an entry in the Cocoon sitemap that associates a pattern with the `ScriptGenerator`. In this example, we used the following, where the "py" file type is recognized by the BSF manager as being associated with Python:

```
<map:match pattern="jython/*.py">
  <map:generate type="script" src="jython/{1}.py" />
  <map:transform src="stylesheets/test/simple-page2html.xsl"/>
  <map:serialize type="html"/>
</map:match>
```

The XML tags written by the Jython script are transformed to HTML using the XSL file shown in Listing 8.4. This is a modification of the XSL file of the same name found in the standard Cocoon distribution.

Listing 8.4 The *simple-page2html.xsl* File

```
<?xml version="1.0"?>
<xsl:stylesheet version="1.0" xmlns:xsl="http://www.w3.org/1999/XSL/Transform">

  <xsl:template match="page">
   <html>
    <head>
     <title>
      <xsl:value-of select="title"/>
     </title>
    </head>
    <body bgcolor="white" alink="red" link="blue" vlink="blue">
     <xsl:apply-templates/>
    </body>
   </html>
  </xsl:template>

  <xsl:template match="para">
   <p align="left">
    <i><xsl:apply-templates/></i>
   </p>
  </xsl:template>

  <xsl:template match="table">
    <table border="2" ><tr><th>Header</th><th>Value</th></tr>
      <xsl:apply-templates/>
    </table>
  </xsl:template>
  <xsl:template match="header" >
    <tr><td><xsl:value-of select="param"/></td>
    <td><xsl:value-of select="value"/></td></tr>
  </xsl:template>

  <xsl:template match="list">
    <ul>
```

```
      <xsl:apply-templates/>
    </ul>
  </xsl:template>
  <xsl:template match="item">
    <li><xsl:apply-templates/></li>
  </xsl:template>
</xsl:stylesheet>
```

The resulting HTML page is shown in Figure 8.1.

Using the Jython Modules

The Jython distribution comes with a large library of functions in packages referred to as modules. These are provided as script files having the characteristic "py" file type.

When run as an interpreter, Jython normally does not have any trouble finding the module library. However, executing under the BSF manager, we have to provide the location explicitly. Here is an example of defining the location of the library in a sitemap `<map:parameter>` tag:

```
<map:generate type="script" src="jython/{1}" >
   <map:parameter name="python.path"
     value="c:/java/jython-2.1/Lib" />
</map:generate>
```

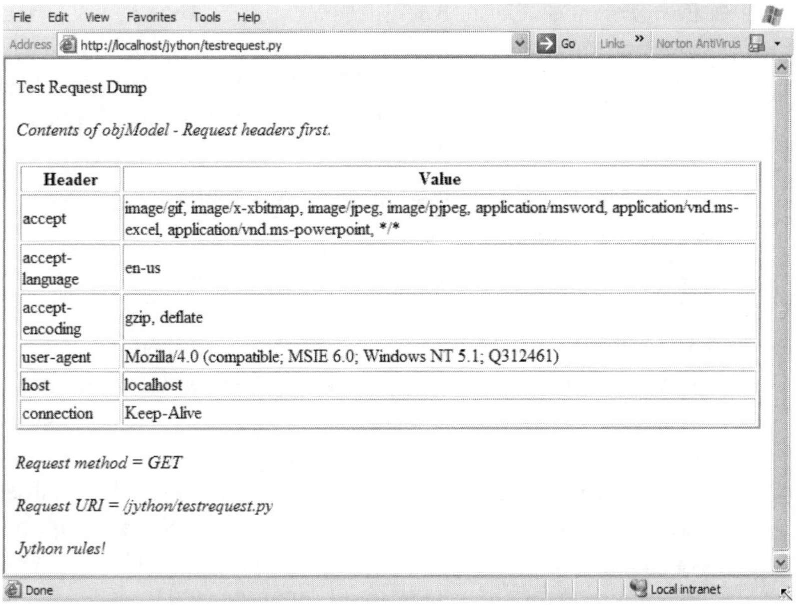

FIGURE 8.1:

A page generated by the `testrequest.py` script

File Edit View Favorites Tools Help

Address http://localhost/jython/testrequest.py

Test Request Dump

Contents of objModel - Request headers first.

Header	Value
accept	image/gif, image/x-xbitmap, image/jpeg, image/pjpeg, application/msword, application/vnd.ms-excel, application/vnd.ms-powerpoint, */*
accept-language	en-us
accept-encoding	gzip, deflate
user-agent	Mozilla/4.0 (compatible; MSIE 6.0; Windows NT 5.1; Q312461)
host	localhost
connection	Keep-Alive

Request method = GET

Request URI = /jython/testrequest.py

Jython rules!

Done Local intranet

In the Jython script, you have to locate this parameter and insert it in the array of paths that Jython uses to look up modules, before attempting to import them. Here is a snippet of Jython code to do this:

```
params   = bsf.lookupBean( "parameters" )
import sys  # that is the Jython standard library, includes sys.path
pth = params.getParameter("python.path")
sys.path.insert(0, pth )
```

Advantages of Jython for Cocoon Programming

Jython really shines as a rapid prototyping environment for Cocoon for the following reasons:

Java library All Java classes are available and may be sub-classed.

Rapid development cycle Because `ScriptGenerator` creates a new BSF environment for every access, there is no edit-compile-reload cycle. You can modify a script and view the new output very quickly.

Disadvantages of Jython for Cocoon Programming

The following disadvantages of Jython should be recognized:

Syntax differences Python syntax takes some getting used to. For example, Python uses level of indentation where Java would use `{ }` code blocks to indicate program organization, and does not terminate statements with "`;`".

Performance Because `ScriptGenerator` creates a new `BSFManager` for every request, all scripting languages will suffer from performance problems in a high-throughput environment. This means that Cocoon is unable to take advantage of compiled versions of scripting languages. Also, because the output is first created as a String, large documents are going to consume lots of memory.

For further study of Python the language and Jython the specific implementation, we recommend the following sites:

```
www.python.org/doc/tut/tut.html
www.jython.org
```

Also take a look at Martin Brown's *XML Processing with Perl, Python, and PHP* (Sybex, 2001) and James Jaworski's *Mastering JavaScript, Premium Edition* (Sybex, 2001).

Jacl

Java Command Language (Jacl) is an interpreter in Java for a subset of the Tool Command Language (Tcl). Tcl started in the Unix world in 1990 as a scripting language written in C for the creation of utility tools. The project to integrate Tcl with Java originated at Sun with the intent of making it the ideal scripting language for Java.

The claims made for Jacl are similar to those made for NetRexx, namely that it is a simpler and faster way to write programs making use of Java classes. One source for information on Jacl is the following website:

```
http://tcl.activestate.com/software/java/
```

The *JSPGenerator*

JavaServer Pages (JSP) can be thought of as a scripting language that allows mixing of HTML tags and Java code. Many websites now make extensive use of JSP despite the fact that this mixture of content, style, and control is difficult to maintain. The `JSPGenerator` directly executes the JSP engine with a specified JSP page and parses the output into SAX events for the pipeline. This is provided to make it easier to convert JSP-based web applications to Cocoon.

Recall that there is also a `JSPReader` class defined in a `<map:reader>` tag. Both the reader and the generator send the current request to the JSP engine. The difference between the two is that the reader outputs characters directly to the response without alteration, whereas the generator creates SAX events that can be further modified in the Cocoon pipeline. If you use the generator, your JSP must generate correct XML and not use shortcut markup. For more information about JSP programming, see *Mastering JSP* (Sybex, 2002).

The Velocity Generator

Velocity is an open-source Java-based template engine housed at `jakarta.apache.org`. This generator provides for supplying request data, Cocoon sitemap context data, and a Velocity template to the template engine. The output of the template engine is then parsed into SAX events.

Velocity uses a Model-View-Controller (MVC) style of development. Any Java code involved in page production is entirely separate from HTML template code. The home website for Velocity can be found here:

```
http://jakarta.apache.org/velocity/index.html
```

Velocity is very similar to the better-known WebMacro project. You can find out more about WebMacro at the following URL:

```
www.webmacro.org
```

The Directory Generator Group

The `DirectoryGenerator` and its descendents make it easy to produce web pages that let users navigate in a file system. A typical use would be for sites with many downloadable files. When combined with descriptive text from an XSLT transformation or by aggregating multiple sources, you can create a nice-looking download page like this one at the Cocoon website:

```
http://xml.apache.org/cocoon/dist/
```

DirectoryGenerator

The entry for DirectoryGenerator in the <map:generators> section of a sitemap typically looks like this:

```
<map:generator name="directory"
   logger="sitemap.generator.directory"
   label="content,data"
   src="org.apache.cocoon.generation.DirectoryGenerator"/>
```

The following snippet from a Cocoon sitemap shows one way of using the Directory-Generator:

```
<map:match pattern="**/">
   <map:generate type="directory" src=""/>
   <map:transform src="stylesheets/system/directory2html.xsl"/>
   <map:serialize/>
</map:match>
```

The beginning of the sequence of SAX events created by the DirectoryGenerator is shown in Listing 8.5 translated back into XML. Note how the first <dir:directory> tag establishes the dir namespace with the xmlns:dir attribute.

Listing 8.5 The XML Equivalent of the SAX Events from the *DirectoryGenerator*

```
<?xml version="1.0" encoding="UTF-8" ?>
<dir:directory name="ROOT" lastModified="1019006303236"
   date="4/16/02 8:18 PM" requested="true"
   xmlns:dir="http://apache.org/cocoon/directory/2.0">
<dir:directory name="books" lastModified="1016399001235"
   date="3/17/02 3:03 PM" />
<dir:directory name="docs" lastModified="1016284048789"
   date="3/16/02 7:07 AM" />
<dir:directory name="documentation" lastModified="1016284051352"
   date="3/16/02 7:07 AM" />
<dir:directory name="i18n" lastModified="1016284064661"
   date="3/16/02 7:07 AM" />
<dir:file name="index.xml" lastModified="1016331664718"
   date="3/16/02 8:21 PM" />
```

The directory2html.xsl stylesheet formats this XML as a table, inserting href links so that the page may be used to navigate through the file system. Note that only the date attribute from the XML is used and the lastModified attribute is ignored, as shown by the first few lines of the resulting HTML in Listing 8.6.

Listing 8.6 Part of the HTML Created by the directory2html Stylesheet

```
<html xmlns:dir="http://apache.org/cocoon/directory/2.0">
<head>
<META http-equiv="Content-Type" content="text/html; charset=UTF-8">
<title>ROOT</title>
</head>
<body bgcolor="#ffffff">
<h1>Directory Listing of ROOT</h1>
<table border="0">
<tr>
<td><a href="../"><i>parent directory</i></a></td>
</tr>
<tr>
<td>   </td>
</tr>
<tr>
<td><a href="books/"><i>books</i></a></td><td>3/17/02 3:03 PM</td>
</tr>
<tr>
<td><a href="cocoon.xconf">cocoon.xconf</a></td>
<td>3/19/02 6:16 AM</td>
</tr>
<tr>
<td><a href="cocoon.xconf.bak">cocoon.xconf.bak</a></td>
<td>3/16/02 7:07 AM</td>
</tr>
<tr>
<td><a href="docs/"><i>docs</i></a></td>
<td>3/16/02 7:07 AM</td>
</tr>
```

The `DirectoryGenerator` class has four configuration options:

`depth` An integer representing how far to go down the directory structure, where the value of 1 means only the starting directory. Note that the `directory2html.xsl` file that comes with Cocoon does not support formatting of more than one level.

`dateFormat` A format string following the conventions of the `SimpleDateFormat` class in the `java.text` package.

`include` A string containing a "regular expression" pattern that will be applied to the file names. The regular expression syntax used is that for the `RE` class in the `org.apache.regexp` package. Bare bones documentation can be found at the following website:

`http://jakarta.apache.org/regexp/apidocs/org/apache/regexp/RE.html`

`exclude` A regular expression string used to exclude files from the listing.

ImageDirectoryGenerator and *MP3DirectoryGenerator*

These generators are similar to `DirectoryGenerator` but add specific information. For instance, the `ImageDirectoryGenerator` adds height and width information for files of "GIF" or "JPEG" type. Naturally each file in the directory must be opened and read to determine this information so `ImageDirectoryGenerator` and `MP3DirectoryGenerator` will be slower than the straight `DirectoryGenerator`.

The *FileGenerator*

Typically `FileGenerator` is the default generator because it can read and parse an XML document from a file. However, the name is a misnomer because `FileGenerator` is not limited to reading files. Because it is used so frequently, the `FileGenerator` class implements the `Cacheable` interface, and the sitemap entry for the class specifies various pool parameters as shown in this example:

```
<map:generator name="file"
      logger="sitemap.generator.file"
      label="content,data"
      src="org.apache.cocoon.generation.FileGenerator"
      pool-max="32" pool-min="16" pool-grow="4"/>
```

The `FileGenerator` takes as input any object that implements the `Source` interface defined in the `org.apache.cocoon.environment` package. Writing a custom `Source` is yet another way to get your specialized data into a Cocoon pipeline. A `Source` simply has to implement the methods shown in Table 8.3.

TABLE 8.3: Methods in the Source Interface

Method	Returns	Used for
`getLastModified()`	`long`	Last modification date or 0 if it can't be determined
`getContentLength()`	`long`	Content length or –1 if it can't be determined
`getInputStream()`	`java.io.InputStream`	To read a byte stream from the source
`getInputSource()`	`org.xml.sax.InputSource`	A standard SAX input source
`getSystemId()`	`java.lang.String`	A unique identifier for the class

The `FileGenerator` gets a `Source` from a `SourceResolver` passed to it in the setup method when the pipeline is being created to handle a particular request. For example, in the following pipeline entry, the `SourceResolver` would decide that the `src` attribute in the `<map:generate>` tag represents a local file relative to the Cocoon root directory and would generate an `InputSource` to read it:

```
<map:match pattern="sample-*">
  <map:generate src="docs/samples/sample-{1}.xml"/>
```

```
    <map:transform src="stylesheets/simple-samples2html.xsl"/>
    <map:serialize/>
  </map:match>
```

On the other hand, the following pipeline entry would cause the SourceResolver to generate a URLConnection because it recognizes the "http://" protocol:

```
  <map:match pattern="slashdot/slashdot.xml">
    <map:generate src="http://slashdot.org/slashdot.xml"/>
    <map:transform src="stylesheets/news/slashdot.xsl"/>
    <map:serialize/>
  </map:match>
```

Sources and Pseudo-Protocols

In addition to supporting sources such as files and URLs, Cocoon also supports sources that are addressed with a protocol-like syntax, as shown in Table 8.4. This is a very powerful concept. It allows you to draw on a variety of resources with the same syntax as used for reading a file.

TABLE 8.4: Currently Available Pseudo-Protocols

Protocol	Refers to
"cocoon:/"	a pipeline from the current sitemap
"cocoon://"	a pipeline from the root sitemap
"context://"	a resource using the servlet context
"resource://"	resource from the context classloader
"xmldb:"	interpret URL as a XML:DB query and read retrieved data as the source

The following snippet of pipeline from the Cocoon 2.0.2 sitemap shows how the "xmldb:" pseudo-protocol is used:

```
  <map:match pattern="xmldb/**">
    <map:match pattern="xpath" type="request-parameter">
      <map:generate
       src="xmldb:xindice://localhost:4080/db/{../1}#{1}"/>
      <map:serialize type="xml"/>
    </map:match>
    <map:generate src="xmldb:xindice://localhost:4080/db/{1}"/>
    <map:serialize type="xml"/>
  </map:match>
```

When an XMLDBSource object is used in a FileGenerator pipeline, it carries out the following steps:

1. Connect to the database.
2. Extract the query from the URL.

3. Perform the query.
4. Generate SAX events representing the results.

Subsequent transformer and serializer steps must then be applied to create the final version in the desired format.

Utility Generators

This section discusses three generators that work from specific file formats to get data into a pipeline. The `FragmentExtractorGenerator` processes a selected set of SAX events from the pipeline. The `HTMLGenerator` converts an HTML document to XHTML. The `ServerPagesGenerator` generates XSP script pages.

FragmentExtractorGenerator

This generator works in combination with the `FragmentExtractorTransformer`. The transformer removes a selected set of SAX events from the pipeline so they can be processed by this generator. Here is the sitemap entry for the generator:

```
<map:generator label="data" logger="sitemap.generator.extractor"
   name="extractor"
   src="org.apache.cocoon.generation.FragmentExtractorGenerator"
/>
```

The sitemap entry for the matching transformer follows:

```
<map:transformer logger="sitemap.transformer.extractor"
   name="extractor"
   src="org.apache.cocoon.transformation.FragmentExtractorTransformer"
/>
```

In operation, the transformer removes selected nodes from a SAX stream and builds a DOM that is stored in a static variable held by the generator. The transform substitutes a new XML element that identifies the stored data.

A request for the image causes the generator to put the SAX event data into another pipeline. This pipeline uses a serializer that can convert the SVG markup into a format commonly recognized in browsers, such as png.

The main use for this process is in offline document generation to separate SVG image data from a document, but it can also be used online, as in this pipeline snippet from the Cocoon distribution:

```
<map:match pattern="welcome-svg">
   <map:generate src="docs/samples/samples.xml"/>
   <map:transform src="stylesheets/svg-samples2html.xsl"/>
   <map:transform type="extractor"/>
   <map:transform src="stylesheets/fragment-extractor.xsl"/>
   <map:serialize/>
</map:match>
```

In this example, the `svg-samples2html.xsl` stylesheet introduces SVG codes to draw the lines with code that looks like this:

```
<svg:g style="stroke: black; stroke-width: 2px;">
  <svg:line x1="5" y1="5" x2="8" y2="5"/>
  <svg:line x1="5" y1="5" x2="5" y2="15"/>
</svg:g>
```

Each group of SVG tags is grabbed by the transformer and handed to the generator, inserting image tags where the SVG tags were. In the resulting HTML, each of the image tags look like the following example, with a different number for each separate image:

```
<img xmlns:fe="http://apache.org/cocoon/fragmentextractor/2.0"
   border="0"
   src="welcome-svg-images/18062f-ed79e5be75--7fff.png">
```

As you can see, the browser will make a request for the image that will match the following sitemap entry:

```
<map:match pattern="welcome-svg-images/*.png">
  <map:generate src="{1}" type="extractor"/>
  <map:serialize type="svg2png"/>
</map:match>
```

This request will fire off the `ExtractorGenerator`, which retrieves the stored events that represent the SVG image markup using that unique number. The generator feeds these events to the `svg2png` serializer that delivers the binary image back to the browser, resulting in a display that looks like Figure 8.2. Needless to say, all of this computation takes a substantial amount of time, so one would not want to dynamically generate images that could easily be provided as static files.

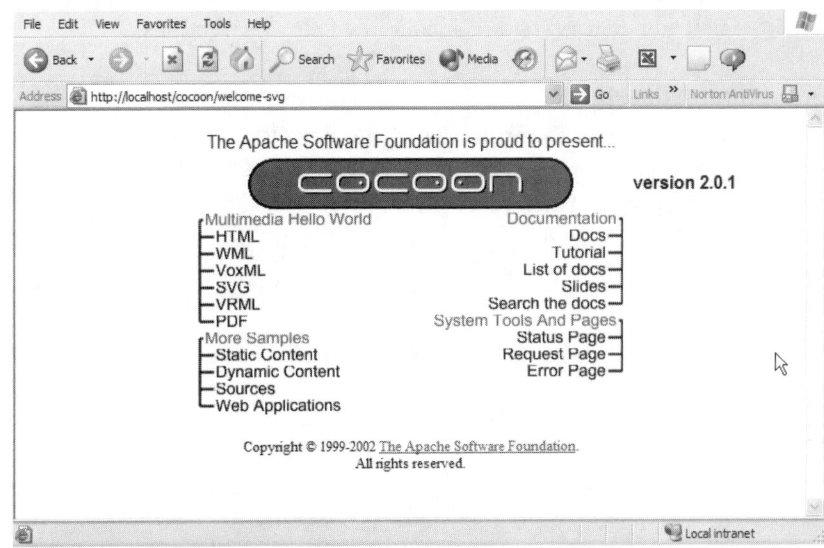

FIGURE 8.2: The example page containing generated SVG images

HTMLGenerator

The `HTMLGenerator` reads an HTML-formatted document and converts it to XHTML compatibility using the JTidy package on the fly. Passing the data through JTidy is necessary because typical HTML pages are not well formed by XML rules.

This generator could be useful as an intermediate step in remodeling an existing site, either to get existing pages into the Cocoon pipeline or as an offline operation to clean up ill-formatted HTML pages. For more information about XHTML, see Ed Tittel's *Mastering XHTML, Premium Edition* (Sybex, 2001).

ServerPagesGenerator

This generator is primarily used with XSP script pages. A typical example sitemap using `ServerPagesGenerator` follows:

```
<map:match pattern="xsp-plain/*">
  <map:generate type="serverpages" src="docs/samples/xsp/{1}.xsp"/>
  <map:serialize/>
</map:match>
```

There is one optional parameter for `ServerPagesGenerator`. If specified *`true`*, extra processing is done to ensure that all tags generated by the XSP are properly closed.

```
<map:parameter name="autocomplete-documents" value="true" />
```

The default value is *`false`*; it is much better to ensure that your XSP generates correct tags because this checking step is time-consuming.

Debugging and Performance Tuning

Several generators are related to Cocoon's facilities for debugging and performance tuning. These generators are discussed in the following sections.

ProfileGenerator

The Cocoon `Profiler` interface is used in classes that can gather information on the time consumed in various parts of the pipeline. The Profiler interface and the `ProfileGenerator` are in the `org.apache.cocoon.profiler` package.

To capture profiling data, you must modify the way Cocoon handles the event pipeline. This is accomplished by three modifications in the `cocoon.xconf` configuration file.

NOTE Be sure to save a backup copy of `cocoon.xconf` before attempting these modifications.

First, look at the `<event-pipeline>` section, which normally reads as follows:

```
<event-pipeline
 class="org.apache.cocoon.components.pipeline.CachingEventPipeline"
    logger="core.event-pipeline"
    pool-max="32" pool-min="16" pool-grow="4"/>
```

You should comment that tag out and un-comment the one that reads as follows (note that the line has been wrapped to fit the page):

```
<event-pipeline
 class="org.apache.cocoon.components.profiler.
   ProfilingNonCachingEventPipeline"/>
```

Next, to set up the component that records timestamps as various events flow through the pipeline, you have to un-comment the tag that reads as follows:

```
<sax-connector
  class="org.apache.cocoon.components.profiler.ProfilingSAXConnector"/>
```

Finally, the following tag, presently commented out in `cocoon.xconf`, must be un-commented:

```
<profiler/>
```

Next you must modify the sitemap to include the `ProfileGenerator` in the `<map:generators>` section.

```
<map:generator name="profile"
  src="org.apache.cocoon.components.profiler.ProfilerGenerator"
  label="content" />
```

Finally, you need to have an entry in the pipeline that executes the profile generator and transform the results to a readable HTML page.

```
<map:match pattern="profile">
   <map:generate type="profile" />
   <map:transform type="xslt"
     src="stylesheets/system/profile2html.xsl"/>
   <map:serialize type="html"/>
</map:match>
```

In order to generate an example, we ran the Jython `testrequest.py` example script several times and then ran the profile twice. The page created on the second profile execution is shown in Figure 8.3.

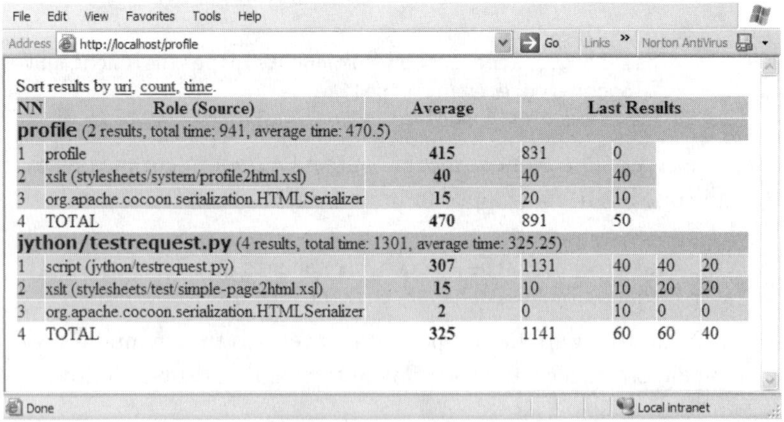

FIGURE 8.3: Example `ProfileGenerator` output

Sort results by uri, count, time.

NN	Role (Source)	Average	Last Results			
profile (2 results, total time: 941, average time: 470.5)						
1	profile	**415**	831	0		
2	xslt (stylesheets/system/profile2html.xsl)	**40**	40	40		
3	org.apache.cocoon.serialization.HTMLSerializer	**15**	20	10		
4	TOTAL	**470**	891	50		
jython/testrequest.py (4 results, total time: 1301, average time: 325.25)						
1	script (jython/testrequest.py)	**307**	1131	40	40	20
2	xslt (stylesheets/test/simple-page2html.xsl)	**15**	10	10	20	20
3	org.apache.cocoon.serialization.HTMLSerializer	**2**	0	10	0	0
4	TOTAL	**325**	1141	60	60	40

StatusGenerator

This generator essentially dumps the current state of the Cocoon system as XML. Such parameters as total memory available to the JVM, current memory used, and a list of cached objects can be very helpful in debugging. The entry for this generator in the sitemap looks like this:

```
<map:generator name="status"
    logger="sitemap.generator.status"  label="data"
    src="org.apache.cocoon.generation.StatusGenerator"/>
```

A typical pipeline entry using the `StatusGenerator` uses the `status2html.xsl` stylesheet to format output as shown in the following:

```
<map:match pattern="status">
  <map:generate type="status" />
  <map:transform type="xslt" src="stylesheets/system/status2html.xsl"/>
  <map:serialize type="html"/>
</map:match>
```

RequestGenerator

This handy generator can extract much of the data in an HTML request into an XML format. In addition to the request parameters and headers, the configuration parameters are displayed, making this an ideal debugging tool for questions related to the actual content of a request. A typical entry for the `RequestGenerator` in the `<map:generators>` section of the sitemap is as follows:

```
<map:generator name="request"
     logger="sitemap.generator.request"
     label="data"
     src="org.apache.cocoon.generation.RequestGenerator"/>
```

Creating a Custom Generator

Now let's look at creating a generator customized to a particular data source. The data source we will be using is the XML formatted survey script described in Chapter 7 of *Java Developer's Guide to E-Commerce with XML and JSP* (Sybex, 2001), by William Brogden and Chris Minnick. For more information about the book, or to take an example survey, go to the following website:

```
www.lanw.com/books/javaxml
```

A custom generator is required for several reasons. The most significant are that the user path through the survey depends on previous answers, and we have to make provision for recording the answers. We look only at the custom generator in this section.

In many cases, the best way to approach design of a custom generator is to work backward from the elements of the desired presentation. In this case, the main thing we have to create is a form with either "radio-button" or "checkbox"-style selection elements and a submit button. We also need to show the survey question text. In a commercial application there would also be graphics, and other information on the page, but for purposes of this discussion we will aim at a very plain page. An example of the presentation we are aiming for is shown in Figure 8.4.

FIGURE 8.4: Presentation of a survey question

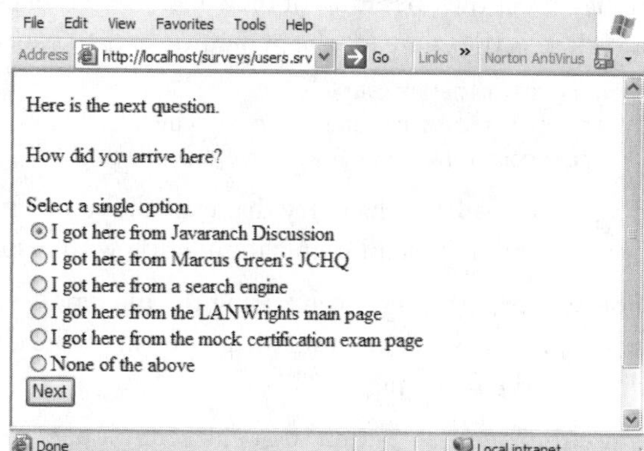

Listing 8.7 shows the fragment of the total survey XML script that contains the data for this question. We will have to create a generator to read this style of data and create SAX events. We will also have to create an XSL script that can create the desired HTML form.

Listing 8.7 Script for a Single Question

```
<Ques id="entry:1" type="QMC" >
  <Qtext>How did you arrive here?</Qtext>
<Qopt val="a">I got here from Javaranch Discussion</Qopt>
<Qopt val="b">I got here from Marcus Green's JCHQ</Qopt>
<Qopt val="c">I got here from a search engine</Qopt>
<Qopt val="d">I got here from the LANWrights main page</Qopt>
<Qopt val="d">I got here from the mock certification exam page</Qopt>
<Qopt val="e">None of the above</Qopt>
</Ques>
```

A further complication is introduced by the fact that questions are organized in blocks of questions that are presented in sequence. Certain answers can cause the survey to branch to a different block. For example, a survey response indicating that the user is familiar with XML might cause a branch to a question asking the user to indicate how many XML-related books he or she owns.

Sitemap Entries for the *SurveyGenerator*

It will be easier to understand the SurveyGenerator code if we first describe the sitemap entries that affect the operation of the code. We set up everything related to surveys as a sub-sitemap. Here is the entry for the generator in the <map:generators> section:

```
<map:generator name="survey"
     logger="sitemap.generator.survey"
     src="com.lanw.csurvey.SurveyGenerator"/>
```

The pipeline <map:match> entry that calls the survey generator is shown in Listing 8.8. There are several important points to mention with respect to this listing.

- In the <map:match> tag, we are using the file type "srv" in the matching pattern to indicate that a request requires survey processing. The single "*" tells the sitemap engine to hold on to the filename.
- We use the "request" action to get all request parameters into the sitemap environment.
- The first <map:parameter> tag tells the sitemap engine that we will be passing parameters to the generator.
- In the <map:generate> tag, the src attribute is filled in with the wildcard filename from the <map:match> tag. The "{../1}" notation is required because the <map:generate> tag is inside the <map:act> </map:act> element.
- The generator gets passed several parameters.
- The <map:transform> for logging has been commented out. This was used during debugging to record all generated SAX events in a separate log file.

- The final transformation step uses a file named `qformat.xsl`. We will be looking at the contents of this file later.
- Serialization is the default HTML serialization.

Listing 8.8 The Pipeline Entry for Surveys

```
<map:match pattern="*.srv">
  <map:act type="request" >
    <map:parameter name="parameters" value="true" />
    <map:generate type="survey" src="{../1}" >
      <map:parameter name="survey" value="users" />
      <map:parameter name="handler" value="{../1}.srv" />
      <map:parameter name="srcfile"
        value="c:/CocoonBook/QGenerator/XMLdocs/ecombookpage.xml" />
      <map:parameter name="workpath"
        value="c:/JavaProj2002/CocoonBook/QGenerator/XMLdocs" />
    </map:generate>
  </map:act>
<!-- uncomment the log transform for debugging
  <map:transform type="log" >
     <map:parameter name="logfile"
        value="c:/Tomcat401/logs/debuglog.txt" />
     <map:parameter name="xlogfile"
        value="c:/Tomcat401/logs/xdebuglog.txt" />
     <map:parameter name="append" value="yes" />
  </map:transform>
-->
    <map:transform type="xslt" src="stylesheets/qformat.xsl" />
    <map:serialize />
</map:match>
```

With the operating environment for our custom generator established, let's look at what Cocoon generators have to do.

Requirements for a Generator

A convenient starting point for a custom generator is the `AbstractGenerator` class in the `org.apache.cocoon.generation` package. You will find the `AbstractGenerator` class in the parentage of many of the generators we have discussed in this chapter. The following diagram from the Cocoon API for this class shows where `AbstractGenerator` fits in the Java class hierarchy.

```
java.lang.Object
  |
  +--org.apache.avalon.framework.logger.AbstractLoggable
      |
      +--org.apache.cocoon.xml.AbstractXMLProducer
          |
          +--org.apache.cocoon.generation.AbstractGenerator
```

When working with Cocoon classes, we always have to keep in mind the interfaces that are implied by the class hierarchy. For example, we might create our custom generator like this:

```
public class SurveyGenerator extends AbstractGenerator
```

In that case, we would pick up the `Generator` interface from `AbstractGenerator`, which is defined like this:

```
public abstract class AbstractGenerator extends AbstractXMLProducer
   implements Generator
```

The `Generator` interface gets us two more interfaces because it is defined like this:

```
public interface Generator extends XMLProducer,
   SitemapModelComponent
```

Furthermore, `SitemapModelComponent` extends `Component`, which is just a marker interface in the `org.apache.avalon.framework.component` package. We inherit the `XMPProducer` and `Recyclable` interfaces from the `AbstractXMLProducer` class, which is defined like this:

```
public abstract class AbstractXMLProducer extends AbstractLoggable
     implements XMLProducer, Recyclable
```

From the `AbstractLoggable` class, we inherit the `Loggable` interface. All of the above means that our custom generator class will inherit all of the following interfaces:

```
org.apache.avalon.framework.component.Component
org.apache.component.generation.Generator
org.apache.avalon.framework.logger.Loggable
org.apache.avalon.excalibur.pool.Poolable
org.apache.avalon.excalibur.pool.Recyclable
org.apache.cocoon.sitemap.SitemapModelComponent
org.apache.cocoon.xml.XMLProducer
```

We also inherit some important methods and variables. For example, the `AbstractXMLProducer` class has the following method that attaches the `XMLConsumer` object, which will get the SAX events that the generator creates:

```
public void setConsumer(XMLConsumer consumer) {
    this.xmlConsumer = consumer;
    this.contentHandler = consumer;
    this.lexicalHandler = consumer;
}
```

The `setConsumer` method is called during pipeline setup. In our example, this will either be a `"log"` transformer or an `"xslt"` transformer, as shown in Listing 8.8.

The *SurveyGenerator* Code

Now that we have discussed the requirements for our custom generator, we can get to the actual source code. Listing 8.9 shows the import statements, class declaration, static variables, instance variables, and constructor. Note the `AttributesImpl` variables. This class, from the `org.xml.sax.helpers` package, is used to hold attributes during the generation of a SAX event indicating start of an element.

Listing 8.9 Start of the *SurveyGenerator* code

```
package com.lanw.csurvey ;

import org.w3c.dom.* ;
import org.xml.sax.SAXException ;
import org.xml.sax.helpers.AttributesImpl ;

import org.apache.cocoon.ProcessingException ;
import org.apache.cocoon.generation.AbstractGenerator ;
import org.apache.cocoon.environment.SourceResolver ;
import org.apache.cocoon.environment.Request;
import org.apache.avalon.framework.parameters.* ;

import java.io.IOException ;
import java.util.Map ;

public class SurveyGenerator extends AbstractGenerator {

   // following used for namespace in SAX events
   static final String URI="http://www.lanw.com/surveygenerator" ;
   static final String PREFIX="srv" ;

   private org.w3c.dom.Document theDom ;
   private String workPath ; // for dom and results
   private String theSurvey ; // complete file
   private org.w3c.dom.Node nowBlock, nowNode ;
   private boolean terminal = false ; // true if the block is terminal
   private String title ;
   private String actionStr ; // goes into form
   private org.apache.cocoon.environment.Request request ;

   private org.w3c.dom.NodeList blockNodeList ;
   // that is all the Nodes that are <Block> type

   private AttributesImpl attr, handlerAttr ;

   // the constructor with optional debug message
   public SurveyGenerator(){
    // System.out.println("SurveryGenerator created");
   }
```

The Pipeline Setup Phase

The `setup` method is called during the pipeline setup phase of the processing of a request. It is required by the `SitemapModelComponent` interface. Listing 8.10 shows the `setup` method for our custom generator. The first step in `setup` is to call the `setup` method in the parent class. This call sets the `resolver`, `objectModel`, `src`, and `parameters` variables in the parent class.

Variables indicating the source of the survey, the path where the results are to be stored, etc., are set from the `Parameters` object passed to the `setup` method by the sitemap engine. Note how the string named `actionStr` is used in the call to the `addAttribute` method of the `handlerAttr` variable. Attributes held in `handlerAttr` will be used later in writing the tag that starts the question form.

From the `objectModel` variable we retrieve the `request` object. This is not an `HttpServletRequest` but Cocoon's wrapper for the actual request received by the Cocoon servlet. In a real application the `request` would contain either parameters to start the survey or answers to a previous survey question.

We get the survey script data from a class called `SurveyLibrary`. For the survey generator, the script is in XML `Document` object form, but the data source could just as easily be a database or a plain text file. The `SurveyLibrary` class is discussed later in this chapter.

Listing 8.10 The *setup* Method

```
    // setup gets called every time a generator
    // is to be called in a pipeline
  public void setup( SourceResolver resolver, java.util.Map objectModel,
         String src, Parameters par )
         throws ProcessingException, SAXException, IOException {
    super.setup( resolver, objectModel, src, par );
    try {
      workPath = par.getParameter("workpath");
      theSurvey = par.getParameter("srcfile");
      actionStr = par.getParameter("handler") ;
      request = ( org.apache.cocoon.environment.Request )
           objectModel.get("request");
      handlerAttr = new AttributesImpl();
      handlerAttr.addAttribute("","action","action","CDATA",actionStr);
    }catch(ParameterException pe){
      throw new ProcessingException( "missing parameters " +
        theSurvey + " " + actionStr + " " + pe );
    }
    SurveyLibrary lib = SurveyLibrary.getLibrary();
    theDom = lib.getDOM( theSurvey ) ;
    Element E = theDom.getDocumentElement(); // the root
    blockNodeList = E.getElementsByTagName("Block");
    recordAndDecide();
  }
```

The last line in the setup code is a call to a recordAndDecide method. In the real application that method would record results from the previous question and decide which question to present next. Because this process is not relevant to the discussion of generators, we have substituted a simple fake method as shown in Listing 8.11. This listing also shows the generate method that is required by the Generator interface.

After the setup method is done, it is the generate method that is called next. Here are the steps that generate carries out.

1. A call to startDocument method of the contentHandler. Recall that the contentHandler is a transformer that was attached to the generator during pipeline setup. The contentHandler variable is in the AbstractXMLProducer class that our generator inherits from. The startDocument method is one of the basic SAX "event handler" methods specified in the org.xml.sax.ContentHandler interface. This must always be the first ContentHandler method called.
2. A call to startPrefixMapping establishes the fact that subsequent tags will have the specified namespace.
3. A call to start creates the opening <questionnaire> tag. Note that we have to supply an empty AttributesImpl in this call.
4. A call to genQuest will generate the tags representing the entire question.
5. A call to end with the "questionnaire" parameter creates the closing </questionnaire> tag.
6. A call to endPrefixMapping removes the namespace.
7. A call to endDocument terminates SAX event creation.

Listing 8.11 **The *SurveyGenerator* Code Continued**

```
    // in the real application this interprets the request,
    // records the response to
    // the previous question, and decides which question to ask next.
  private void recordAndDecide(){
      setTestQ( 0 ); // fake for testing
  }

  public void generate() throws java.io.IOException,
      org.xml.sax.SAXException,
      org.apache.cocoon.ProcessingException {
    // System.out.println("generate called");  // for debug
    this.contentHandler.startDocument();
    this.contentHandler.startPrefixMapping(PREFIX,URI);
    attr = new AttributesImpl();
    start("questionnaire", attr ); // empty att
    genQuest();
```

```
    end("questionnaire");
    this.contentHandler.endPrefixMapping(PREFIX);
    this.contentHandler.endDocument();
  }
```

Now let's look at the genQuest method that generates the events making up the body of the question. As shown in Listing 8.12, data for a question comes from an XML Element named nowNode. This was previously set by the setTestQ in the recordAndDecide method. After various attributes have been extracted from nowNode, the <qtext> element is written in the following sequence:

1. A call to start with the "qtext" name and the attr object creates the opening tag. The attr object is an empty AttributesImpl, so if rendered in XML the opening tag is simply "<qtext>" without any attributes.
2. A call to data sends the entire question text.
3. A call to end creates the closing "</qtext>" tag.

Don't worry about the start, data, and end methods right now; we will get to them shortly. The next statements in genQuest proceed to write a "startform" tag with attributes that include the question qid string and the "handler" URL that got originally placed in handlerAttr back in the setup method in Listing 8.10. Next, individual tags for each question option are written by calling the doOption method. Finally the closing "startform" tag is written.

Listing 8.12 The *genQuest* Method of *SurveyGenerator*

```
    // nowNode known to be a <Ques>
  public void genQuest( )throws SAXException {
    Element E = (Element) nowNode ;
    String qid = E.getAttribute("id") ;
    String type = E.getAttribute("type");
    String lim  = E.getAttribute("limit");
       // System.out.println("genQuest, id=" + qid );
       // Uncomment above for debugging
    NodeList nm = E.getElementsByTagName("Qtext");
      // skip empty Qtext
    if( nm.item(0).getFirstChild() != null ){
        start( "qtext", attr );
        data( getChildrenText( (Element) nm.item(0)) );
        end( "qtext" );
    }
    NodeList opm = E.getElementsByTagName("Qopt");
    int optCt = opm.getLength();
    attribute( handlerAttr, "quesid", qid );
    start("startform", handlerAttr );
```

```
      attribute( attr, "type",type);
      attribute( attr, "ct", Integer.toString(optCt) );
      attribute( attr, "limit", lim );
      start("optType", attr );
      end("optType");
      for( int i = 0 ; i < optCt ; i++ ){
         doOption( opm.item(i), type );
      }
      end("startform");
   }
```

We are going to break the narrative discussion of `SurveyGenerator` at this point to show you in Listing 8.13 the XML equivalent of the SAX "events" that the generator created. This is the data that will be fed down the pipeline. Here are some important points to notice:

- The `srv:questionnaire` element establishes the `srv` namespace that is used for all remaining tags.
- The `srv:optType` element contains `type`, `ct`, and `limit` attributes.
- Each `srv:option` element contains a `type` and an `opt` attribute.

Listing 8.13 The Content of the Generated SAX Events with Long Lines Wrapped to Fit the Page

```
<?xml version="1.0" encoding="UTF-8" ?>
<srv:questionnaire xmlns:srv="http://www.lanw.com/surveygenerator">
  <srv:qtext>How did you arrive here?</srv:qtext>
  <srv:startform action="users.srv" quesid="entry:1">
    <srv:optType type="QMC" ct="6" limit="" />
    <srv:option type="QMC" opt="a">I got here from Javaranch
Discussion</srv:option>
    <srv:option type="QMC" opt="b">I got here from Marcus Green's
JCHQ</srv:option>
    <srv:option type="QMC" opt="c">I got here from a search
engine</srv:option>
    <srv:option type="QMC" opt="d">I got here from the LANWrights main
page</srv:option>
    <srv:option type="QMC" opt="d">I got here from the mock
certification exam page</srv:option>
    <srv:option type="QMC" opt="e">None of the above</srv:option>
  </srv:startform>
</srv:questionnaire>
```

Now let's continue the `SurveyGenerator` class discussion. Listing 8.14 shows the `doOption` method. The sequence of operations, which should be familiar by now, gets some parameters from the data source that will become attributes in the `"option"` tag. Note the handling of the `"branch"` attribute: if an option leads to a branch in the survey, we include it; if not, no `"branch"` attribute is written.

Listing 8.14 The *SurveyGenerator* Code Continued

```
    // opN is from node list of <Qopt> - options
  private void doOption( Node opN, String type )throws SAXException {
    Element opE = (Element) opN;
    String val = opE.getAttribute("val") ;
    String branch = opE.getAttribute("branch");
    String content = getChildrenText( opE );
    attribute( attr, "type", type );
    attribute( attr, "opt", val );
    if( branch != null && branch.length() > 0 ){
        attribute( attr, "branch", branch );
    }
    start("option", attr );
    data( content );
    end("option" );
  }
```

Listing 8.15 shows some of the utility methods used to set the variable nowNode to the current question.

Listing 8.15 The *SurveyGenerator* Source Code Continued

```
  private Node setQnodeInBlock( int n ){
    Element e = (Element) nowBlock ;
    NodeList nl = e.getElementsByTagName("Ques");
    nowNode = nl.item( n );
    return nowNode ;
  }

  private void setTestQ( int n ){
    nowBlock = blockNodeList.item(n);
    if( nowBlock == null ){
       System.out.println("Error 1 setting up first question.<br>");
       return ;
    }
    if( setQnodeInBlock( 0 )== null ){
       System.out.println("Error 2 setting up first question.<br>");
       return ;
    }
    checkBlockType((Element)nowBlock ); // sets the terminal flag
  }

  // look at the type attribute in <Block> element - sets terminal flag
  private void checkBlockType( Element e ){
    String tmp = e.getAttribute("type");
    terminal = tmp.equals("terminal");
  }
```

The final set of utility methods is shown in Listing 8.16. The `getChildrenText` method collects all of the text contents of an element. Normally this will be from a single text node, but if the text contains characters that have significance in XML, it will have to be in a CDATA section. When writing a survey script containing CDATA sections, it is easy for an author to accidentally introduce extra empty text nodes, as in the following example in which the `<Qopt>` tag contains two text nodes in addition to the CDATA node:

```
<Qopt val="g">
<![CDATA[A Programmer's Guide to Java Certification -
 Mughal &amp; Rasmussen]]>
</Qopt>
```

The `attribute`, `start`, `end`, and `data` methods shown in Listing 8.16 are convenience methods that we have copied from `RequestGenerator`. Note that the `start` method clears the `AttributesImpl` object so that it can conveniently be reused.

Listing 8.16 **Some Utility Methods in *SurveyGenerator***

```
private String getChildrenText( Element e ){
  StringBuffer sb = new StringBuffer();
  NodeList nl = e.getChildNodes();
  for( int i = 0 ; i < nl.getLength() ; i++ ){
       sb.append( nl.item(i).getNodeValue() );
  }
  return sb.toString();
}

  // handy event building methods based on Cocoon RequestGenerator code
private void attribute(AttributesImpl attr, String name, String value){
    attr.addAttribute("",name,name,"CDATA",value);
}

private void start(String name, AttributesImpl attr)
       throws SAXException {
  super.contentHandler.startElement(URI,name,PREFIX+":"+name,attr);
  attr.clear();
}

private void end(String name) throws SAXException {
  super.contentHandler.endElement(URI,name,PREFIX+":"+name);
}

private void data(String data)  throws SAXException {
  super.contentHandler.characters(data.toCharArray(),0,data.length());
}

public String toString() {
  StringBuffer sb = new StringBuffer("SurveyGenerator ");
  return sb.toString() ;
}
```

```
// must null all references to the data and the specific request
public void recycle(){
  super.recycle();
  request = null ;
  theDom = null ;
  nowBlock = nowNode = null ;
}
} // end of the SurveyGenerator class
```

That takes care of the SAX event generation; now let's look at the next step.

The XSLT Transformation for Surveys

The next step in the pipeline is transformation using the `"xslt"` transformer working with a XSL script. Listing 8.17 shows the start of the script used to create the HTML example shown in Figure 8.4 (see the "Creating a Custom Generator" section). A detailed discussion of the operation of XSL is beyond the scope of this book. For more information, see Chuck White's *Mastering XSLT* (Sybex, 2002). Basically, the first `<xsl:template>` tag creates the enclosing HTML. Filling out the body is accomplished by the `<xsl:apply-templates>` tag, which invokes further instructions, shown in Listing 8.18.

Listing 8.17 **The *qformat.xsl* File**

```
<?xml version="1.0"?>

<xsl:stylesheet version="1.0"
   xmlns:xsl="http://www.w3.org/1999/XSL/Transform"
   xmlns:srv="http://www.lanw.com/surveygenerator">
  <xsl:output indent="no" method="html"/>

  <xsl:template match="/">
   <html>
    <head>
     <title>Experimental questionnaire presentation.
     </title>
    </head>
    <body bgcolor="white" alink="red" link="blue" vlink="blue">
    <p>Here is the next question.</p>
     <xsl:apply-templates/>
    </body>
   </html>
  </xsl:template>
```

The `<xsl:template>` instructions in Listing 8.18 match various XML elements that describe the question input form and create HTML based on information these elements contain.

Listing 8.18 The *qformat.xsl* File Continued

```
<xsl:template match="srv:qtext">
 <p align="left" ><xsl:value-of select="." /></p>
</xsl:template>

<xsl:template match="srv:startform">
 <form method="GET" action="{@action}" >
   <xsl:apply-templates/>
  <input type="hidden" name="quesid" value="{@quesid}" />
  <input type="SUBMIT" name="action" value="Next" />
  </form><br />
</xsl:template>

<!-- we also have option count "ct" and "limit"  attributes
    which could be used to add information -->
<xsl:template match="srv:optType" >
  <xsl:if test="@type = 'QMC'" >Select a single option.<br />
  </xsl:if>
  <xsl:if test="@type = 'QMCM'" >Select all applicable options.<br />
  </xsl:if>
</xsl:template>

<xsl:template match="srv:option" >
  <xsl:if test="@type = 'QMC'" >
    <input type="radio" name="option" value="{@opt}" />
      <xsl:value-of select="." /><br />
  </xsl:if>
  <xsl:if test="@type = 'QMCM'" >
    <input type="checkbox" name="option" value="{@opt}" />
      <xsl:value-of select="." /><br />
  </xsl:if>
</xsl:template>

</xsl:stylesheet>
```

The final step in the pipeline is a simple HTML serializer, typically the default serializer in Cocoon sitemaps. The result is the HTML page presented in Figure 8.4 (see the "Creating a Custom Generator" section). Naturally, a complete survey application would contain additional code to provide for saving the answers and controlling the flow of questions.

Summary

Generators are used at the start of a Cocoon pipeline to convert some input into a stream of SAX events that can be transformed in the pipeline to a final output format. The remainder of the pipeline does not have to be concerned with where the original data comes from so this simple concept turns out to be remarkably powerful.

Cocoon comes with generators suitable for converting data from many sources. In addition to converting data files, generators can extract data from the host operating system, as seen with the various directory generators. Generators can also grab data from existing web server resources such as JavaServer Pages documents.

In this chapter, we have demonstrated custom generators using both custom Java programs and scripting languages. Although slower than compiled programs, scripting languages such as Jython are particularly well suited to rapid prototyping of Cocoon applications. The capability of using a variety of data formats and a variety of scripting languages in generators makes Cocoon extremely flexible.

CHAPTER 9

Configuration for Debugging and Optimization

- Tips for Debugging
- Optimizing the Cocoon 2 System

The overall management of a Cocoon 2 site is accomplished with the sitemap and configuration files. The configuration files control the resources that are available to the framework and can be used to optimize the site. This chapter explores several tips and techniques for debugging and optimizing a Cocoon server. Most of the error messages that can be seen in a browser window are Java exceptions, and a strong understanding of Java exception messages is essential to debugging a Cocoon application. It is also necessary to have a broad understanding of the different Cocoon components because the error messages will name these components.

In addition to the `cocoon.xconf` and `sitemap.xmap` file, the `logkit.xconf` file is a very important configuration file that can be used to generate log files that hold error details. These log files can then be used in conjunction with the on-screen errors to track down the errors in the applications.

We also describe a custom transformer that can be used to monitor the flow of SAX events in the pipeline by logging the events to a user-defined log file. This custom transformer is the `XLogTransformer`, which is an extension of the `LogTransformer` provided in the Cocoon distribution.

After the application has been cleared of bugs and is ready to be deployed in a production environment, it becomes necessary to make modifications to the configuration files to improve the speed of processing the application. Several changes can be made to the `sitemap.xmap`, `logkit.xconf`, and `cocoon.xconf` files that significantly improve the performance of the application. Caching of static pages is another way to make a significant performance improvement to a Cocoon application.

Tips for Debugging

Application development in any framework that uses prefabricated components is challenging. This is because the developer invariably does not have a detailed knowledge of the internals of the components and is relying on the API documentation to aid in the development of the system. This is true for the Cocoon system too. Because Cocoon is built on Java, errors are reported in the format of the Java exception stack trace.

When the Cocoon system encounters an error, the exception is reported to the browser screen and the developer can use this error message to begin debugging. More often than not, the error message in the browser window does not have any details to assist the developer. In this case, the developer has access to other aids to assist in the debugging process.

The Cocoon system has an elaborate logging system that generates many files that log the details of running the application. The logging facility is based on LogKit, which was described in detail in Chapter 3, "A Review of the Essential Technologies," in the section on the Avalon framework. This chapter discusses how the logging facility is configured and used when debugging applications. Later on we also describe the steps for creating a custom logging component and its use in an application.

Logging in Cocoon

The LogKit toolkit is configured using the `logkit.xconf` file. This file resides in the `webapps\cocoon\WEB-INF` directory and defines the components and parameters of the logger. Listing 9.1 shows the factories or component definitions that are used for logging and are defined in the configuration file.

Listing 9.1 The Factories Definitions in the *logkit.xconf* File

```
<?xml version="1.0"?>
<logkit>
  <factories>
    <factory type="priority-filter"
class="org.apache.avalon.excalibur.logger.factory.PriorityFilterTargetFactory"/>
    <factory type="servlet"
class="org.apache.avalon.excalibur.logger.factory.ServletTargetFactory"/>
    <factory type="cocoon"
class="org.apache.cocoon.util.log.CocoonTargetFactory"/>
  </factories>
```

The `logkit.xconf` file is an XML file and the elements and their values define the configuration parameters of the toolkit. As defined in Chapter 3, the `LogTarget` is one of the basic components of LogKit, which consumes `LogEvents`. Listing 9.1 defines three factories:

`PriorityFilter` A `PriorityFilter` can be used to filter out messages of a particular priority before forwarding it to the destination. The specific `LogTarget` defined is the `PriorityFilterTargetFactory`.

`Servlet` The `ServletTargetFactory` consumes `LogEvents` that deal specifically with the servlet.

`Cocoon` The `CocoonTargetFactory` consumes `LogEvents` that deal specifically with the Cocoon servlet.

These components will be given detailed parameters and attributes in other sections of the configuration file.

Formatting the Output of a *LogTarget*

The output of a `LogTarget` has to be formatted if the data has to be serialized to the file system. This is achieved using a specific Formatter component such as the `PatternFormatter`. The output of the Formatter is a String object formatted based on the `LogEvent` received. The format specifier for the `PatternFormatter` is based on the C language `printf` function.

The Formatter specifier is String, which names the parameters and stipulates the pattern to be used. The following code snippet defines a format and shows a sample output for that format:

```
format: "%7.7{priority} %5.5{rtime} [%{category}]: %{message}\n"
output: DEBUG   123   [network.interceptor.connected]: This is a debug message
```

The code snippet shows an example format string which writes out exactly seven characters of the value in the *priority* field, exactly five characters of the value in the field named *rtime*, which is the time since the application was started, and variable length values in the *category* and *message* fields. The example output line for this formatter is shown in the second line of the preceding code snippet.

Subsequent code listings highlight specific formatters for different `LogTargets` in the `logkit.xconf`. The configuration information for each of these targets appears in the `<targets>` element of the file as follows:

```
<targets>
  <cocoon id="core"
     ...
   </cocoon>

  <cocoon id="sitemap"
     ...
   </cocoon>

  <cocoon id="access"
     ...
   </cocoon>

   <priority-filter>
     ...
   </priority-filter>
</targets>
```

Listings 9.2, 9.3, 9.4, and 9.5 give the details of each target element. The following are the configuration parameters common to all four targets. The Formatter specifies that the following fields of the `LogEvent` will be written to the log file.

Priority This is the name of the priority level of the message being logged. The five priorities are as follows:

- DEBUG

- INFO
- WARN
- ERROR
- FATAL_ERROR

Time This is the time when the message was logged based on the system time.

Category Also called *Channels* or *Facilities*, is the name of a subdivision of the logging namespace to give a finer control on the logging.

Uri The URI string that caused this event to be logged.

Thread The identifier of the specific thread in the Cocoon application.

Class:short The class name of the component.

Message The message that was available in the field in the `LogEvent`.

Throwable The details of the exception, if one was thrown.

The configuration details of a target also specify if the data is appended to an existing log file or written over. The rotation of the log files can be set based on maximum size or fixed time duration. In the targets, the size is set at 100MB and the time is one hour. All log files will be saved in the `WEB-ING/logs` directory in the Cocoon folder.

Listing 9.2 shows the details for the `core` Cocoon application. In addition to the common parameters just listed, this target specifies the name of the log file to be `core.log`.

Listing 9.2 The Target Element of the *logkit.xconf* File for *id=core*

```
<cocoon id="core">
  <filename>${context-root}/WEB-INF/logs/core.log</filename>
  <format type="cocoon">
    %7.7{priority} %{time}   [%{category}] (%{uri})
%{thread}/%{class:short}: %{message}\n%{throwable}
  </format>
  <append>true</append>
  <rotation type="revolving" init="1" max="4">
    <or>
      <size>100m</size>
      <time>01:00:00</time>
    </or>
  </rotation>
</cocoon>
```

Listing 9.3 shows the details for the `sitemap` target. This target specifies the log file to be `sitemap.log`.

Listing 9.3 The Target Element of the *logkit.xconf* for *id=sitemap*

```
<cocoon id="sitemap">
  <filename>${context-root}/WEB-INF/logs/sitemap.log</filename>

  <format type="cocoon">
    %7.7{priority} %{time}   [%{category}] (%{uri})
%{thread}/%{class:short}: %{message}\n%{throwable}
  </format>
  <append>true</append>
  <rotation type="revolving" init="1" max="4">
    <or>
      <size>100m</size>
      <time>01:00:00</time>
    </or>
  </rotation>
</cocoon>
```

Listing 9.4 shows the details for the access target. This target specifies the log file to be `access.log`.

Listing 9.4 The Target Element of the *logkit.xconf* for *id=access*

```
<cocoon id="access">
  <filename>${context-root}/WEB-INF/logs/access.log</filename>
  <format type="cocoon">
    %7.7{priority} %{time}   [%{category}] (%{uri})
%{thread}/%{class:short}: %{message}\n%{throwable}
  </format>
  <append>true</append>
  <rotation type="revolving" init="1" max="4">
    <or>
      <size>100m</size>
      <time>01:00:00</time>
    </or>
  </rotation>
</cocoon>
```

Listing 9.5 shows the details for the specialized `LogTarget`, which is the priority-filter target. The log-level specifies the priority level, which is `ERROR` in this example. The output is written to the `error.log` file.

Listing 9.5 The Priority-Filter Target

```
<priority-filter id="error" log-level="ERROR">
  <cocoon>
    <filename>${context-root}/WEB-INF/logs/error.log</filename>
    <format type="cocoon">
      %7.7{priority} %{time}   [%{category}] (%{uri})
%{thread}/%{class:short}: %{message}\n%{throwable}
    </format>
    <append>true</append>
    <rotation type="revolving" init="1" max="4">
      <or>
        <size>100m</size>
        <time>01:00:00</time>
      </or>
    </rotation>
  </cocoon>
</priority-filter>
```

The `categories` element subdivides the logging namespace into named sections. In doing so we can achieve a finer granularity in the logging. In addition to dividing the namespace, we can set different levels of logging within a particular category. Listing 9.6 shows the categories defined in our `logkit.xconf`.

Listing 9.6 The *categories* Definition in *logkit.xconf*

```
<categories>
  <category name="core" log-level="DEBUG">
    <log-target id-ref="core"/>
    <log-target id-ref="error"/>
  </category>

  <category name="sitemap" log-level="DEBUG">
    <log-target id-ref="sitemap"/>
    <log-target id-ref="error"/>
  </category>

  <category name="access" log-level="DEBUG">
    <log-target id-ref="access"/>
    <log-target id-ref="error"/>
  </category>
</categories>
```

When the Cocoon application is launched, the loggers are activated and the log files are created. These files are kept open for the duration the application is active and every relevant event is written to the log file. Figure 9.1 shows the directory containing the log files.

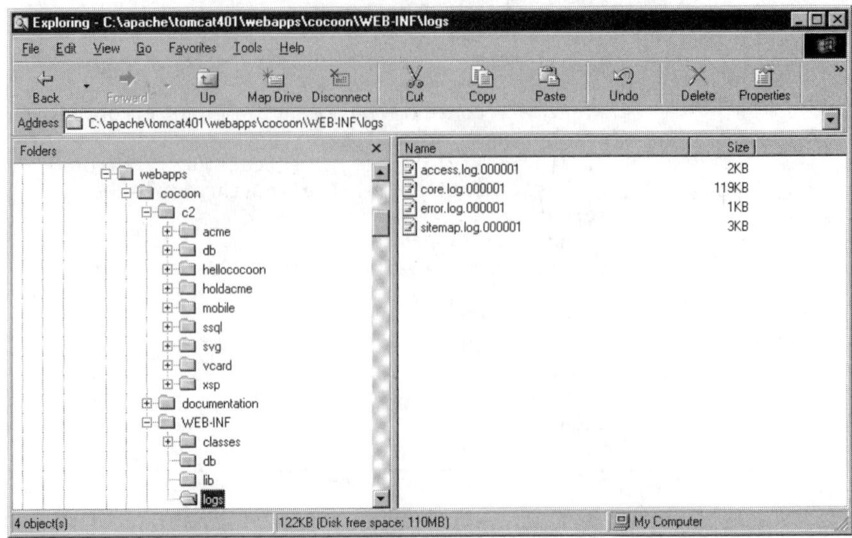

FIGURE 9.1: The directory with the log files

The log files for each target can be seen with their rotation number (000001). The rotation allows logs from previous sessions to be saved after a restart, thereby preserving information from previous runs of the application.

Figure 9.2 shows a section of the `core.log` file. The events logged in this file are related to the launching of the main Cocoon application.

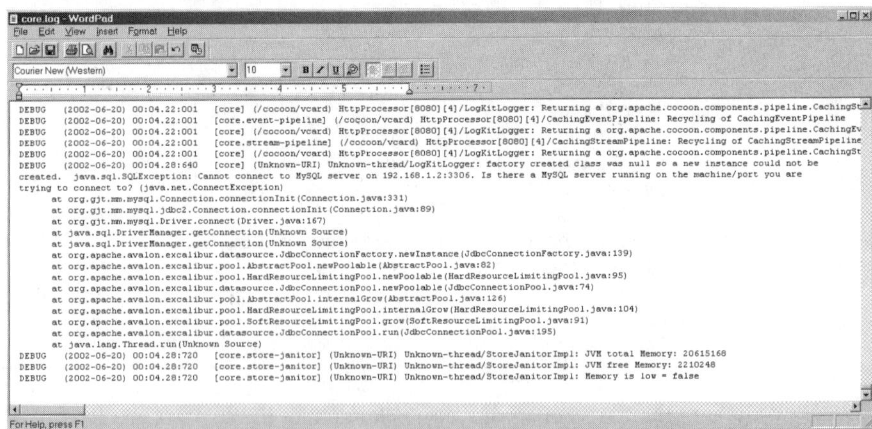

```
DEBUG   (2002-06-20) 00:04.22:001   [core] (/cocoon/vcard) HttpProcessor[8080][4]/LogKitLogger: Returning a org.apache.cocoon.components.pipeline.CachingSt
DEBUG   (2002-06-20) 00:04.22:001   [core.event-pipeline] (/cocoon/vcard) HttpProcessor[8080][4]/CachingEventPipeline: Recycling of CachingEventPipeline
DEBUG   (2002-06-20) 00:04.22:001   [core] (/cocoon/vcard) HttpProcessor[8080][4]/LogKitLogger: Returning a org.apache.cocoon.components.pipeline.CachingEv
DEBUG   (2002-06-20) 00:04.22:001   [core.stream-pipeline] (/cocoon/vcard) HttpProcessor[8080][4]/CachingStreamPipeline: Recycling of CachingStreamPipeline
DEBUG   (2002-06-20) 00:04.22:001   [core] (/cocoon/vcard) HttpProcessor[8080][4]/LogKitLogger: Returning a org.apache.cocoon.components.pipeline.CachingSt
DEBUG   (2002-06-20) 00:04.28:640   [core] (Unknown-URI) Unknown-thread/LogKitLogger: factory created class was null so a new instance could not be
created.  java.sql.SQLException: Cannot connect to MySQL server on 192.168.1.2:3306. Is there a MySQL server running on the machine/port you are
trying to connect to? (java.net.ConnectException)
	at org.gjt.mm.mysql.Connection.connectionInit(Connection.java:331)
	at org.gjt.mm.mysql.jdbc2.Connection.connectionInit(Connection.java:89)
	at org.gjt.mm.mysql.Driver.connect(Driver.java:167)
	at java.sql.DriverManager.getConnection(Unknown Source)
	at java.sql.DriverManager.getConnection(Unknown Source)
	at org.apache.avalon.excalibur.datasource.JdbcConnectionFactory.newInstance(JdbcConnectionFactory.java:139)
	at org.apache.avalon.excalibur.pool.AbstractPool.newPoolable(AbstractPool.java:82)
	at org.apache.avalon.excalibur.pool.HardResourceLimitingPool.newPoolable(HardResourceLimitingPool.java:95)
	at org.apache.avalon.excalibur.datasource.JdbcConnectionPool.newPoolable(JdbcConnectionPool.java:74)
	at org.apache.avalon.excalibur.pool.AbstractPool.internalGrow(AbstractPool.java:126)
	at org.apache.avalon.excalibur.pool.HardResourceLimitingPool.internalGrow(HardResourceLimitingPool.java:104)
	at org.apache.avalon.excalibur.pool.SoftResourceLimitingPool.grow(SoftResourceLimitingPool.java:91)
	at org.apache.avalon.excalibur.datasource.JdbcConnectionPool.run(JdbcConnectionPool.java:195)
	at java.lang.Thread.run(Unknown Source)
DEBUG   (2002-06-20) 00:04.28:720   [core.store-janitor] (Unknown-URI) Unknown-thread/StoreJanitorImpl: JVM total Memory: 20615168
DEBUG   (2002-06-20) 00:04.28:720   [core.store-janitor] (Unknown-URI) Unknown-thread/StoreJanitorImpl: JVM free Memory: 2210248
DEBUG   (2002-06-20) 00:04.28:720   [core.store-janitor] (Unknown-URI) Unknown-thread/StoreJanitorImpl: Memory is low = false
```

FIGURE 9.2: The `core.log .000001` file

Figure 9.3 shows a section of the `access.log` file. The events logged in this file pertain to accessing the resources specified in the pipelines defined in the sitemap.

Figure 9.5 shows a section of the `error.log` file. As can be seen, all `LogEvents` with a priority of either `ERROR` or `FATAL_ERROR` are written to this file.

Figure 9.4 shows a section of the `sitemap.log` file. The events logged pertain to the components defined in the sitemap.

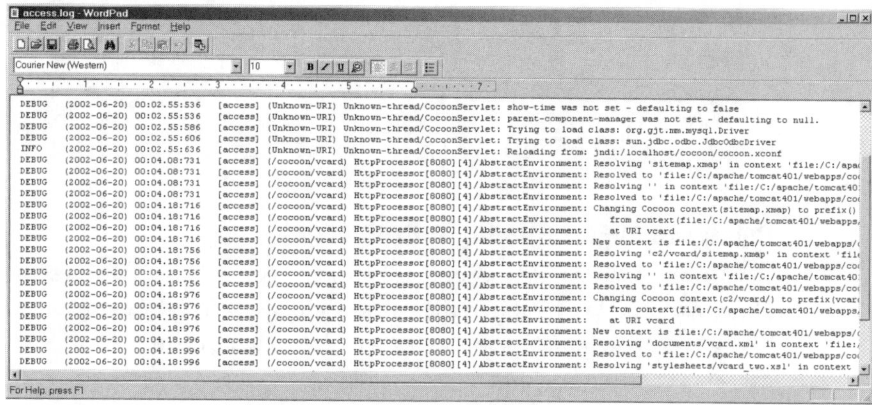

FIGURE 9.3: The `access.log.000001` file

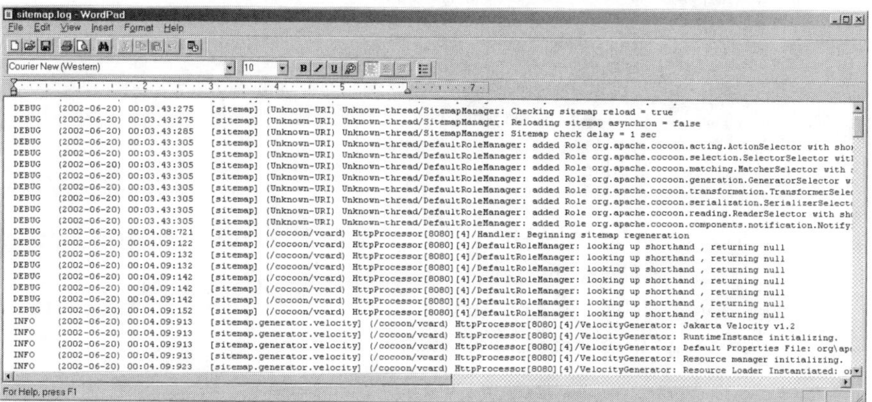

FIGURE 9.4: The `sitemap.log.000001` file

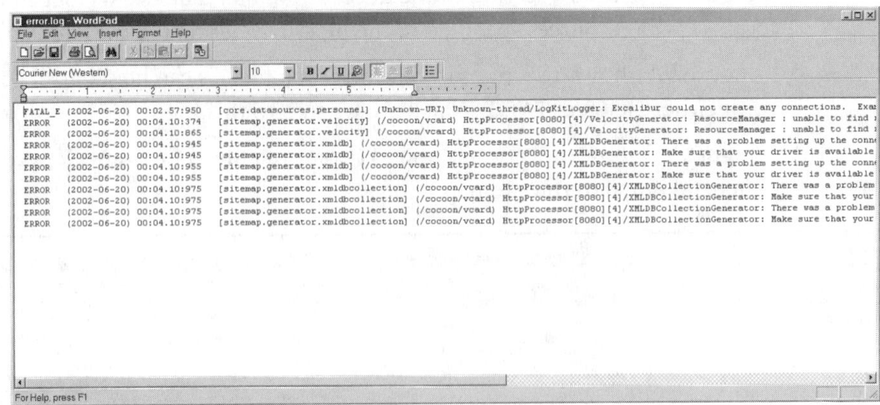

FIGURE 9.5: The error.log .000001 file

Using the Logs to Debug a Problem

In Chapter 2, "Uses of Cocoon," we presented an example to access a database on the Cocoon server. We modified the cocoon.xconf file in the example to access a remote database server to demonstrate using logs to debug a problem. The modified jdbc element of the cocoon.xconf file is shown in Listing 9.7.

Listing 9.7 The *jdbc* Element in the *cocoon.xconf* File

```
<jdbc name="remote_pool">
  <pool-controller min="5" max="10"/>
  <dburl>jdbc:mysql://192.168.1.2/mydb</dburl>
  <user>root</user>
  <password></password>
</jdbc>
```

When the browser tries to access the URL http://192.168.1.3:8080/cocoon/c2sql, the application hangs and never gets launched. To debug the problem, we started looking at all the log files, beginning with the core.log. Listing 9.8 shows an error message in the core.log file shown in Figure 9.2.

Listing 9.8 An Error Message in the *core.log* File

```
java.sql.SQLException: Cannot connect to MySQL server on 192.168.1.2:3306. Is
there a MySQL server running on the machine/port you are trying to connect to?
(java.net.ConnectException)
     at org.gjt.mm.mysql.Connection.connectionInit(Connection.java:331)
     at org.gjt.mm.mysql.jdbc2.Connection.connectionInit(Connection.java:89)
     at org.gjt.mm.mysql.Driver.connect(Driver.java:167)
     at java.sql.DriverManager.getConnection(Unknown Source)
     at java.sql.DriverManager.getConnection(Unknown Source)
```

Listing 9.8 indicates that the Cocoon servlet itself did not initiate the connection to the database when the server was started. The problem did not get noticed during startup and only became an issue when the browser tried to access the database from a Cocoon application defined in the sitemap.

Starting the MySQL database running on the 192.168.1.2 server rectified the problem. Next, we verified that the database was accessible by remote machines using a SQL client on the application server. The Tomcat server had to be stopped and restarted for the Cocoon servlet to establish the JDBC connection to the database server. The application URI was submitted and the application was launched and executed correctly.

We would like to emphasize that in order to effectively debug a problem in a Cocoon application, it is necessary to make use of all available aids. These include any error messages displayed in the browser window and all four log files created by the Cocoon application. Additional resources, such as Tomcat server log files, which are located in the `tomcat/logs` directory, can be used in conjunction with system monitoring applications to verify connectivity to remote servers and client browsers. If available, tools such as network sniffers and monitors can also be used to assist in the monitoring and debugging during development or when running in production mode.

Spying on the Pipeline

In Chapter 5, "Logic Control: The Sitemap," we introduced the `LogTransformer` class provided in the Cocoon distribution that can be used to assist in the debugging of the pipeline processes. This transformer writes a log containing a short representation of the SAX events as they pass through the pipeline. The `LogTransformer` reports only the events passing through it and does not modify them.

We did not find a tool for conveniently reporting the other information available to pipeline components. It seemed logical to extend `LogTransformer` for that purpose so we can track both SAX events and the additional information. The following are the steps to create the new component and configure it to be used in an application:

1. Define and create the XLogTransformer class.
2. Deploy the new class file.
3. Add the new component definition.
4. Use the transformer in an application pipeline.

The source code and compiled class can be obtained from the support website for this book. We step through the preceding list in reverse order for the benefit of the reader who wants to see the `XLogTransformer` in action. The Java class will be described in detail after the discussion on configuration steps.

Using the Transformer in an Application Pipeline

When used in a sitemap, the `XLogTransformer` accepts configuration parameters giving filenames to use for logging both the SAX events and the additional information. Listing 9.9 shows the `transform` element in the pipeline that uses the `XLogTransformer` component.

Listing 9.9 The *<map:transform>* Element in the Pipeline

```
<map:transform type="log">
   <map:parameter name="logfile"
       value="c:/Tomcat401/logs/debuglog.txt" />
   <map:parameter name="xlogfile"
       value="c:/Tomcat401/logs/xdebuglog.txt" />
   <map:parameter name="append" value="yes" />
</map:transform>
```

As we discussed in the section on the `LogTransformer` in Chapter 5, the `append` parameter controls whether or not the new data is added to or written over in the log files, every time the pipeline is activated. We have used the same format in `XLogTransformer`.

Adding the New Component Definition

The new transformer can be introduced into a pipeline by modifying the log transformer entry in the `<map:transformers>` area of the sitemap to point to our new transformer class as follows:

```
<map:transformer name="log"
         logger="sitemap.transformer.log"
         src="com.lanw.cocoon.util.XLogTransformer"/>
```

Deploying the New Class File

In this example, we have created just one Java file. After the class file is compiled, it must be deployed within the Cocoon application.

Defining and Creating the *XLogTransformer* Class

The new `java` class extends the functionality of the existing `LogTransformer` class. Listing 9.10 shows the start of the `XLogTransformer` code.

Listing 9.10 Start of the *XLogTransformer* Code

```
package com.lanw.cocoon.util ;

import org.apache.cocoon.transformation.LogTransformer ;

import org.apache.avalon.framework.parameters.Parameters;
import
```

```
org.apache.avalon.framework.parameters.ParameterException;

import org.apache.cocoon.ProcessingException;

import org.apache.cocoon.environment.SourceResolver;
import org.apache.cocoon.environment.http.HttpRequest;
import org.apache.cocoon.environment.Cookie ;

import org.xml.sax.Attributes;
import org.xml.sax.Locator;
import org.xml.sax.SAXException;

import java.io.FileWriter;
import java.io.PrintWriter ;
import java.io.IOException;
import java.util.*;

public class XLogTransformer extends LogTransformer {

  PrintWriter xlog = null ;
  String xlogfilename ;
  boolean append ;
```

The methods inherited from the `LogTransformer` class take care of the logging of SAX events. We have added variables to handle the new log file, and a specialized version of the `setup` method. The `setup` method is specified in the `SitemapModelComponent` interface in the `org.apache.cocoon.sitemap` package.

Before any data is passed down a pipeline, Cocoon prepares the pipeline by calling the `setup` method of each pipeline component. As shown in Listing 9.11, after calling the `setup` method of the parent class, the initial part of our setup method creates a `PrintWriter` that gets the output.

Listing 9.11 The *setup* Method

```
public void setup(SourceResolver resolver, Map objectModel,
      String source, Parameters parameters)
         throws ProcessingException, SAXException, IOException {
  super.setup( resolver, objectModel, source, parameters );
  if (xlog == null) {
     String appends = parameters.getParameter("append", null);
     xlogfilename = parameters.getParameter("xlogfile", null);
     if ("yes".equals(appends)) {
          append = true;
     } else {
          append = false;
     }
     try {
```

```
// Check for null, use System.out if logfile is not specified.
    if(xlogfilename != null) {
       xlog = new PrintWriter(
          new FileWriter(xlogfilename, append ));
    } else {
        xlog = new PrintWriter(
         new FileWriter(java.io.FileDescriptor.out));
    }
 } catch (IOException e) {
      throw new ProcessingException( "XLogTransformer setup "
       + e );
 }
}
```

The remainder of the setup method, as shown in Listing 9.12, provides for examining objects passed to setup in the objectModel variable. Although many of these objects could be of interest in a debugging situation, our example only looks in detail at the object stored under the name of "request." Information on other objects is simply dumped as the result of the object's toString method.

Listing 9.12 The *setup* Method Continued

```
String[] names = parameters.getNames();
xlog.println("XLogTransformer setup - Parameter ct: "
   + names.length );
try {
  for( int i = 0; i < names.length ; i++ ){
     xlog.println( names[i] + " = "
        + parameters.getParameter( names[i] ) );
  }
  xlog.println("objectModel size: " + objectModel.size() );
  Object[] keys = objectModel.keySet().toArray() ;
  for( int i = 0 ; i < keys.length ; i++ ){
     String key = (String)keys[i];
     Object val = objectModel.get( key );
     if( key.equals("request") &&
         val instanceof HttpRequest ){
       dumpRequest( (HttpRequest )val );
     }
     else {
       xlog.println( key + " = " + val.toString() );
     }
  }
}catch( ParameterException pe ){
    xlog.println("Hit " + pe );
}
xlog.flush();
}
```

In the `objectModel` variable, the object held under the "request" key is an `HttpRequest` from the `org.apache.cocoon.environment.http` package. This is not necessarily the object implementing `HttpServletRequest` as created by a servlet host, because Cocoon also has to operate in an offline mode. However, the Cocoon version implements the `HttpServlet-Request` interface so the code to extract values, as shown in Listing 9.13, will be familiar to servlet programmers. The `cookie` objects are also special Cocoon versions that implement the usual cookie methods.

Listing 9.13 Method to Output Request Contents

```
void dumpRequest( HttpRequest req ){
   String name, value ;
   Object obj = null ;
   xlog.println("Dump of HttpRequest");
   Cookie[] cookies = req.getCookies();
   if( cookies == null || cookies.length == 0 ){
     xlog.println("No Cookies");
   }
   else {
     for(int i = 0 ; i < cookies.length ; i++ ){
       name = cookies[i].getName();
       value = cookies[i].getValue();
       xlog.println("Cookie " + name + " = " + value );
     }
   }
   Enumeration e = req.getAttributeNames();
   while( e.hasMoreElements() ){
     name = (String)e.nextElement();
     obj = req.getAttribute( name );
     xlog.println("Attribute " + name + " = " + obj );
   }
   e = req.getParameterNames();
   while( e.hasMoreElements() ){
     name = (String)e.nextElement();
     value = req.getParameter( name );
     xlog.println("Parameter " + name + " = " + value );
   }
}
```

Finally, note that `XLogTransformer` has a `destroy` method as shown in Listing 9.14. This ensures that any log files created are properly closed.

Listing 9.14 The *destroy* Method Ensures the File Is Properly Closed

```
public void destroy() {
   try {
    super.destroy();
    if( xlog != null ) xlog.close();
```

```
        } catch (Exception e) {
          System.out.println( "XLogTransformer destroy " + e);
        }
    }
```

We recorded the results of running the surveys generator using the sitemap shown in Chapter 8, "Content Generators," Listing 8.8. Answering a question results in a request URL such as the following that encodes the response parameters:

```
http://localhost/surveys/users.srv?option=c&quesid=entry%3A1& action=Next
```

Listing 9.15 shows what `XLogTransformer` recorded from the activation of the surveys pipeline caused by this request. The `Dump of HttpRequest` section shows the extraction of the request parameter values.

Listing 9.15 Results from *XLogTransformer* Monitoring Surveys Pipeline

```
XLogTransformer setup - Parameter ct: 3
append = yes
xlogfile = c:/Tomcat401/logs/xdebuglog.txt
logfile = c:/Tomcat401/logs/debuglog.txt
objectModel size: 8
httpresponse = org.apache.catalina.connector.HttpResponseFacade@495daa
profiler = org.apache.cocoon.components.profiler.ProfilerData@6c1f9e
response = org.apache.cocoon.environment.http.HttpResponse@fe89a
notifying-object =
   org.apache.cocoon.components.notification.SimpleNotifyingBean@6fdca5
context = org.apache.cocoon.environment.http.HttpContext@2ecb09
request = org.apache.cocoon.environment.http.HttpRequest@7f0a34
Dump of HttpRequest
No Cookies
Parameter quesid = entry:1
Parameter option = c
Parameter action = Next
httprequest = org.apache.catalina.connector.HttpRequestFacade@1b50a1
httpservletcontext =
   org.apache.catalina.core.ApplicationContextFacade@4ab40a
```

Cleaning Out the Cache

Occasionally, when developing an application, caching comes in the way of debugging a problem. Although there is no fixed symptom to indicate the problem is in the components that have been cached, it often manifests itself as erratic behavior when accessing the URL across different invocations. Simply stopping and restarting the Tomcat application server does not rectify the situation. When such a problem occurs it is necessary to clean the cache out completely and let Cocoon recompile the modified sitemaps. Figure 9.6 shows the location of the `work` directory and the subdirectories within.

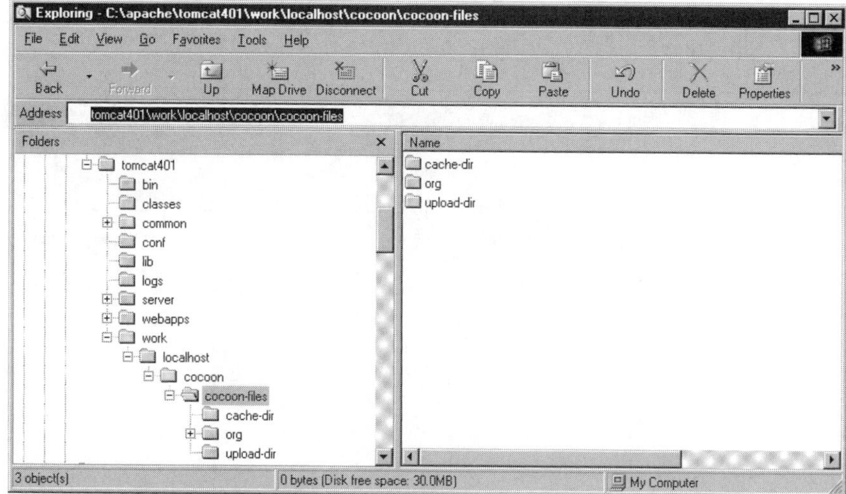

FIGURE 9.6: The Cocoon `work` directory

The `cocoon-files` subdirectory is of special interest and contains two directories of significance to this discussion. The `cache-dir` is the location of all the cached components. Figure 9.7 shows the contents of the `cache-dir`, which holds just a few cached components on our development server. In a production server, there will be many more components in this subdirectory.

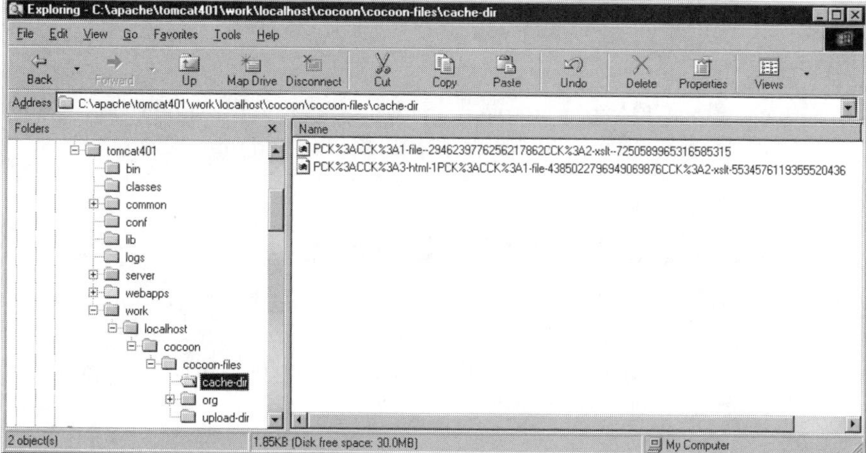

FIGURE 9.7: The contents of the `cache-dir` directory

When the Tomcat server is launched, the sitemaps are compiled into `java` classes and saved in the `work` directory. These `java` classes are placed in the `org.apache.cocoon.www` package. Figure 9.8 shows the contents of the `org` subdirectory in which all the compiled sitemaps are saved. We have chosen to expand the subdirectory of the acme application to show the contents that would typically be present in this directory.

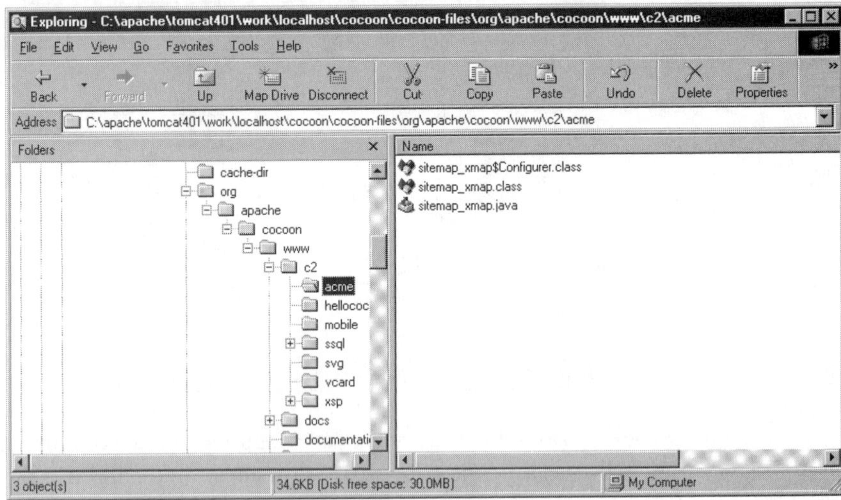

FIGURE 9.8: The `org` directory with the compiled sitemaps

During development and testing, if you encounter any erratic behavior when running a particular application, the contents of the specific sitemap subdirectory in the `org` hierarchy should be deleted. Additionally, the contents of the entire `cache-dir` should also be cleaned out before restarting the Tomcat server. When the server starts, the sitemap for that application will be recompiled and the contents of the `cache-dir` will be refreshed. It would be a good practice to clean out the entire `work` directory on a server before performing any quality assurance (QA) testing to eliminate problems in the subdirectories that may arise during development that may have gone unnoticed and unresolved.

Optimizing the Cocoon 2 System

Cocoon is not the best choice for applications that can be implemented in plain HTML pages and require minimal or no dynamic data. There are several other simpler technologies, such as Java Servlets and JSP, that can be used to achieve very good performance and have a shorter development cycle.

After carefully analyzing the requirements of your application and deciding that Cocoon is the best possible choice, you would embark on a formal design and implementation process to develop your application. An important part of this process is application debugging. We covered many important tips and techniques for debugging in the previous section, all of which give rise to server performance degradation when running the application. Once an application is completely debugged, tested, and deployed, it becomes necessary to start implementing some performance enhancements to the Cocoon server as well as the application modules themselves. This section examines some of the steps that can be adopted during analysis, design, implementation, and execution that can help enhance the performance of your Cocoon application.

Modifying the Tomcat Configuration File

The performance of your Cocoon server can be greatly enhanced by making more virtual memory available for use by the JVM (Java Virtual Machine) that is used by the server. In all our examples, we have used the Apache Tomcat server and so we will describe the steps needed to increase the amount of virtual memory available to the Tomcat JVM. Please consult the documentation for the specific server you are using to deploy the Cocoon servlet for details on increasing the amount of virtual memory available to the server.

In the case of Tomcat 4.*x*, the configuration file named `catalina.bat` (for a Microsoft Windows deployment) or `catalina.sh` (for a Unix deployment) are located in the `bin` directory of the Tomcat 4.*x* installation. In Tomcat 3.2.*x*, the names of the configuration files used are `tomcat.bat` (for the Microsoft Windows environment) or `tomcat.sh` (for the Unix environment). The following are the lines of code to be added at the top of the respective files. We show the line to be added to the configuration file for a memory size of 1024MB. Depending on the size of physical memory available on the server, you can experiment with different values, such as 256MB, 512MB, and 2048MB.

The following code will be added to the `catalina.bat` file in a Microsoft environment:

```
set CATALINA_OPTS = -mx1024m
```

The following code will be added to the `catalina.sh` file on a Unix server:

```
CATALINA_OPTS = -mx1024m
```

The following code will be added to the `tomcat.bat` file in a Microsoft environment:

```
set TOMCAT_OPTS = -mx1024m
```

A Unix server will have the following line added to the `tomcat.sh` file:

```
TOMCAT_OPTS = -mx1024m
```

Modifying the *cocoon.xconf* File

The sitemap element in the `cocoon.xconf` file is used to configure how the Cocoon servlet uses the main sitemap configuration file. The following code snippet shows the settings for an application that has been deployed in a production environment:

```
<sitemap file="sitemap.xmap"
         logger="sitemap"
         reload-method="asynchron"
         check-reload="no"/>
```

The `check-reload` attribute of the sitemap element shown in the preceding code determines whether the sitemap will be reloaded if changes are made to the sitemap on the production servers. If set to *no*, the sitemap is generated only once at startup and subsequent changes to the sitemap and any subsitemap for the application is ignored.

Furthermore, in a production environment, the `reload-method` is set to *asynchron*. This is done for safety and the sitemap will never be reloaded because the `check-reload` has been set to *no*.

The purpose of these changes to the `cocoon.xconf` file is to make sure the users accessing the application do not encounter performance problems caused by the server recompiling a modified sitemap during runtime. If maintenance changes are made to the sitemap, the server needs to be stopped and restarted to ensure that the new sitemap is compiled just once.

Modifying the *sitemap.xmap* File

The sitemap for a given application defines the processing pipeline. This sitemap does not need to change when the application has been deployed in a production environment. Each `mount` element in the main sitemap must be modified to ensure that the sitemaps are compiled just once at startup. The following code snippet highlights the modifications in the main sitemap for the acme application demonstrated in Chapter 2.

```
<map:mount uri-prefix="acme"
           check-reload="no"
           reload-method="asynchron"
           src="c2/acme/"/>
```

The attributes of the `mount` element have the same values as the attributes of the `sitemap` element in the `cocoon.xconf` file. Setting the `reload-method` to *asynchrony* and the `check-reload` to *no* guarantees that the subsitemap is compiled only once at startup. Any modifications made to the subsitemap on the production server will be ignored until the server is stopped and restarted.

Modifying the *logkit.xconf* File

The section on debugging discussed the benefits of logging in detail. Tomcat and the Cocoon applications allow logging of a lot of information from various parts of the Cocoon system. However, logging causes a serious drain on system resources. The instances of the logger create `String` messages, which is a very expensive process in most programming languages.

In addition to disk space for storing the log, the applications suffer performance degradation when the server logs details to multiple files. Most of the information stored in files is redundant, but is also a valuable asset for tracking down problems. Once the application has been deployed, redundant logging of information is a drain on valuable resources and can be turned off. As described in the section on debugging, there are five priority levels for logging, as follows:

- DEBUG
- INFO
- WARN
- ERROR
- FATAL_ERROR

Each instance of the logger in a Cocoon application has a priority assigned to it in the configuration file. Furthermore, the use of categories subdivides the logging namespace and allows for a finer grain control of the logging levels. If a hierarchy of loggers is created, the child logger inherits the priority level of the parent unless it is explicitly overridden in the configuration file.

The logger then displays or writes details of a `LogEvent` that is greater than or equal to that priority level. For example, if the priority level was set to `INFO`, then a `LogEvent` with priority level of `DEBUG` will be suppressed and all other `LogEvents` will be saved to the log file. Listing 9.16 shows the `categories` element of the `logkit.xconf` file with the log-level set to `ERROR`.

Listing 9.16 The *categories* Configuration in *logkit.xconf*

```
<categories>

  <category name="core" log-level="ERROR">
    <log-target id-ref="core"/>
    <log-target id-ref="error"/>
  </category>

  <category name="sitemap" log-level="ERROR">
    <log-target id-ref="sitemap"/>
    <log-target id-ref="error"/>
```

```
    </category>

    <category name="access" log-level="ERROR">
      <log-target id-ref="access"/>
      <log-target id-ref="error"/>
    </category>

  </categories>
```

The discussion on debugging introduced priority filtering using specialized `LogTarget` components. Listing 9.5 showed all the details of a priority-filter on the `CocoonTarget-Factory` component. Listing 9.17 highlights only the sections that are significant for performance tuning.

Listing 9.17 A Priority Filter Definition in *logkit.xconf*

```
<priority-filter id="error" log-level="ERROR">
  <cocoon>
     ...
  </cocoon>
</priority-filter>
```

We have set all the priority levels in the `logkit.xconf` file to *ERROR*. As discussed in the section on setting priorities, this causes the Cocoon application to log only those events that have a priority of `ERROR` or `FATAL_ERROR`, thereby reducing the level of resource consumption by the logger, resulting in significant improvement in the performance when running the applications.

Pooling and Caching in Cocoon

Performance is adversely affected when the server cannot service the request load with the available pool of components. When a pool size is too small, the server has to swap the available resources between the requests, which results in a lot of overhead. This problem can be alleviated by properly sizing the pools. This can be achieved by tuning the values in the `cocoon.xconf` and `sitemap.xmap` files. Listing 9.18 shows attributes for configuring pooling on two of the important components in Cocoon. The `CachingEventPipeline` produces a character stream at the output by connecting generators and transformers, whereas the `CachingStreamPipeline` produces a character stream either by using a `Reader` or by connecting an `EventPipeline` to a serializer component.

Listing 9.18 The Pool Attributes in *cocoon.xconf*

```
<stream-pipeline
class="org.apache.cocoon.components.pipeline.CachingStreamPipeline"
logger="core.stream-pipeline"
pool-max="32"
pool-min="16"
pool-grow="4"/>

<event-pipeline
class="org.apache.cocoon.components.pipeline.CachingEventPipeline"
logger="core.event-pipeline"
pool-max="32"
pool-min="16"
pool-grow="4"/>
```

Each of the elements shown in Listing 9.18 defines the following:

`pool-max` The maximum number of component instances in the pool.

`pool-min` The minimum number of component instances in the pool.

`pool-grow` The number of instances of the components by which the pool size should grow.

Pool sizes can also be configured in the main `sitemap.xmap` file. Listing 9.19 shows examples of pool attributes in generators, transformers, and serializers.

Listing 9.19 The Pool Attributes in *sitemap.xmap*

```
<map:generators default="file">

<map:generator name="file"
logger="sitemap.generator.file"
label="content,data"
src="org.apache.cocoon.generation.FileGenerator"
pool-max="32"
pool-min="16"
pool-grow="4"/>

</map:generators>

<map:transformers default="xslt">

<map:transformer name="xslt"            logger="sitemap.transformer.xslt"
src="org.apache.cocoon.transformation.TraxTransformer"
pool-max="32"
pool-min="16"
pool-grow="4">
</map:transformer>
```

```
</map:transformers>

<map:serializers default="html">

<map:serializer name="xml"
mime-type="text/xml"
logger="sitemap.serializer.xml"
src="org.apache.cocoon.serialization.XMLSerializer"
pool-max="32"
pool-min="16"
pool-grow="4"/>

</map:serializers>
```

In the examples just listed, the pool sizes were chosen based on estimates of request loads. In practice, however, it might be difficult to predict in advance what sizes to choose and the numbers will have to be modified based on a study of the logs to determine what part of the application is in greater demand and suffering from limited instances of the components in the pool. The rule to follow is that the pool sizes should be greater than the total number of instances used to service the load at any given time so that there is at least one free component in the pool when all requests are being serviced. As an example, consider an application that will service 250 simultaneous user requests. If the application has one pipeline that uses one file generator, two XSLT transformers, and one XML serializer, the pool sizes to service all requests will be 250 file generators, 500 XSLT transformers, and 250 XML serializers. The pool sizes in the `sitemap.xmap` as shown in Listing 9.19 can be set at least one more than each of these numbers, i.e., 251 file generators, 501 XSLT transformers, and 251 XML serializers. It should be noted that Cocoon will instantiate these components only when needed. After servicing the request, the component will be saved in the pool for future use.

Deciding What Gets Served from Cache

Once the document or other resource has been saved in cache, Cocoon needs to correctly identify a client request for that same resource so that the request can be serviced from the cache. To do this, Cocoon must verify whether the request for that particular resource is equivalent to what is stored in the cache. The following are some of the criteria used by Cocoon to determine request equivalence:

- Verify the browser identity using the HTTP User Agent parameter
- Verify the target server name
- Verify the target port number
- Verify the request headers
- Verify the protocol scheme used (e.g., HTTPS, HTTP, etc.)
- Verify the remaining URI, which includes the query string

Optimizing and Compiling XSPs

In Chapters 6, "Introducing XSP Usage," and 7, "XSP Logicsheets," we provided details and best practices for designing and implementing XSPs. If an application consists of XSPs that will see significant user loads, this could be a serious performance issue. To alleviate the problem it is important to study the log files and identify the XSPs that are used heavily and pre-compile them into generators.

One suggested way would be to let Cocoon compile the XSPs into class files. These will be saved in the following directory: `tomcat/work/..../org/apache/cocoon/www/userxsp.class`, where `userxsp.class` is the compiled XSP file. The compiled generator can then be added to the sitemap as shown in the following:

```
<map:generator
  type="userXSP"
  src="org.apache.cocoon.www.userxsp"/>
```

The generator can then be used in the sitemap as follows:

```
<map:generate type="userXSP"/>
```

For larger applications, this provides a significant improvement in performance and it is well worth the time and effort involved in following the steps for the heavily used XSPs. For smaller applications, especially where only a minimum amount of work is performed by the XSP, it may not provide a very significant performance improvement and may not be worth the effort involved to convert the XSPs into generators.

General Recommendations for Application Design

The following are suggestions and recommendations that have been gleaned from the Cocoon websites and mailing lists. An up-to-date list of performance tips can be found at `http://xml.apache.org/cocoon/performancetips.html`. The following information expands a few of the most significant items from the list that are relevant to the discussion on Cocoon. Feel free to experiment with some of the other suggestions regarding operating systems and Java Virtual Machines (JVM).

Processing a Cocoon request in a pipeline is very slow and is responsible for the slow response experienced by the end user making the request. The following are some guidelines to be considered when designing a web application that will influence the decision on using Cocoon or going with a different approach.

- Dynamic data cannot be completely cached. So dynamic data should be used in sections of the web application only when required.
- Parts of the website that will always contain static content should be rendered in HTML or pre-rendered. This applies to SVG images, PDF reports, or results of database queries.

- Some dynamic data that does not change frequently should be pre-generated by batch process, depending on the schedule the data changes, and should be saved as static content.
- Static content does not need to be served by Cocoon or even the same application server. The static content can reside on a remote server or another virtual web server responding on a different port. A transparent proxy can be used to separate the requests and forward them to the correct destination server.
- A transparent proxy is one that can intercept a web request without the client being aware of it. Transparent proxies can be used to serve up static content, thereby making a marked improvement in the performance.
- Limit the size of the document to be cached. The process of caching a document for the first time is time-consuming and a drain on system resources.
- When using the `CachingPipeline`, it is important to set the cache size to an optimum level depending on the available virtual memory on the system. If the size of the cache is too small, then the benefits of caching will not be evident because the entire document cannot be saved in the cache.
- The log files should be used to verify that the resources that have been cached are being served from cache.
- The free memory and heap size parameters can be optimized in the `cocoon.xconf` file to use the maximum available resources. If the values are not carefully chosen, it may have an adverse effect on the performance.
- Because Cocoon is based on Java, there is great demand on system resources for a typical enterprise application that will service multiple users. As part of the process for designing and implementing such an application, it is important to do a proper analysis of the hardware and software resources and factor those needs into the design of the application. One of the most important choices that will affect system performance is the choice of an operating system and the hardware on which it runs. All flavors of Unix support the JVMs that use native threads. This helps medium to large multiuser applications that rely on threading. For small to medium size applications, other operating systems such as Windows 2000 or NT could suffice.
- Having a large amount of physical memory and a larger allocated swap space on disk helps improve the overall performance of an application.
- The hard disk technologies used also affect the performance of the application server. A general rule would be to choose faster SCSI technologies over the more common ATA drives.
- For very large applications that have a substantially large number of concurrent users, a discreet load balancing solution should be implemented. The load balancer acts as a front end to marshal the user request to two or more Cocoon servers. This solution can be used to improve overall performance of the application from a user's point of view.

Summary

Debugging an application developed in Cocoon can be a challenge. Fortunately, Cocoon has an elaborate logging mechanism based on the Avalon LogKit project. The salient features of the LogKit mechanism are as follows:

`LogEvents` The events that are generated by the components in the pipeline that will be logged.

`LogTargets` The components that consume the `LogEvents`.

`Priorities` There are five priority levels to designate the severity of the `LogEvent`. These five are `DEBUG`, `INFO`, `WARN`, `ERROR`, and `FATAL_ERROR`.

`Priority filters` These are special `LogTargets` that can be used to filter out `LogEvents` and direct them to specific destinations.

`Formatters` These are used to format the output string, which will contain details of the fields in the `LogEvent`.

`Categories` For fine-grain control on the logging process, the logging namespace is subdivided to create a hierarchy of loggers called *categories*.

The `logkit.xconf` configuration file is used to select and configure features of the Cocoon logging mechanism. There are several log files created when Cocoon is running:

`core.log` This log contains event information related to launching the Cocoon application.

`access.log` This log contains event information related to accessing resources in the application.

`sitemap.log` This log contains events related to the sitemaps.

`error.log` This log contains events that have priority levels of either `ERROR` or `FATAL_ERROR`.

Depending on the fields in the `LogEvents`, the logs might contain redundant information; however, to effectively debug an application and solve many of the problems, it is necessary to reference all the log files and correlate the information contained in them. In addition to the logs defined by Cocoon, special logs can be created using user defined components that can log details of the SAX events flowing in the pipeline. We created a simple extension to the `LogTransformer` called `XLogTransformer` to dump out details of the pipeline events.

To solve erratic behavior of the sitemaps during development, clean out the `work` directory on the server before restarting the application.

Once the application has been debugged and tested, it can be optimized for performance before being deployed in a production environment. The following is a list of steps that can be adopted to increase performance of the application:

1. Increase the virtual memory size in the Tomcat configuration file.
2. Disable reloading of the sitemap in `cocoon.xconf`.
3. Disable reloading of the subsitemaps in the `sitemap.xmap`.
4. Set all priorities to *ERROR* in the `logkit.xconf`.
5. Set the pool sizes on all pipeline components.
6. Set the pool sizes on generators, transformers, and serializers.

In addition to these steps, the following are some of the best practices when designing an application with Cocoon:

- The application should be designed to have clear demarcations between static and dynamic content.
- Dynamic content that does not change frequently can be cached; but for the most part, dynamic content cannot be cached completely.
- Static content can be served up by a separate web server whether it is running locally or remotely.
- Transparent proxies can be used to intercept the user request and forward it to the appropriate server serving static content or running Cocoon.
- The size of the documents to be cached must be manageable because the process of caching is time-consuming and a drain on resources.
- The size of the cache should be chosen to be able to save the largest document that will be cached.
- The free memory and heapsize parameters in the cache must be adjusted carefully to reflect actual system resource availability.
- The physical hardware for the server and the operating system should be carefully chosen as part of the overall system design keeping performance in mind.
- The log files should be examined carefully to check for indications that Cocoon is in fact serving cached resources.
- XSPs that are used heavily and do a significant amount of work in the application should be pre-compiled and used in the sitemap.

CHAPTER 10

Patterns of Presentation

- Patterns in Web Programming
- Moving Simple Sites to Cocoon
- The Portal Pattern
- The Forms Problem
- The Wiki and Blog Phenomena
- Client Capability

In the context of programming, *patterns* are descriptions of problems and solutions that have been found to recur again and again. Probably the most widely read and discussed book about programming in recent years is *Design Patterns: Elements of Reusable Object-Oriented Software*, by Erich Gamma, Richard Helm, Ralph Johnson, and John Vlissides (Addison-Wesley, 1994). Many programmers have found that browsing in this book can inspire them to write better code.

The success of *Design Patterns* has inspired many authors to seek out patterns in many areas of programming with mixed results. A web search for programming patterns will now get you a huge harvest. Because web programming is an immature branch of programming in general, it is not surprising that there is no compilation of patterns for web design that has the universal quality of the *Design Patterns* book. However, we are going to attempt to point out some common features.

Keeping in mind that *separation of concerns* is a major Cocoon design principle, we have decided to separate considerations of patterns into two areas: *presentation* in this chapter and *generation* in the next. We are not going to be dogmatic about the form used to discuss topics; rather, we hope that the discussion will aid new Cocoon programmers in making use of the powerful tools that the Cocoon approach offers.

Patterns in Web Programming

A recent effort to define patterns in web programming was an essay written in early 2000 by Nathan Wallace. The text is available on the Web at the following URL:

```
www.e-gineer.com/articles/design-patterns-in-web-programming.phtml
```

Wallace remarked that it is difficult to determine the proper level of abstraction when trying to discover web-programming patterns. The pattern that Wallace developed in greatest detail he called "Filter." The intent of this pattern is to "provide a mechanism for conditionally executing code at the start or end of each page request."

We are sure that you immediately recognize that this pattern is one of the basic concepts in Cocoon. At the start of request processing, pipelines have matcher, selector, and action components that recognize appropriate requests and perform preliminary calculations. At the end of request processing, pipelines have transformers and serializers to perform operations on the response content.

Other areas of web programming that Wallace felt could yield usable patterns are data entry and maintenance, authentication, and error handling. Because the focus of this chapter is presentation, we will address data entry, in particular the use of XForms.

Moving Simple Sites to Cocoon

Chapter 2, "Uses of Cocoon," discussed some of the organizational features of a relatively simple website being served by Cocoon. To support this organization, your present simple website will probably require some reorganization. Based on our experience with migrating a relatively simple site, we think that the process deserves some extended discussion.

In our case, the site had accumulated a number of features over the years as various webmasters tackled the problem. The following points seem worthy of discussion:

- Moving a site to Cocoon offers an excellent opportunity to reorganize and simplify certain elements. By rationalizing the use of stylesheets and JavaScript scripts, your reorganized site will be easier to maintain and respond more rapidly.
- You should not try to accomplish the move in a single quantum leap. In this chapter we describe a stepwise process that you may find helpful.

You are probably tired of hearing us say the title of the following section, but here it is anyway.

Separating Presentation from Content

For most websites, various aspects of presentation have worked their way into the underlying HTML over the years. Particularly pernicious is use of `FONT` tags in documents converted to HTML by Microsoft Word. A good first step in converting a site to Cocoon is to clean up the use of HTML style elements.

Cascading Style Sheets (CSS) provide the perfect mechanism for you to move HTML-rendering style information into separate files. If your site has several different styles in use, that's OK—just use a subsitemap to define the pipelines that use those styles. One great advantage of using CSS is that browsers can cache the contents, so your pages will load more rapidly after the first viewing. With a separate CSS stylesheet, incorporating the information is as simple as having your XSLT stylesheet include a line like this in the `<head>` area:

```
<link rel="stylesheet" type="text/css" href="/lanwstyle.css" />
```

Separating style elements from content is the first step in making your content accessible to a wide variety of browsers. See the "Client Capability" section later in this chapter for information on how to determine the browser capabilities for a particular request. However, this process is pretty complicated, so your first effort should concentrate on the styles for the average web browser.

The other simplification you can perform is removal of common JavaScript methods to a separate file. As with CSS stylesheets, you will then be able to control which script is loaded at the XSLT transformation stage of the Cocoon pipeline. The "Sunspot" sample provided with Cocoon 2.0.2 has the following excellent example of matching the XSL script to the capabilities of the user's browser:

```
<map:match pattern="sunspotdemo-portlets">
    <map:generate type="sunSpot"/>
    <map:select type="browser">
        <map:when test="explorer">
            <map:transform src="sunspotdemo/styles/portalHTML.xsl"/>
        </map:when>
        <map:when test="netscape">
            <map:transform src="sunspotdemo/styles/portalHTML-Netscape.xsl"/>
        </map:when>
        <map:otherwise>
            <map:transform src="sunspotdemo/styles/portalHTML.xsl"/>
        </map:otherwise>
    </map:select>
    <map:transform type="encodeURL"/>
    <map:serialize/>
</map:match>
```

The subject of exactly how to take advantage of XSLT processing is beyond the scope of this book. For more details on XSLT processing, refer to *Mastering XSLT*, by Chuck White (Sybex, 2002). It's an excellent tutorial and reference of 905 pages.

Conforming to Standards

Another important step in converting an existing site is to ensure that the pages you are going to convert conform to standards. A clean page will be much easier to convert to XML and much easier to transform with XSLT.

Cleaning up your HTML can either be done locally with JTidy or with the validation service at the W3C site. The free utility can be used to test HTML, XHTML, and CSS stylesheets. This service accepts either full text of the HTML or a URL pointing to it on the Web. The starting point for validation of HTML is the following URL:

```
http://validator.w3.org/
```

The starting point for validation of stylesheets is this:

```
http://jigsaw.w3.org/css-validator/
```

The validator can detect bad usages such as `<img>` tags without `alt` descriptions, attributes without quotes, and the improper use of case in tags and attributes. Although cleaning up accumulated bad usages can be time-consuming, it will pay off in the end.

NOTE JTidy is a Java version of the Tidy utility. The original Tidy was written by Dave Raggett, and was hosted at the W3C site, but the task of expanding Tidy and moving it to a variety of languages and platforms has moved to Sourceforge: `http://tidy.sourceforge.net`

Recall from Chapter 8, “Content Generators,” that the HTMLGenerator passes HTML through JTidy to ensure that it can emit well formed SAX events. Therefore, every Cocoon installation already has the JTidy jar available in the WEB-INF/lib directory, although it may have a name that includes a version, such as jtidy-04aug2000r7-dev.jar. Unfortunately, we don’t have the space here to go into all of the configuration parameters used by Tidy and JTidy. The following command line shows an extremely simple execution of JTidy with an error report going to the errs.txt file and the index.html file being patched in place:

```
java -jar JTidy.jar -f errs.txt -m index.html
```

Here is the list of the errors reported by that run:

```
Tidy (vers 4th August 2000) Parsing "index.html"
line 9 column 28 - Warning: missing </a> before <h2>
line 10 column 35 - Warning: discarding unexpected </a>
line 20 column 1 - Warning: trimming empty <p>
line 46 column 1 - Warning: missing </a> before <h2>
line 59 column 1 - Warning: missing </a> before <h2>
line 71 column 52 - Warning: unescaped & or unknown entity "&Drop"
line 80 column 1 - Warning: <img> lacks "alt" attribute
line 90 column 1 - Warning: missing </ul>

index.html: Document content looks like HTML 3.2
8 warnings/errors were found!
```

The alt attribute should be used to give a short description of an image; longer descriptions should be given with the longdesc attribute, which takes a URL linked to the description. These measures are needed for people using non-graphical browsers.

For further advice on how to make your pages accessible, see www.w3.org/WAI/GL. You may also want to try www.cast.org/bobby/ which is a free Web-based service for checking URLs for accessibility.

HTML and CSS specifications are available from www.w3.org. To learn more about Tidy see www.w3.org/People/Raggett/tidy/. Send bug reports to Dave Raggett care of html-tidy@w3.org. Lobby your company to join W3C, see www.w3.org/Consortium.

Usability Standards

It is an unfortunate fact that many web presentation design innovations that are very popular are completely unusable for people with disabilities. Although there are specialized browsers and browser add-ons for users with limited vision that can speak the text found on a page, that does not help if the page does not provide text alternatives to fancy interface components.

It is a strongly felt sentiment by many of the Web pioneers that content on the Web should be accessible to all, regardless of disability. To support that effort and provide advice on how to ensure usability, the W3C has created the Web Accessibility Initiative. The following site can get you started:

```
www.w3.org/WAI/
```

Commercial websites in the United States may be subject to the provisions of the Americans with Disabilities Act. Although most enforcement issues have related to physical facilities, recently there has been work on applicability of standards to the Web. This has been accelerated by the 1998 amendment to the Rehabilitation Act, which has a specific section, Section 508, devoted to accessibility to electronic information systems. The revised act went into effect in June 2001.

Although the Act is restricted to requirements for federal government purchases of equipment and services, it obviously has wider significance. An excellent summary of the requirements can be found at the Information Technology Industry Council website. The Voluntary Product Accessibility Template, which allows a vendor to assess the extent to which a product meets the guidelines, can be found at the following URL:

```
www.itic.org/policy/508/vpat.html
```

The following list summarizes the most important points for web designers. You will undoubtedly recognize that many of these are well known suggestions for good web page design patterns. Now, however, designers are required to follow them in products sold to the United States Federal Government:

- A text equivalent for every non-text element shall be provided (e.g., via “alt,” “longdesc,” or in element content).
- Equivalent alternatives for any multimedia presentation shall be synchronized with the presentation.
- Web pages shall be designed so that all information conveyed with color is also available without color, for example from context or markup. Foreground and background color choices must provide sufficient contrast.
- Documents shall be organized so they are readable without requiring an associated stylesheet.
- Redundant text links shall be provided for each active region of a server-side image map.
- Client-side image maps shall be provided instead of server-side image maps except where the regions cannot be defined with an available geometric shape.
- Row and column headers shall be identified for data tables, and markup shall be used to associate data cells and header cells for data tables that have two or more logical levels of row or column headers.

- Frames shall be titled with text that facilitates frame identification and navigation.
- When pages utilize scripting languages to display content, or to create interface elements, the information provided by the script shall be identified with functional text that can be read by Assistive Technology.
- When electronic forms are designed to be completed online, the form shall allow people using Assistive Technology to access the information, field elements, and functionality required for completion and submission of the form, including all directions and cues.
- A method shall be provided that permits users to skip repetitive navigation links.
- When a timed response is required, the user shall be alerted and given sufficient time to indicate more time is required.
- A text-only page, with equivalent information or functionality, shall be provided to make a website comply with the provisions of this part, when compliance cannot be accomplished in any other way. The content of the text-only page shall be updated whenever the primary page changes.

Cocoon to the Rescue

Although these requirements look formidable, the basic Cocoon tools can help at every step. If you have already thought about how to make your pages usable on devices other than the standard desktop browser, you are well on the way.

This capability is exactly what the designers of Cocoon have made great progress toward achieving. However, having the capability and implementing it are two different things. The following site provides a utility for checking a given URL for compliance with the 508 standard:

`http://bobby.cast.org/html/en/index.jsp`

You will probably be shocked to see how many accessibility flaws this utility finds in your web page. The Cocoon home page at `http://xml.apache.org/cocoon` does not come out well, with over 100 flaws mentioned when we checked it.

We are sure you realize that the tools Cocoon provides will be a great help in converting a site to meet accessibility standards. In fact, you can accomplish this at the same time as you are formatting your XML data sources for use with the rapidly expanding number of wireless web-enabled devices.

The Portal Pattern

One of the most commercially successful presentation patterns on the Web these days is typically called a "portal." The motive driving portal design is to make a site so useful that it becomes part of every user's web browsing day.

Portals are characterized by the following:

- Standardized arrangement of elements using either tables or frames (but frames are going out of style)
- Customized data presentation based on user preferences
- Intensive use of JavaScript for rollover actions
- Advertising
- Extensive in-house and out links
- Reducing load time with compact HTML

Everybody is familiar with such portals as Yahoo and Amazon, so we decided to show an example of portal presentation from a less well known site. Figure 10.1 shows a recent startup page at the following URL:

`www.theserverside.com/home/index.jsp`

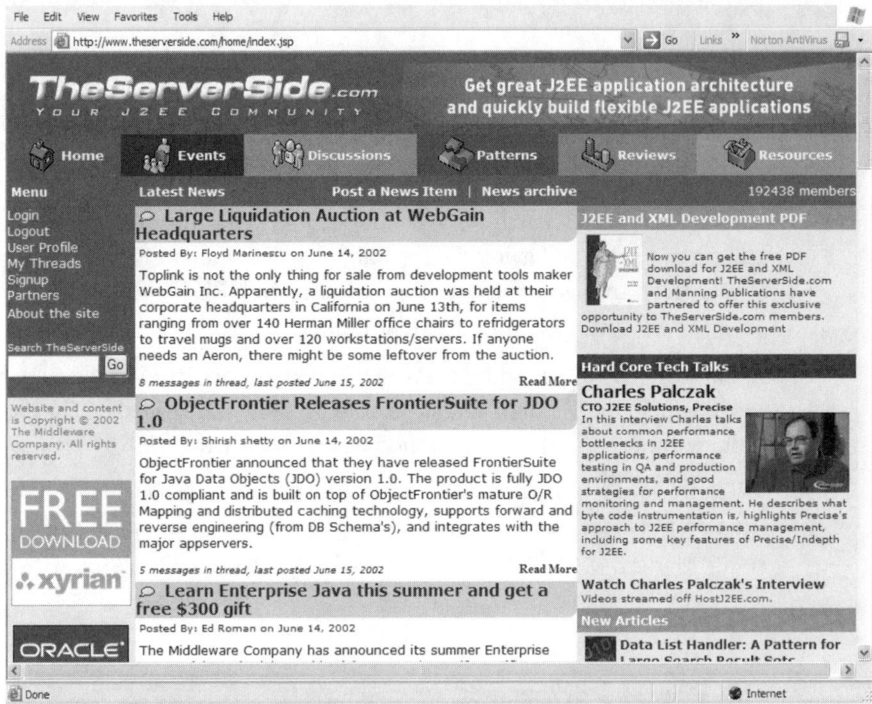

FIGURE 10.1: A startup page with typical portal presentation

If you select to view the source of a typical portal page, it is quite a confusing mish-mash of HTML tags, so we are going to continue this discussion with a skeleton that is a lot easier to understand. The appearance of this skeleton is shown in Figure 10.2.

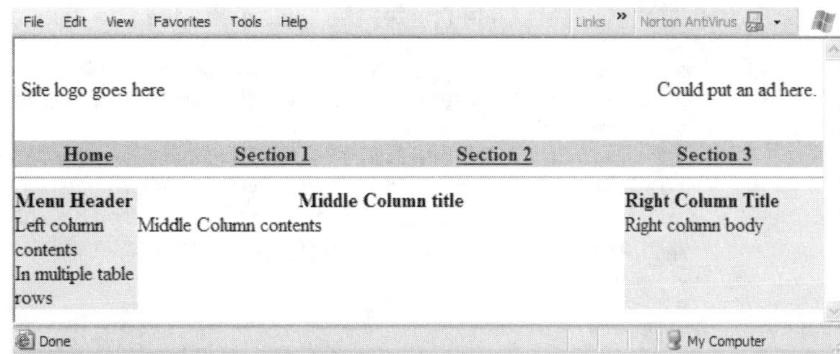

FIGURE 10.2: A vastly simplified portal style page

Listing 10.1 shows the start of the HTML for this skeleton portal. Note that this code links to a stylesheet instead of mixing style information with the content. This makes maximum use of the browser cache capability and reduces page load time, an important consideration if you want people to use the page frequently. Normally a banner would have images, but we have left the image code out to emphasize the table structure.

Listing 10.1 The HTML to Start the Skeleton Page Creates a Full-Width Site Banner.

```
<!DOCTYPE HTML PUBLIC "-//W3C//DTD HTML 4.0 Transitional//EN">

<html>
<head>
<title>The Portal Title</title>
<meta http-equiv="Content-Type" content="text/html;
    charset=iso-8859-1">
<link rel="stylesheet" type="text/css" href="somestyle.css" >

</head>
<body>

<!-- site logo and banner ad get a table -->
<table border="0" cellspacing="0" cellpadding="5" width="100%">
 <tr>
  <td >
      Site logo goes here
  </td>
  <td align="right" >
   Could put an ad here.
  </td>
  </tr>
</table>
```

In a typical portal, links to various main sections of the site are arranged under the main site banner. Visually stimulating graphics are typically used here, but we have simplified, as shown in Listing 10.2 for the purposes of this discussion.

Listing 10.2 This Code Creates the Links under the Site Banner.

```
<!-- main section links get a full width table -->
<table border="0" cellspacing="0" width="100%" bgcolor="#99EEEE" >
  <tr valign="middle" align="center">
     <td><b><a href="/home.xml">Home</b></td>
     <td><b><a href="/section1/index.xml">Section 1</b></td>
     <td><b><a href="/section2/index.xml">Section 2</b></td>
     <td><b><a href="/section3/index.xml">Section 3</b></td>
  </tr>
</table>
```

Listing 10.3 shows the code that creates the main body of the page as a table organized as a single row with three columns. Each column is then made up of additional tables.

Listing 10.3 This HTML Creates the Main Body of the Page.

```
<!-- the remaining page body is a table in 3 columns.
    Each column contains a table of two rows, the first
    row is the header, the second row for the body of the column.
-->
<hr />
<table border="0" cellspacing="0" cellpadding="0" width="100%" >
  <tr>
  <!-- left column is narrow -->
  <td valign="top" width="15%" align="left" bgcolor="#EEEEEE" >
    <table border="0" cellpadding="0" cellspacing="0" width="100%" >
      <tr>
        <td valign="middle" ><b>Menu Header</b>
        </td>
      </tr>
      <tr>
        <td align="left" valign="top" >
        <!-- a table could be used here to organize links, search, signin form
etc. -->
          Left column contents
        </td>
      </tr>
      <tr><td>In multiple table rows</td>
      </tr>
    </table>
  </td> <!-- End left column -->
  <!-- middle column gets whats left from left and right -->
  <td valign="top" width="*" >
```

```
    <table border="0" cellpadding="0" cellspacing="0" width="100%">
      <tr><td valign="top" align="center" ><b>Middle Column title</b></td>
      </tr>
      <tr><td valign="top" align="left" > Middle Column contents</td>
      </tr>
    </table>
  </td><!-- End middle column -->

    <!-- start right column -->
  <td valign="top" width="25%" align="left" width="150" bgcolor="#EEEEEE" >
     <table border="0" cellpadding="0" cellspacing="0" width="100%" >
        <tr><td valign="top" ><b>Right Column Title</td>
        </tr>
        <tr><td valign="top" align="left">
         Right column body </td>
        </tr>
    </table>
  </td>
</tr>
</table> <!-- end table of three columns -->

</body>
</html>
```

By this point you have probably realized that Cocoon provides the perfect basic tool for assembling a portal page in the map:aggregate function. As described in Chapter 5, "Logic Control: The Sitemap," this function acts like a generator that assembles a flow of XML events from multiple pipeline fragments. The basic pipeline structure to assemble our skeleton aggregates the various elements from named pipeline fragments:

```
<map:match pattern="/" >
<map:aggregate element="page"
       ns="http://mysite/myportal" >
  <map:part element="banner"
      src="cocoon:/portal/banner.xml"
      ns="http://mysite/portal/banner" />
  <map:part element="mainmenu"
      src="cocoon:/portal/mainmenu.xml"
      ns="http://mysite/portal/banner" />
  <map:part element="leftcol"
      src="cocoon:/leftcol/contents.xml"
      ns="http://mysite/leftcol/contents" />
  <map:part element="center"
      src="cocoon:/newsitems/items.xml"
      ns="http://mysite/newsitems/items" />
  <map:part element="rightcol"
      src="cocoon:/reviews/reviews.xml"
      ns="http://mysite/reviews/review" />
```

```
</map:aggregate>
<map:transform src="stylesheets/finalportal.xsl" />
<map:serialize />
</map:match>
```

Each component of the final page can be rendered differently because each part comes from a different namespace. Naturally, aggregation is only one of many approaches for which the great flexibility of Cocoon provides. Another possibility is provided by the proposed "portlet" standard.

Portal Standardization

There have been many proprietary mechanisms for creating portal style presentation. Among Java web application server vendors, there is interest is creating a standard API for portals as part of the J2EE specification. There have been several proposals for Portlet APIs submitted to the Java Community Process. The only one currently under serious consideration is JSR 168. You can find out the current status of this proposal at:

```
http://jcp.org/jsr/detail/168.jsp
```

The proposed schedule for development of this specification calls for the first public draft to be released in the Fall of 2002. Participants in the development of this proposed API include BEA, IBM, Sun, Oracle, and SAP. Goals of the project include the following:

- A simple API
- Support for multiple client types
- Support for localization and internationalization
- An API similar to the Servlet API

A related standardization effort is JSR 127, sometimes called JavaServer Faces. The intent of this project is to develop standard JSP tags and Java classes to simplify building web-based user interfaces. The Portlet specification would become part of this total picture.

In our opinion, the weakness of these standardization efforts is that they place too much emphasis on using JSP tag libraries and not enough on XML representation of data structures. In other words, *this approach fails to separate presentation from content.*

The Jetspeed Project

One implementation of the Portlet API can be found at yet another Apache organization project, Jetspeed. Jetspeed is a sub-project of the Jakarta project. Basically, it uses a servlet to integrate data from portlets using XML technology. The home site is at the following URL:

```
http://jakarta.apache.org/jetspeed/site/index.html
```

The Jetspeed project provides facilities that enable a user to design a home page by selecting predefined portlets from a form. Jetspeed provides for defining the available portlet components in an XML-based system called the Portal Structure Markup Language (PSML). PSML is similar in some respects to Cocoon's sitemap XML in that it defines the possible components of a portal page. Instead of a pipeline, each registered user has an XML file that defines the components that will go into a page. Jetspeed includes stylesheet information for various presentations so that a user could get the same basic portal page on both a desktop PC and a wireless device.

Jetspeed is an obvious candidate for integration into the Cocoon framework. The system for letting a user build a custom portal page is very powerful and should be easy to use in Cocoon. Unfortunately, at the present time, there is no ongoing effort to do this. The Cocoon developers seem to be concentrating on the Sunspot project.

The Sunspot Project

Another portal-related project in the Apache organization is Sunspot. This is a commercially developed portal that has been donated to the Cocoon project. As of this writing, Sunspot is in the early stages of development. Here is an example pipeline segment for a Sunspot portal from the Cocoon 2.0.2 distribution:

```
<map:match pattern="sunbank-portal">
  <map:act type="sunRise-auth"/>
      <!-- for getting the sunSpot configuration -->
      <map:parameter name="handler" value="sunshinehandler"/>
      <map:parameter name="application" value="sunBank"/>
    <map:generate type="sunSpot"/> <!-- generate the portal view -->
    <map:transform src="sunbank/styles/portalHTML.xsl"/>
     <!-- presentation in HTML -->
    <map:serialize/>
  </map:act>
</map:match>
```

It appears likely that Sunspot will become the primary portal system using Cocoon. Figure 10.3 shows the initial entry screen for the Sunspot demo provided with Cocoon 2.0.2.

The Forms Problem

Many commercial and noncommercial websites have to get user input for various reasons. The basic capability is created by HTML forms that use the CGI standard to package form data and communicate with a server. The basic HTML forms technology leaves a lot to be desired:

- Forms have very little control over user input.
- Forms mix presentation and business logic.
- Form creation methods designed for HTML on standard Web browsers are not easy to translate to other environments, such as PDAs.

FIGURE 10.3: An example Sunspot portal entry page

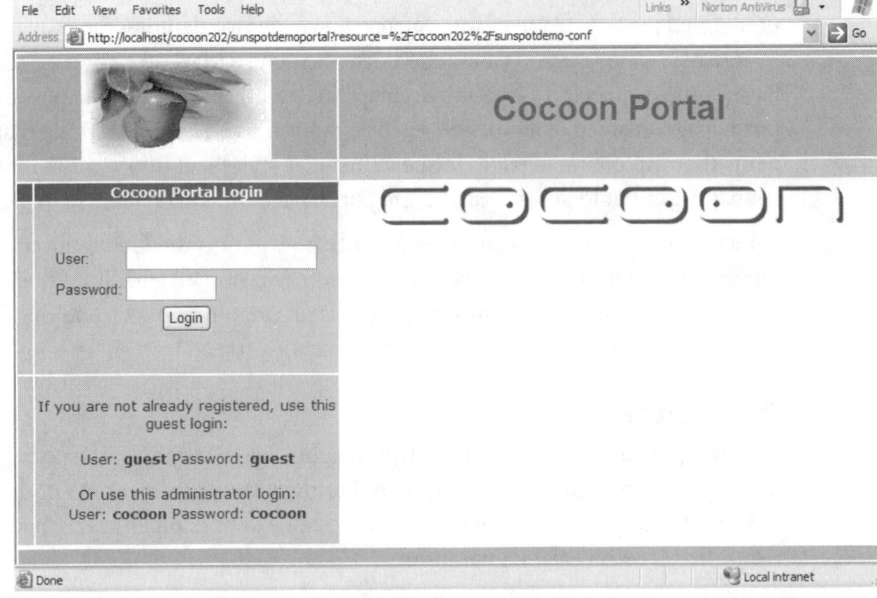

NOTE One of the most successful open-source Java projects to deal with forms is called Struts. This is a sub-project of the Jakarta project in the Apache organization. Struts makes extensive use of JavaServer Pages technology and custom taglibs. It appears to us that Struts would be difficult to integrate with Cocoon. If you want to learn more about Struts, here is the website: `http://jakarta.apache.org/struts/`

The conventions for entering data into a form on an HTML web page grew up as part of a Common Gateway Interface (CGI) in the early days of the Web when forms processing on the server was typically accomplished by Perl scripts executing as a process separate from the server.

- It is up to a web designer to create the form that a business process needs, which means that the designer has to closely coordinate with a business process.
- It is up to a programmer to extract the information from the submitted form, decide if it is in the correct format, and provide for redisplay of the form to the user with messages if it is not.
- If the designer and the programmer try to provide error checking on the web page, they end up with a mess of hard-to-understand JavaScript.
- Getting the same input from a wireless PDA or phone means starting all over again from scratch.

Coming up with a rational solution to the problem has been tackled by the XForms working group at the W3C.

XForms: XML-Based Forms

Like many other technologies that have come together in the Cocoon project, an XML-based standard for forms handling has matured at just the right time to be incorporated in Cocoon. This technology is called XForms, and is the subject of a standardization effort at the W3C. XForms attempts to rationalize form design and separate the presentation from the business logic.

It is the intent of the specification that web browsers will eventually work with forms defined with XForms logic instead of HTML forms. Obviously, we are a long way from that goal with present browsers, and the XForms documentation recognizes this by suggesting how a transition to XForms might take place. It is the feeling of the Cocoon design community that by adopting as much as possible of the XForms standard at the present time, Cocoon users will be prepared for future developments.

The XForms specifications are currently in the "last call working draft" state and are presumably rather stable. The latest W3C specification can be found here:

```
www.w3.org/TR/xforms/
```

As this is being written, integration of XForms into Cocoon is in a beta development stage and will probably not appear in a release version until Cocoon 2.1. However, the general pattern for use of XForms seems well established. A list of implementations of various aspects of XForms in a variety of languages can be found here:

```
www.w3.org/MarkUp/Forms
```

As with everything XML, progress on XForms is intimately associated with other XML projects, such as XML Schemas, XHTML, the Web Accessibility Initiative, and Style Sheets. This means that standardization efforts take a lot of time and developers may be tempted to ignore the standards and develop approaches on their own.

How XForms Relates to Presentation

The intent of XForms is to allow a form creator to specify a model in XML that can be used to generate forms for user input in HTML, XHTML, WML, or any other technology that might come along. The same model should then be usable for converting submitted data into XML and basic checking of validity of the data. A complete XForms model is not simple—it requires an XML formatted description of the input fields combined with an XML Schema defining the values these fields can take. By using the same schema for form input that would be used in further XML processing of the data, we ensure that user input is in the right format.

In HTML forms, the input presentation for each input item is specified as a specific HTML element with known characteristics during user input. For example, a single-line text-entry field might be defined with this code:

```
<input type="text" name="lastName" size="20"
    maxlength="40" value="" />
```

Any accompanying caption information would have to be added with additional HTML markup. Furthermore, input items are always enclosed in a form tag that defines a set of inputs that will be presented at one time. Thus, there is no flexibility for displaying the input items according to the limitation of the display device.

The XForms user interface definition of forms controls does not specify an enclosing form element. Presentation of controls can be adapted to the capabilities of the display device. The current XForms specification document gives this example of a form specification with multiple controls:

```
<selectOne ref="as">
  <caption>Select Payment Method</caption>
  <choices>
    <item>
      <caption>Cash</caption><value>cash</value>
    </item>
    <item>
      <caption>Credit</caption><value>credit</value>
    </item>
  </choices>
</selectOne>

<input ref="cc"><caption>Credit Card Number</caption>
</input>
<input ref="exp"><caption>Expiration Date</caption>
</input>
<submit submitInfo="submit"><caption>Submit</caption>
</submit>
```

For presentation of an HTML form based on this sort of specification, the developer must create an XSL transformation that translates the information types into interface components. Fortunately, the specification requires that every control must have an associated caption. Obviously this will be a big help in meeting the accessibility criteria discussed earlier in the section "Usability Standards."

Submission of Data

In an environment that fully implements XForms, data from the preceding form would be submitted as an XML element using the reference attributes like the following:

```
<instanceData>
   <as>credit</as>
```

```
    <cc>123456789012345</cc>
    <exp>2001-08</exp>
  </instanceData>
```

In other words, the goal of the XForms project is to be in XML from start to finish. Given the present state of the Web, the prospect for direct handling of XForms for forms processors is several years off, so Cocoon has to take a compromise path.

Cocoon's XmlForms Project

The version of XForms for Cocoon is called XmlForms. As of this writing, XmlForms is in the alpha stage of development, for release with Cocoon 2.1, so we can't give firm details. Generally speaking, each form has a corresponding XML document describing each input item following the XForms convention.

The type of information required for each input data item comes from an XML Schema description of the data. This schema gives flexible control over what will be accepted in the input and what will be rejected.

As presently envisioned, development and deployment of a form under XmlForms would take the following steps:

1. Use XMLForm markup to create a document naming the various elements of the form.
2. Validate against an XML Schema.
3. Create a Java class in the JavaBean style with "set and get" methods matching the various elements of the form. An instance of this class will be filled with form data.
4. Create a Java class extending the `AbstractXMLFormAction` class to handle initial processing of a submitted form.
5. Incorporate the new action and associated components into the sitemap.

NOTE A "how to" document for XmlForms is under development, and can be found at `http://xml.apache.org/cocoon/howto/xmlform-wizard/howto-xmlform-wizard.html`.

As you can see, XmlForms as it presently stands is far from the ideal of putting all of the configuration details into XML because it requires custom Java elements. However, the potential is there to have the Java class creation automated by tools.

The Wiki and Blog Phenomena

Highly personal web pages and diaries have been a feature of the Web for years. However, because creating web pages involves some technical knowledge, these personal pages have generally been done by users involved in the graphic arts or computing industries. Recently there has been a rebirth of interest in these forms of personal expression as *blogs* and *wikis* started appearing. With respect to presentation, both wikis and blogs use a very simple style well suited to creation by Cocoon.

A Blog in Cocoon

The idea of a personal web page has been revitalized by the "blog" craze. Short for "web log," the rise of sites that offer facilities for blog creation have made it possible for non-technically savvy users. An example commercial site is here:

`www.blogspot.com`

An implementation in Cocoon, called CocoBlog, can be found in action here:

`www.beblogging.com/blog/`

A nice discussion on the technology behind "blogging" with Cocoon can be found at this site:

`www.need-a-cake.com/stories/2002/02/15/bloggingWithCocoon.html`

Generally speaking, data flow for both blogs and wikis follows the flow shown in Figure 10.4, the main difference being that wikis can have multiple contributors.

FIGURE 10.4: Data flow for a blog or wiki

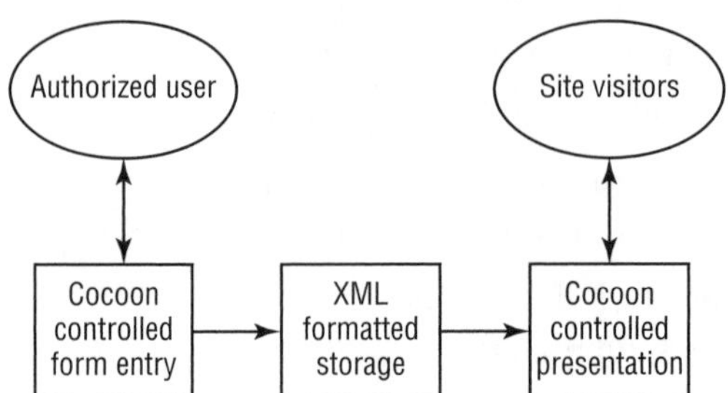

A Wiki in Cocoon

In contrast to a blog, a wiki (Hawaiian for quick) invites entries from the world at large on a variety of topics. The user presentation is quite simple, as shown in Figure 10.5. The Cocoon Dictionary Wiki invites the Cocoon community to submit their own definitions at this URL:

`www.anyware-tech.com/wikiland/`

Handling user entries as XML in this system comes naturally to Cocoon. More information and a free download of the wikiLand application are available here:

`http://rossel.free.fr/`

FIGURE 10.5: An example wiki user interface

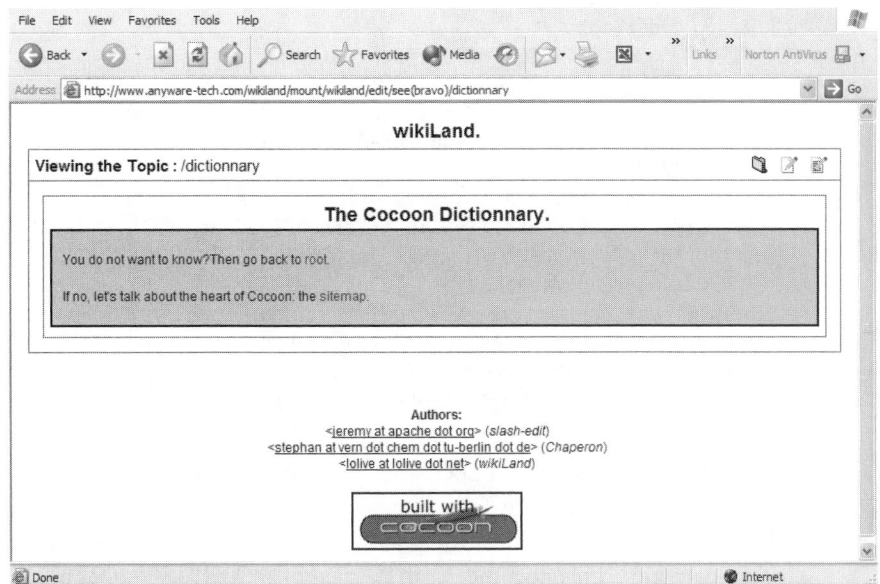

Client Capability

The days when a web designer only had to worry about presentation on a few browsers on full-size screens are long gone. Now, in addition to the desktop and laptop, there are a variety of formats and capabilities from Palm Pilots to Java-capable cellular phones. Furthermore, the legal requirements for accessibility by disabled users will undoubtedly create new browser capabilities.

A lot of work by the industry, particularly Hewlett-Packard, has been devoted to coming up with a practical way of describing the capabilities of a particular platform so that web servers can generate appropriate output. This effort has led to something called a Composite Capabilities/Preference Profile or CC/PP. Naturally, the W3C has a working group on the topic. For the current status on this project, go to this site:

www.w3.org/Mobile/CCPP/

For example, the following is a portion of the capabilities profile of an Ericsson cellular phone. Using this information, a Cocoon application could know that the user will be able to see color-coded text, and use the appropriate XSLT script:

```
<prf:ScreenSize>101x80</prf:ScreenSize>
 <prf:Model>T68R1</prf:Model>
```

```
<prf:InputCharSet>
    <rdf:Bag>
        <rdf:li>ISO-8859-1</rdf:li>
        <rdf:li>US-ASCII</rdf:li>
        <rdf:li>UTF-8</rdf:li>
        <rdf:li>ISO-10646-UCS-2</rdf:li>
    </rdf:Bag>
</prf:InputCharSet>
<prf:ScreenSizeChar>15x6</prf:ScreenSizeChar>
<prf:BitsPerPixel>8</prf:BitsPerPixel>
<prf:ColorCapable>Yes</prf:ColorCapable>
<prf:TextInputCapable>Yes</prf:TextInputCapable>
<prf:ImageCapable>Yes</prf:ImageCapable>
<prf:Keyboard>PhoneKeypad</prf:Keyboard>
<prf:NumberOfSoftKeys>0</prf:NumberOfSoftKeys>
<prf:Vendor>Ericsson Mobile Communications AB</prf:Vendor>
```

HP Labs has released an open-source project called DELI that is now part of the Cocoon release package. Basically, DELI works by recognizing elements of the user-agent HTTP header in a request, and returning an XML Document object that encodes the display device characteristics. This document can be used in an XSL stylesheet to select the appropriate formatting for a particular page. Naturally, any Cocoon server making use of DELI will have to maintain a database of devices.

Summary

Although converting an existing website to Cocoon can be a chore, think of it as an opportunity to clean house and replace a collection of bad usages with the best possible practices. This will pay off in a number of ways: The future evolution of your site will be easier; you will be prepared for the inevitable changes in web browser technology; and your site will be more accessible to disabled users.

Given that the Cocoon project was originally started as a web-publishing tool, it is not surprising that the tools it offers for controlling presentation are excellent. This is noticeable whether you are putting together a portal-style site or something simpler.

Cocoon offers a unifying vision of separating content creation in XML from flexible presentation controlled by the sitemap. This vision has attracted the developers of many open-source projects so if you develop for Cocoon, you have an ever-increasing range of presentation technologies available.

CHAPTER 11

Patterns of Content Generation

- Cocoon and J2EE
- Cocoon and Loosely Coupled Systems
- Web Services and SOAP
- Data Sources
- Business Logic

This chapter discusses the patterns and practices that Cocoon provides to tackle problems of content generation in relation to various industry standards and best practices. We also indulge in some speculation as to where Cocoon could be useful in some evolving technologies.

The main unique features of Cocoon are all in relation to its origin as a web publishing system. The Cocoon developers have not yet tried to create unique approaches to business systems, preferring to make use of industry standards as much as possible. For example, Cocoon follows the emerging standards for XML database-like functions such as the XPath, XQuery, and XPointer standards, and fits easily into the J2EE application server environment.

Cocoon and J2EE

The dominant paradigm in Java-based web servers has been firmly established by Sun's Java 2 Enterprise Edition (J2EE). This set of standard APIs is supported by all of the major web server software vendors except Microsoft. Figure 11.1 shows a typical view of the components of a J2EE system.

FIGURE 11.1: Components of a J2EE web application server

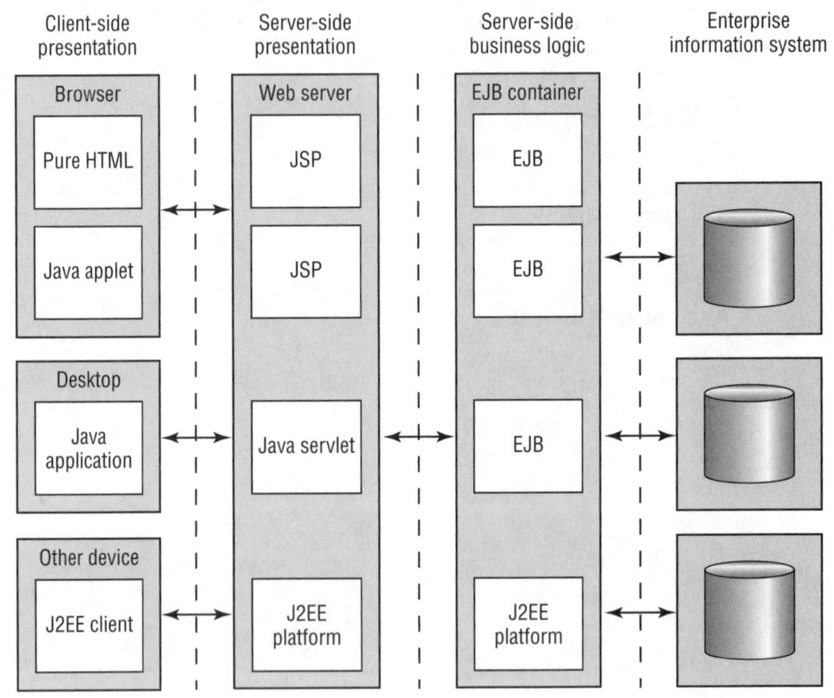

Cocoon fits into this picture as taking over the "Server-Side Presentation" component functions. Due to the clean separation between "Server-Side Business Logic" and the presentation functions, and because Cocoon already operates in a Java Servlet environment, using Cocoon with Enterprise JavaBeans presents little problem.

Cocoon's pipeline-based matching of requests with the proper handling components is much more flexible than the URL-based servlet and JSP matching used in standard J2EE servers. A dominant pattern (called "model 2") in servlet-based systems is to have a single servlet receive all requests in a given application, perform some calculations, and forward the request to the proper JSP or servlet. Passing of data is limited to modifications of the request. Cocoon essentially provides this functionality with actions, matchers, and selectors that not only supplement the request, but also modify sitemap variables.

J2EE emphasizes JSP for presentation, with tag libraries to provide separation of business logic from the straight HTML content. Although there is a tag library for XSLT transformation, there are no capabilities similar to Cocoon's ability to plug multiple transformations together in a pipeline. JSP is also limited in that it works only with character output. This means that generation of binary output, such as images, has to be generated by a different mechanism, whereas Cocoon pipelines can easily generate binary or character data with the same mechanisms.

J2EE passes data from user input to Enterprise JavaBeans (EJB), which use standard JDBC methods for business logic operations and connecting with relational databases. The J2EE server environment manages bean caches for reuse without programmer intervention.

When using Cocoon with J2EE, application designers can choose many alternatives for interaction with Enterprise JavaBeans. Generators, transformers, and/or XSP scripts are all quite usable in this context.

On the client presentation side of Figure 11.1, Cocoon obviously has all of the built-in capabilities for dealing with a variety of client-side devices. We anticipate that Cocoon or Cocoon-like approaches that combine XML and XSLT will become much more widely used in J2EE applications in the future.

Cocoon and the Model-View-Controller Pattern

The Model-View-Controller pattern is one of the first patterns to be recognized as a convenient architecture for computer applications. It emerged in early work with graphical user interfaces and the Smalltalk language at Xerox PARC. The concept proved so useful that you have probably run into it many times and are tired of hearing the explanation, but here it is again. These are the components:

Model The model represents the business data and the business logic by which the data is read or changed.

View A view is a particular rendering of the contents of a model. There can be many different views of the same model.

Controller A controller is responsible for interpreting user actions in terms of the model and view.

The MVC approach is frequently used in architectures of J2EE applications. For example, see this discussion at Sun:

```
http://java.sun.com/blueprints/patterns/j2ee_patterns/model_view_controller/
index.html
```

You may find MVC convenient when trying to describe Cocoon to other programmers. Jumping right into explaining pipelines may be a little overwhelming. You might start with the following points:

Model Cocoon makes no assumptions about models. As long as data can be translated to XML, it does not matter whether the underlying data model is a relational database, serialized Java objects, a simple file system, or a more exotic data source.

View Cocoon provides superior flexibility in the rendering of a view because of the flexibility of plugging together transformers and serializers. Because of this flexibility, it is relatively easy to provide views to a wide variety of user interfaces.

Controller Logical control is provided by actions, matchers, and selectors that control the selection of a pipeline, retrieval of data, and rendering of a view.

NOTE For in-depth coverage of J2EE, we recommend *Enterprise Java 2, J2EE 1.4 Complete* (Sybex, 2002).

JBoss—the Open-Source J2EE Server

By far the most widely used open-source J2EE-compatible web application server is JBoss. JBoss is a full-function web application server that is rapidly becoming a major influence among Java developers. JBoss beat out BEA and IBM to sweep the JavaWorld's 2002 Editors' Choice Award for Best Java Application Server.

Hundreds of thousands of Java programmers have downloaded JBoss for free from `www.jboss.org`.

The Cocoon installation instructions include a section on installing with JBoss. In the past there have been some problems related to XML parser versions, but these appear to have been resolved and installation is straightforward otherwise.

Cocoon and Loosely Coupled Systems

A classical (if we can use the term) web application using J2EE is a tightly coupled system. If the EJB-related computing load is distributed over multiple processors, they are tightly coordinated. Cocoon developers need to be aware that there is another possible approach to organizing web applications. Adapting your programming style and practices to the world of loosely coupled systems is as much of a jump as moving from single-user desktop applications to Java servlets, so be prepared for some mind-stretching ideas.

Loosely coupled systems are not a new thing for Sun, which has always had the slogan "the network is the computer." The wisdom of this approach becomes more apparent as the degree of interconnection between computing devices, and the number of devices, increases.

Generally speaking, as the number of components in a system increases, the probability that one or more components is not working correctly approaches unity. Loosely coupled messaging systems are much more tolerant of partial failure. The rise in importance of messaging systems on corporate networks has led to a new class of network application, Message-Oriented Middleware (MOM).

The most significant problem for loosely coupled systems is finding a common format for exchanging data. Previous attempts such as CORBA (Common Object Request Broker Architecture) were notorious for the complexity involved. You will not be surprised to learn that XML is rapidly becoming a widely accepted solution to this problem.

The most common objection to XML message formats is that they are bulky and inefficient in terms of information transferred per byte of message. This undeniable disadvantage is offset by the widespread availability of powerful Java tools for XML and the fact that XML is readable by both humans and machines. Now Cocoon adds ease of manipulating and reformatting XML data.

Java Message Service

Java Message Service (JMS) is a messaging API for asynchronous exchange of data messages within a network or between networks. Starting with version 1.3, JMS has been a part of the J2EE package with "message-driven beans." A working implementation and a tutorial can be found at `http://java.sun.com/products/jms/`.

Asynchronous messaging is very important within large enterprises because it can provide reliable communication between the wide variety of systems in a typical corporation. Corporate uses go far beyond the obvious typical e-mail and scheduling applications. IBM's MQ series of messaging software is one of the leading examples of enterprise messaging. The Sun implementation of JMS was designed in cooperation with major vendors to interface with various commercial messaging systems.

Message Service Architecture

There are two basic message exchange patterns. With point-to-point messaging, a message is directed at a single user, whereas with publish-subscribe messaging, a message is available to all who subscribe to a particular topic. A topic is simply a name known to the messaging system that can be set up to control access to particular topics.

The participants in a message system never address each other directly—all messages flow through message servers that are responsible for authentication, persistent storage, and message forwarding. The advantages of communication by JMS over communication by more direct means are as follows:

Messaging is asynchronous All participants in a message system do not have to be online. However, they must be registered with the message system as subscribing to a particular topic.

Messaging is fault tolerant Message servers can adjust to network loads and route around network problems.

Messaging is secure Message servers can impose security precautions without regard for the applications served.

Cleanup can be automatic After a specified lifetime, messages are automatically removed from the system.

A JMS message consists of a header containing addressing information and a body. There are five types of content that a body can represent, including any serializable Java object. The type of interest to Cocoon programmers is the `TextMessage`, where the content is a Java `String` and thus can be an XML document or fragment.

An example of a message service for which Cocoon could easily provide a front end would be a corporate chat system based on web browsers. Chat systems can provide much more flexible communication within a corporation than e-mail or physical meetings. With Cocoon providing presentation for a variety of devices, a chat system can become a useful tool for group collaboration.

JavaSpaces

The JavaSpaces concept is based on an academic research project called Linda at Yale University that got started in 1982. Researchers from that project have been working at Sun on JavaSpaces and the related Jini distributed computing project. There is also a similar project at IBM called TSpaces.

The basic idea is that participants in a JavaSpace interact by writing and reading objects into the space. In a web application, an object written into a space might represent a request for information from a database or a customer's order to be filled. Other participants in the space would be waiting for an object representing a task that they can work on. Figure 11.2 suggests how you might envision the operation of a JavaSpace.

FIGURE 11.2: Processes exchanging data through a JavaSpace

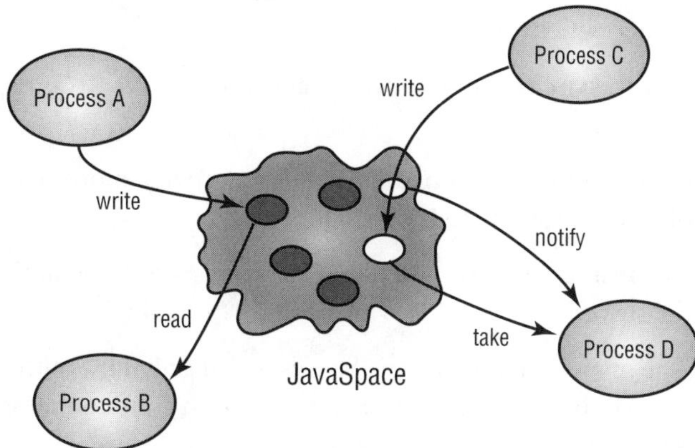

The following operations can be conducted in a JavaSpace:

- Write an object to the space.
- Read a copy of an object from the space.
- Take an object from the space.
- Get a notification that an object has been written to the space.

The system is loosely coupled because the web application does not know the location of other participants—it only needs to know how to contact the space. The processor that maintains the space is responsible for persistent storage of objects.

It is important to realize that a participant in a JavaSpace could be just about any process. For example, a web application creating a portal page (with Cocoon of course) could read current news items or stock quotes from a space. Another participant might be an e-mail service program that picks up mailing jobs written into the space by a shopping cart program.

JavaSpaces allow a system designer to separate business logic operations that may be more efficient with dedicated hardware from user interface systems such as web servers on cheaper hardware. For example, a single computer carrying out credit approval could service many different web applications through a JavaSpace.

JavaSpaces lend themselves to automatic load balancing because they are inherently loosely coupled. For example, if the credit approval load became too great for a single process, the administrator of the space could add another one without any reconfiguration.

The JavaSpaces mechanism for distributed processing improves upon JMS in several ways:

Retrieval by template matching Rather than subscribing to a topic, a participant submits an object of the type that it wants to read from the system. The variable values that this object contains operate as a template. When a qualified object is found, it is returned to the participant.

Truly asynchronous Participants do not have to be registered for a topic to retrieve an object.

Controlled persistence JavaSpaces provide more-detailed control over the persistence of an object in the space.

Event notification Participants can register to be notified when an object is written to the space.

The main limitation of JavaSpaces is that only Java objects can be stored in a space. In contrast, JMS text messages are compatible with common messaging systems without any language specificity.

Web Services and SOAP

We are sure you have been hearing a lot about web services and how the concept will revolutionize the way people use the web. You can think of web services as just another form of distributed computing that provides a potential data source for Cocoon processing. Any website that grabs content from another, such as the news aggregation example in the Cocoon 2.0.2 samples, is using a web service, but the industry is now using the term more specifically. As the industry applies the term, a web service now involves the following elements:

Service lookup Using a public directory and an API such as UDDI (Universal Description, Discovery, and Integration) or ebXML (electronic business XML), you can locate a publicly offered web service. The directory data guides you to a WSDL (Web Services Description Language) file. If you can find a WSDL file any other way, you do not need to use a lookup directory.

Detailed service description The programming details required to connect to a service are encoded in a WSDL service description. This XML formatted data can in many cases be automatically turned into the Java classes needed to communicate with the service.

Message exchange Web services messages are encoded with the SOAP (Simple Object Access Protocol) XML syntax. SOAP messages can be exchanged via any protocol, but HTTP is the most common.

In action, a web application such as a portal might use a SOAP message to request current data for anything from a stock price to the availability of rooms at a resort. Naturally, because SOAP messages are formatted in XML, they are easily processed in Cocoon pipelines.

Getting a SOAP Stock Quote

This discussion skips the service lookup function because there is a huge collection of public SOAP services at the following site:

```
www.xmethods.net
```

The "Delayed Stock Quote" service has an information page from which we can download the rather lengthy WSDL description of the delayed stock quote service. From this WSDL, we can determine that there is a method called `getQuote` that takes a string input of a ticker symbol and returns a float output of the most recent price.

The Cocoon 2.0.2 samples contain an example of using an XSP script to obtain a stock quote from this service. The following is the XSP code that constructs the remote procedure call message sent to the SOAP server at the xmethods.net site.

```
<soap:call url="http://services.xmethods.net:80/soap">
   <ns1:getQuote xmlns:ns1="urn:xmethods-delayed-quotes">
   <soap:enc/>
   <symbol xsi:type="xsd:string"
     xmlns:xsi="http://www.w3.org/1999/XMLSchema-instance"
     xmlns:xsd="http://www.w3.org/1999/XMLSchema">
    <xsp-request:get-parameter name="symbol"/></symbol>
   </ns1:getQuote>
</soap:call>
```

This XSP script causes the creation of a SOAP message that is sent to the server via an HTTP connection. The contents are XML that looks like the following:

```
<SOAP-ENV:Envelope
   xmlns:SOAP-ENV="http://schemas.xmlsoap.org/soap/envelope/"
   xmlns:xsi="http://www.w3.org/1999/XMLSchema-instance"
   xmlns:xsd="http://www.w3.org/1999/XMLSchema">
 <SOAP-ENV:Body>
 <ns1:getQuote xmlns:ns1="urn:xmethods-delayed-quotes"
    SOAP-ENV:encodingStyle="http://schemas.xmlsoap.org/soap/encoding/">
  <symbol xsi:type="xsd:string">IBM</symbol>
 </ns1:getQuote>
</SOAP-ENV:Body>
</SOAP-ENV:Envelope>
```

The server interprets this message and determines the method that is called. The input string is parsed out of the `<symbol>` tag and the method is called with that parameter. The returned value is encoded in a SOAP-formatted message that looks like the following:

```
<SOAP-ENV:Envelope
   xmlns:SOAP-ENV="http://schemas.xmlsoap.org/soap/envelope/"
   xmlns:xsi="http://www.w3.org/1999/XMLSchema-instance"
   xmlns:xsd="http://www.w3.org/1999/XMLSchema">
<SOAP-ENV:Body>
<ns1:getQuoteResponse xmlns:ns1="urn:xmethods-delayed-quotes"
   SOAP-ENV:encodingStyle="http://schemas.xmlsoap.org/soap/encoding/">
<return xsi:type="xsd:float">70.51</return>
</ns1:getQuoteResponse>
</SOAP-ENV:Body>
</SOAP-ENV:Envelope>
```

The `<return>` tag value can then be used in the formatting of a Cocoon output page, as shown in Figure 11.3.

FIGURE 11.3:

The SOAP stock quote sample result

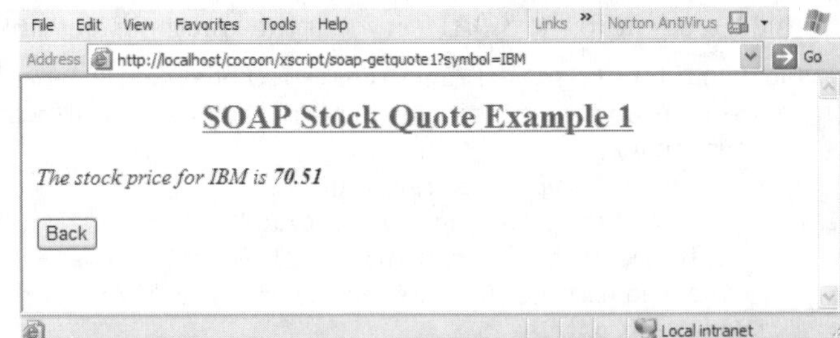

Support for SOAP Programming

There is currently a lot of activity in the field of web services in general and SOAP programming in particular. Utilities have been developed that greatly simplify the creation of WSDL files that match Java classes, thus saving developers a lot of tedious and error-prone coding. One pioneering product is the GLUE system, whose home website is as follows:

```
www.themindelectric.com
```

The main open-source projects for SOAP are, not surprisingly, proceeding under the Apache Software Foundation. The initial project, Apache SOAP, is highly developed and stable in version 2.3.1 as of this writing. This project is based on using DOM models internally, so it is not suitable for large SOAP messages.

The Axis project is intended to avoid memory consumption difficulties by using SAX processing (that should sound familiar to Cocoon developers). As of this writing, the Axis project is in a beta release. The Apache SOAP and Apache Axis projects are reachable from the following URLs:

```
http://xml.apache.org/soap/index.html
http://xml.apache.org/axis/index.html
```

NOTE The recent book, *SOAP Programming with Java,* by Bill Brogden (Sybex, 2002) has much more on using SOAP.

Data Sources

In a J2EE application server, Enterprise JavaBeans (EJB) are interposed between the "Server-Side Presentation" and the "Enterprise Information Systems." For applications with a moderate number of users, many developers feel that EJB is unnecessary and that direct connection to databases is quite practical.

Generally speaking, Cocoon applications typically use databases in the following:

Actions Typical use of an action would be user validation by looking up passwords or otherwise operating on request data. Recall that actions modify the sitemap environment, but they do not create content.

Generation with XSP We showed examples in Chapters 6, "Introducing XSP Usage," and 7, "XSP Logicsheets."

SQLTransformers In this usage, the events generated in a pipeline define the parameters of the query that provides data to fill in a document.

Relational Databases and JDBC

As a Java application, Cocoon can make use of the well-developed JDBC API for connection to relational databases. JDBC is of course the standard used in J2EE servers as well. JDBC-compatible drivers are available for all of the major commercial relational databases and open-source databases. For more about JDBC, See Chapter 9, "Database Connectivity (JDBC)" of *Enterprise Java 2, J2EE Complete* (Sybex, 2002).

Data from Stored Objects

Although the relational database and SQL have dominated the commercial database scene for many years, Cocoon programmers should not automatically assume that SQL is the best solution. XML documents can describe hierarchies that are deep and complex, and not easy to represent in a relational database.

This section looks at some alternatives based on concepts of storing and retrieving objects. Some of these alternatives, such as serialized Java objects, are already well accepted as a standard Java practice. Others are still experimental; we think one or more are likely to be showing up as standard practices soon.

Serialized Java Objects

A vital part of the Java language is the capability of creating a representation of a Java object as a stream of bytes with the object serialization classes. There are several interfaces and classes in the `java.io` package that have to do with serialization:

`Serializable` This interface is used to mark classes that can be serialized. If you attempt to read or write an object that does not implement this interface, you get an exception.

`ObjectOutputStream` Objects of this class are created with an `OutputStream` that may write to a file, internal buffer, or socket. An `ObjectOutputStream` can write simple primitives or a complex object composed of many other objects, as long as they all implement `Serializable`.

`ObjectInputStream` As you might expect, this object reverses the output process and creates an object from a stream.

Java object serialization can be astonishingly simple. For example, we have a servlet application that administers mock Java certification exam questions. The object that stores the test results as the user takes the test implements `Serializable` and contains only `String` objects and arrays of primitives. All that is required to save the state of a test in progress is to execute the following code in the `TestSession` class, where `fs` is a `File` object that has been created with a unique filename.

```
ObjectOutputStream oos = null ;
try {
   FileOutputStream fos = new FileOutputStream( fs );
   oos = new ObjectOutputStream( fos );
   oos.writeObject( this );
}finally {
   if( oos != null ) oos.close();
}
```

In the reverse procedure, you simply open an `ObjectInputStream` and reconstruct the `TestSession` object. Note that the `readObject` method is defined as returning an `Object` so you have to cast the reference to the right type:

```
try {
  fis = new FileInputStream( fs );
  ois = new ObjectInputStream( fis );
```

```
    ret = (TestSession) ois.readObject( );
  } finally {
        if( ois != null ) ois.close();
  }
```

With methods this convenient, you may be wondering why anybody would need to invent another serialization approach. The reasons are as follows:

- Serialized objects can't be accessed by non-Java programs and are not readable by humans.
- Objects written with `ObjectOutputStream` serialization must have exactly the same class files on the input stream side. Even a slight change in class definition makes stored classes invalid. You might even experience difficulty moving objects between different versions of Java.
- This approach does not provide any higher-order database management functions, such as support for transactions, updates, or lookup keys.

The Java Architecture for XML Binding (JAXB)

Development of the Java Architecture for XML Binding (JAXB) has been an ongoing project under the Java Community Process under JSR-31. A final release of the API and a reference implementation is anticipated shortly. The intent of the project is to provide a system to easily convert back and forth between XML documents and Java objects by creating Java objects that know how to parse their data from XML and write their data to XML.

The latest documentation and reference implementation can be found here:

`http://java.sun.com/xml/jaxb/`

Generation of the Java class code is accomplished by automated methods that read an XML Schema and produce a set of Java classes that are capable of parsing an XML document and create Java objects representing the full structure of the document. These classes provide for manipulating the data and serializing a new XML document.

The generated classes are capable of ensuring that the data representation is valid as defined by the original schema at all times. At the present time, the reference implementation can only work from a standard DTD, but extension to other schema is underway. Furthermore, the code generator is not yet capable of checking all schema restrictions. The procedure for generating classes is as follows:

1. Prepare a DTD for your XML document.
2. Prepare a "binding schema" that uses JAXB syntax to make certain declarations about the XML document that serve as hints to the code generator.

3. Execute the schema compiler with the DTD and binding schema as input. This creates Java source code. Methods in the generated code provide for getting and setting variables that correspond to elements in the XML. These methods use the JavaBeans naming convention so the resulting objects can easily be used in JavaServer Pages documents.
4. Compile the resulting Java source code.

The JAXB API is destined to become part of the normal Java release of XML tools called the XML Pack. This package includes Sun's parser and SOAP-related packages and can be found at the following URL:

`http://java.sun.com/xml/downloads/javaxmlpack.html`

A JAXB Example

As an example of how the JAXB API works, we will develop the classes for working with the questionnaire document used in the `SurveyGenerator` example in Chapter 8, "Content Generators." A questionnaire document consists of an introduction followed by multiple blocks of questions. The blocks provide for adapting a survey to a user by allowing answers to a question to control the next block of questions asked.

Each block contains one or more questions, and each question contains question text followed by multiple options. If a block ends with a `<Terminal>` element, that block may be the final one presented to the user. Here is a skeleton of the questionnaire document used in Chapter 8:

```
<?xml version="1.0" standalone="yes" ?>
<Questionnaire title="Cocoon Page Visitors"
   author="wbb" date="March 25, 2002"
   method="xml" file="resultfile.xml">
<Intro> .. text
</Intro>
<Block name="entry" type="terminal" >
  <Ques id="entry:1" type="QMC" >
    <Qtext>How did you arrive here?</Qtext>
    <Qopt val="a">I got here from Javaranch Discussion</Qopt>
    ......... more <Qopt> elements
  </Ques>
  ...... more <Ques> elements
<Terminal>Thanks for completing the questions!</Terminal>
</Block>
.......... more <Block> elements
</Questionnaire>
```

The first step is the creation of a DTD. We started with a DTD created with the commercial XML Spy utility. With some slight editing, we got the result shown in Listing 11.1.

Listing 11.1 A DTD for Questionnaire Documents

```
<?xml version="1.0" encoding="UTF-8"?>
<!--DTD generated by XML Spy v4.2 U (http://www.xmlspy.com)-->
<!ELEMENT Block (Ques+, Terminal)>
<!ATTLIST Block
    name (entry | yesxml) #REQUIRED
    type CDATA #IMPLIED
>
<!ELEMENT Intro (#PCDATA)>
<!ELEMENT Qopt (#PCDATA)>
<!ATTLIST Qopt
    val CDATA #REQUIRED
    branch CDATA #IMPLIED
>
<!ELEMENT Qtext (#PCDATA)>
<!ELEMENT Ques (Qtext, Qopt+)>
<!ATTLIST Ques
    id   CDATA  #REQUIRED
    type (QMC | QMCM | QTX ) #REQUIRED
>
<!ELEMENT Questionnaire (Intro, Block+)>
<!ATTLIST Questionnaire
    title CDATA #REQUIRED
    author CDATA #REQUIRED
    date CDATA #REQUIRED
    method CDATA #REQUIRED
    file CDATA #REQUIRED
    comment CDATA #REQUIRED
>
<!ELEMENT Terminal (#PCDATA)>
```

The Binding Schema

The JAXB schema compiler requires some additional information in the form of a "binding schema." This is an XML document that defines, among other things, which of the resulting Java classes must be capable of representing the root element of a document. An object with root capability can "unmarshal" its content from an XML document or "marshal" the content to an XML document.

Other elements in the binding schema allow you to control the Java type to which a particular element is converted. For example, you might use a `BigDecimal` type to represent money quantities. By default the schema compiler stores all content as `String` variables.

Listing 11.2 shows the rather simple binding schema we used for this example. The `<options>` element tells the schema compiler to put the resulting classes in a package. Note that we want a block element to be capable of being a root because that would let us assemble a complete questionnaire out of separate block documents. Also note the two <enumeration> elements; these direct the schema compiler to create special constant classes to represent "QuestType" and "BlockType" variables.

Listing 11.2 The Questionnaire Binding Schema

```
<xml-java-binding-schema version="1.0ea" >
<options package="com.lanw.cocoon.xmlbind" />
<element name="Questionnaire" type="class" root="true" />
<element name="Block" type="class" root="true" >
  <attribute name="type" convert="BlockType" />
</element>
<element name="Ques" type="class" >
  <attribute name="type" convert="QuesType" />
</element>
<enumeration name="QuesType" members="QMC QMCM QTXT" />
<enumeration name="BlockType" members="terminal" />
</xml-java-binding-schema>
```

The Resulting Java Classes

The schema compiler is a command-line utility that takes the DTD and the binding schema and generates Java source code. In this example, it generated code for the following classes:

Questionnaire A class to represent an entire questionnaire. It contains a number of private String variables to represent the attributes of the <Questionnaire> element and the <Intro> element, and a collection of Block objects. Methods to get and set the values of the variables are named according to the JavaBeans convention. There are also a variety of methods for validating, marshaling, and unmarshaling; these methods make extensive use of the JAXB library classes.

Block A class to represent a block of questions as a collection of Ques objects. Because we specified root="true" in the schema, marshaling and unmarshaling methods are provided.

BlockType This class provides a static final variable to represent the one allowed value for the block "type" attribute if it appears at all.

Ques A class to represent a single question with various String variables and a collection of Qopt objects representing options.

QuestType This class provides static final variables to represent the three different allowed values for the type attribute of a Ques object.

Qopt A class to represent a single option attached to a Ques object.

Creating a new `Questionnaire` object from an existing document uses one of the static `unmarshal` methods as shown in this example, which uses an `InputStream` as a source for the XML text.

```
static Questionnaire unmarshal(String fname )
     throws IOException,UnmarshalException {
   FileInputStream fis = new FileInputStream( fname );
   Questionnaire aQ = Questionnaire.unmarshal( fis );
   fis.close();
   return aQ ;
}
```

The schema compiler automatically creates a number of these methods for various possible XML sources.

Comparison with DOM

Naturally, you will be wondering what advantages the JAXB approach might have over simply keeping a DOM Document in memory, as we did in the `SurveyGenerator` example of Chapter 8. To find out, we compare the memory use and creation time for 1,000 `Questionnaire` objects compared to 1,000 `Document` objects. The results in Table 11.1 show that the Java objects representation with JAXB is much more memory efficient and slightly faster.

TABLE 11.1: Resources Used by JAXB and DOM

Method	Bytes Per Instance	Time Per Instance
JAXB	11,290	4.07 msec
DOM	128,768	5.61 msec

The Java Data Objects Initiative

Sun has sponsored a Java Community Process effort to define Java Data Objects (JDO) under JSR-12. The purpose of this project is to provide additional functionality far beyond simple reading and writing objects. The Sun JDO project is at the proposed final release stage as of this writing. The present state of the project can be found at the following URL:

`http://jcp.org/aboutJava/communityprocess/first/jsr012/index.html`

Despite the fact that the API is not final, the early version has been integrated into J2EE and picked up by major vendors of Object Database Management Systems (ODBMS).

The central element in a Sun JDO application is the `PersistenceManager`. A `PersistenceManager` object handles all details of storage and supports transactions transparently so that the application does not care whether objects are stored in a relational database, object database, or a flat file.

The `PersistenceManager` also controls query capability. Sun JDO uses queries that conform to the Object Query Language specification by the Object Management Group. This language has a syntax similar to SQL. Queries must specify the Java class of the stored object so they can use the names of instance variables and method calls in the stored objects and some basic numeric operators such as comparisons.

Castor Object Serialization

The Castor JDO project got started a little earlier than the Sun project and is considered by many to be more mature. Right now the Cocoon developers seem to be leaning toward support of Castor rather than the Sun JDO. For example, there is an experimental CastorTransformer that inserts XML serialized from a Castor object into a SAX event stream.

There are several projects of interest under the general ExoLab name. Generally speaking, these are designed for mapping between Java objects, XML documents, SQL tables, and LDAP (Lightweight Directory Access Protocol) directories. The home web page for the ExoLab project is at `www.exolab.org`.

Castor and the Sun JDO use different approaches in spite of the common acronym. Castor JDO is based on storage of object data in relational databases and uses SQL syntax for object recovery. Castor is compatible with common commercial and open-source databases such as Oracle, SQL Server, MySQL, and InterBase.

Business Logic

So far we have talked about architectures for only the data storage aspect of a web application. What has been missing is a discussion of how an application performs logical operations and decision-making. In simple cases, decision-making is accomplished by the logical flow of programs written in Java or a scripting language.

The UML Design Tool

There have been many attempts over the years to create diagramming systems to represent program logic. Recently there has been a general unification of the various systems into the Unified Modeling Language (UML). With this common notation, great strides have been made in developing design tools and encoding of UML data in XML documents. UML is not a programming language as such—it is a design tool. The Object Management Group (OMG) has a good introduction to UML at `www.omg.org/uml/`.

One open-source Java-based tool for working with UML diagrams is the ArgoUML project based at `http://argouml.tigris.org/`.

The ArgoUML tool can import and export UML diagrams encoded in the XML-based exchange format endorsed by the OMG. It can also generate Java code to represent certain portions of the UML diagram logic.

Business Rule Engines

One approach to automated decision-making is called a rule engine. This is a form of expert system that takes a set of rules and applies them to the data representing a problem to come to a decision. In other words, operation of a rule engine is declarative rather than procedural.

Rule engines are common in situations such as credit card authorization automation. For example, a rule might call for special processing if a proposed charge is a large fraction of the remaining cash available. This might be balanced against rules related to the credit history of the user to come to a decision.

There is a pending Java Community Process proposal, JSR094, to come up with a rules engine API for Java. One of the participants in this JSR is IBM, which has a project called "Business Rules for Electronic Commerce," based at the following address:

```
www.research.ibm.com/rules/home.html
```

IBM has developed a Business Rules Markup Language (BRML) that uses an XML format to express rules in a way that is portable between rules systems. CommonRules is a 100% Java library for developing rule-based decision-making. The design emphasizes maximum separation of data and business logic, and portability of rules. The current version can be downloaded from the following website:

```
http://alphaworks.ibm.com/tech/commonrules
```

An example of a business rule engine that could be used in a Cocoon environment is Jess. The Jess system is a 100% Java rule engine and scripting environment. As with most expert systems, the programmer tells the system rules with numerical and logical statements in a specialized syntax. You can learn more about Jess at the following website:

```
http://herzberg.ca.sandia.gov/jess/
```

Note that Jess is not an open-source project.

The purpose behind using XML to state portable rules is to ensure that applications will be able to make publicly available the business rules they use. Presumably this will support the exchange of business data in web services. A short discussion of BRML can be found here:

```
www.oasis-open.org/cover/brml.html
```

Summary

The dominant technology for large-scale Java-based web applications is currently Sun's J2EE for content storage and business logic, with servlets and JSP handling user interactions. Cocoon is well suited to take over some or all of the presentation functions in a J2EE web application in which content comes from Enterprise JavaBeans.

In this chapter, we have also discussed how Cocoon relates to other possible architectures for content generation. In addition to the currently popular web services based on XML using SOAP, Cocoon can easily work with content produced by less well known architectures such as messaging systems. Essentially, any content that can be turned into XML can be presented by Cocoon.

We have seen that Cocoon fits cleanly with many standard and experimental industry practices and pattern usages. Industry trends to more extensive use of XML and related technology in web applications and web services mean that Cocoon will be finding many uses in the future of the Internet.

Appendix A

Resources

- Standards
- Apache Projects
- Tutorials, FAQs, and Other Goodies

Cocoon draws on so many different technologies that it is hard to know when to stop listing resources. We have decided on the following, but any search engine can find lots more.

Standards

Cocoon depends on a large number of different standards promulgated by a variety of organizations, some official and some informal. It is a sign of our times that most of these standards probably have some new version in the works.

XML Standards at W3C

Cocoon has to deal with a large number of standards that are supervised by the W3C. The basic entry point is `www.w3.org`. Here are some of the locations for specific standards:

Cascading Style Sheets (CSS) This page presents general information on W3C activities related to CSS.

`www.w3.org/Style/CSS/`

Hypertext Markup Language (HTML) The starting point to learn about W3C activities related to HTML is:

`www.w3.org/MarkUp/`

XML Protocol (SOAP) SOAP and related standards are handled by the XML Protocols Working Group:

`www.w3.org/2000/xp/Group/`

A SOAP overview is at the following website:

`http://developer.java.sun.com/developer/technicalArticles/xml/webservices/`

SVG This page presents an overview of the Scalable Vector Graphics project:

`www.w3.org/Graphics/SVG/Overview.html`

XForms The intent of this project is to create a way of defining web page forms in XML with a goal of eventually replacing the HTML form–related tags.

`www.w3.org/TR/xforms/`

XML The W3C site describes XML as "the universal format for structured documents and data on the Web." This site summarizes W3C operations related to XML.

`www.w3.org/XML/`

XPath XPath is a language for addressing parts of an XML document; it is used by both XSLT and XPointer. W3C activities related to XPath are summarized at:

`www.w3.org/TR/xpath/`

XPointer, XML Link, and XML Base The W3C has now grouped activities on these three technologies on a single page:

`www.w3.org/XML/Linking`

XSL formatting objects and XSL for Transformations Both are part of the XSL standard but are being developed in separate documents:

`www.w3.org/Style/XSL/`

XQuery The XML Query activity is attempting to define how to make queries into collections of XML documents. This activity is closely related to XPath. Current status of the project can be seen at:

`www.w3.org/XML/Query`

Related XML Standards

SAX The Simple API for XML is a *de facto* standard not related to any industry standards body. It has a new home at this address:

`www.saxproject.org`

JDOM The JDOM API is also a *de facto* standard, although it now has a Java Community Process entry (JSR-102) and will probably become part of the Java XML library in the future.

`www.jdom.org`

XML:DB Another attempt to define an API for making queries into collections of XML documents.

`www.xmldb.org/xapi/`

Java Standards from Sun

Java Language Specification The Java Language Specification is the final authority on the Java language:

`http://java.sun.com/docs/books/jls/`

Java XML Pack Sun now offers all major XML related packages as the "XML Pack," downloadable from the following URL:

`http://java.sun.com/xml/downloads/javaxmlpack.html`

JavaSpaces The innovative system for distributed computing is at the following website:

`http://java.sun.com/products/javaspaces/`

Java Standards from JCP

The Java Community Process (JCP) is Sun's institution for soliciting contributions and suggestions for development of Java APIs. The JCP base website at `http://jcp.org/` has a list of all Java Specification Requests (JSRs) currently active. All of the major APIs of interest to Cocoon programmers are represented. Two of particular interest are the following:

Portlets The Java Community Process group to define a "portlet" portal component API:

`http://jcp.org/jsr/detail/168.jsp`

XML Data Binding Specification Defines an API for compiling an XML schema into one or more Java classes that can parse, generate, and validate documents that follow the schema.

`http://jcp.org/jsr/detail/31.jsp`

Apache Projects

Cocoon draws on numerous projects under the umbrella of the Apache Software Foundation. Many of these projects are undergoing rapid evolution and may affect Cocoon in the future, so you need to keep an eye on them. The most general entry point for the Apache organization is:

`www.apache.org`

The major project divisions of interest to Cocoon users are the Jakarta and XML projects. Under the Jakarta project, we find ANT, Avalon, Commons, and Tomcat sub-projects.

```
http://jakarta.apache.org/ant/
http://jakarta.apache.org/avalon/
http://jakarta.apache.org/commons/
http://jakarta.apache.org/tomcat/
```

Under the Apache XML project we find the primary Cocoon site plus a number of other sub-projects of interest:

```
http://xml.apache.org/batik/
http://xml.apache.org/forrest/
http://xml.apache.org/cocoon/
http://xml.apache.org/fop/
http://xml.apache.org/soap/
http://xml.apache.org/xerces2-j/
http://xml.apache.org/xalan-j/
http://xml.apache.org/xindice/
```

Tutorials, FAQs, and Other Goodies

A clever representation of sitemap structure with excellent graphics, suitable for creating a wall chart:

`http://outerthought.net/sitemap/`

A discussion of authentication techniques:

`http://ziegeler.bei.t-online.de/tecart.html`

A list of some of the most commonly asked questions:

`http://xml.apache.org/cocoon/faq/`

Archives of the Apache mailing lists:

`http://marc.theaimsgroup.com/?l=xml-cocoon-users`

Nicely done tutorials:

`www.cocooncenter.de/cc/documents/resources/request-params/index.html`

Tutorials on XSP usage:

`www.suranyami.com/XSPtutorial/`
`www.plenix.com/xsp/doc/xsp-primer.html`

A weekly summary of links posted to the Cocoon mailing lists:

`www.luminas.co.uk/technology/cocoon/url/`

A content management system in Java making use of Cocoon:

`www.wyona.org`

WebDAV stands for *Web-based Distributed Authoring and Versioning.* It is a set of extensions to the HTTP protocol that allows users to collaboratively edit and manage files on remote web servers. The proposed Portlet API would be compatible with WebDAV.

`www.webdav.org`

Appendix B

Sitemap Tag References

Chapter 5, "Logic Control: The Sitemap," discussed the sitemap elements in logical order; the purpose of this reference is to provide an alphabetical listing to help you distinguish between the various forms of the tags. We created these entries from DTDs derived from various Cocoon version 2.0.2 sitemaps. New tags will undoubtedly be created by the developers for subsequent versions.

map:act One or more map:act elements appear either inside a map:action group or in a pipeline fragment. In the pipeline usage, a map:act element contains other pipeline components that will be executed if the action succeeds. In the map:action usage, a map:act may have an action attribute containing a characteristic name. In a pipeline, a map:act may refer to a map:action set by name, in which case, all of the actions in the set will be executed in order. If all map:act operations fail, the referring map:act fails.

Typically, in a pipeline, map:act has an attribute referring to the name of a map:action and thus the Java class that will be executed. A map:act may contain another map:act element or elements such as map:parameter, map:redirect-to, map:call, map:generate, map:transform, map:serialize, or map:match.

map:action Found within the map:actions tag, it defines an action with attributes giving a name and the Java class implementing the action. A map:action element can contain one or more elements defining the action. Actions typically perform computation and modify sitemap variables. Cocoon provides a very large number of specialized action classes.

map:actions A first-level child of map:components, this element encloses all of the map:action elements. Generally speaking, actions are used to modify sitemap variables and to decide which pipeline fragment is executed.

map:action-set A map:action-set is used to create a named group of map:act elements as a convenience to make constructing pipelines more concise. A map:act reference to a map:action-set in a pipeline causes all actions in the set to be executed.

map:action-sets A first-level child of map:sitemap, this contains one or more map:action-set elements.

map:aggregate This element appears within a pipeline in place of a generator. It acts like a generator by creating a stream of SAX events from multiple sources designated by map:part elements. The sequence of map:part elements controls the order in which the sources are used.

map:call When a map:call element appears in a pipeline, it redirects execution to another Cocoon pipeline as named in a resource attribute. A map:call can appear inside a map:match or map:act. Also see map:resource.

map:components This element encloses all of the component-defining groups—map:generators, map:transformers, map:readers, map:serializers, map:matchers, map:selectors, and map:actions—that will be used in a pipeline. This is typically the first element inside a sitemap document. Each component defined in map:components has a name attribute that will be used in the rest of the sitemap to refer to that component.

map:generate When this tag appears inside a pipeline, it activates a generator and passes it the value of the src attribute string. The generator used will be either the default generator or one named by the type attribute. A map:generate element can occur within map:act, map:resource, or map:match elements in a pipeline. One or more map:parameter elements inside a map:generate can be used to supply parameters to the generator.

map:generator Found inside the map:generators element, this defines a generator with attributes giving a name and the Java class implementing the generator. Cocoon defines a large number of generators.

map:generators A first-level child of map:components, this element encloses one or more map:generator elements. Generators create a stream of SAX events representing content. This tag typically contains a default attribute naming the generator to be used if a map:generate tag does not contain a type attribute.

map:handle-errors This element appears inside a map:pipeline to designate the mechanism for reporting a Java exception that occurs during pipeline processing. The error-handling mechanism effectively creates a generator that generates SAX events encoding the exception report. Typically, a map:handle-errors element would contain a map:transform and map:serialize to format the error data and send it in the response.

map:match A map:match element at the start of a pipeline fragment controls whether or not that fragment is executed by using the pattern supplied as the pattern attribute. The matcher class used is controlled by the type attribute. A map:match can occur inside a map:pipeline, map:act, or another map:match element. A map:match can contain the following elements: map:generate, map:aggregate, map:transform, map:serialize, map:mount, map:redirect-to, map:act, map:read, or map:call.

map:matchers A first-level child of map:components, this element encloses one or more map:matcher elements. Matchers are one of the components used to decide which pipeline fragment is executed. This tag typically contains a default attribute naming the matcher to be used if a map:match tag does not contain a type attribute. Typically, the default matcher looks at the request URL, but there are matchers that can look at many other sitemap parameters.

map:mount This element is used inside a pipeline to turn over flow control to a subsitemap. The src attribute gives the path to a subsitemap.

map:otherwise A map:otherwise element appears inside a map:select element to designate the pipeline fragment that will be executed if all of the map:when elements fail to make a selection. It is the equivalent of default in a Java switch statement.

map:parameter A map:parameter element defines name and value attributes that are used to pass data to a component represented by the enclosing element.

map:part This element appears inside a map:aggregate generator as one source of SAX events. Various attributes define the source and the namespace to be attached to the events.

map:pipeline A map:pipeline element contains the elements describing components that control handling of a request. There are also map:pipeline elements that are marked with the internal-only attribute having the value "*true*"—these pipelines are addressed indirectly. A map:pipeline can contain multiple map:match elements and can contain a map:handle-errors element.

map:pipelines This first-level child of map:sitemap contains one or more map:pipeline elements. The order of map:pipeline elements within map:pipelines is significant because it defines the order in which Cocoon tries to find a pipeline to execute.

map:read This element occurs within a pipeline and controls reading a binary stream of data from a source. Attributes give the source and the MIME type of that source.

map:readers A first-level child of map:components, this element encloses one or more map:reader elements. Because readers have the simple job of transferring binary data to output, frequently only one reader is needed in a sitemap. Typically, this tag contains a default attribute naming the reader to be used if a map:read tag does not contain a type attribute.

map:redirect-to When a map:redirect-to element appears in a pipeline, it stops creation of normal output and causes an HTTP redirect to be sent to the response.

map:resource A map:resource defines a pipeline sequence that can be executed by means of a map:call element in another pipeline. Typically, a resource is used for frequently repeated pipeline fragments. A name attribute supplies the name by which other components refer to the resource.

map:resources A first-level child of map:sitemap, this element contains one or more map:resource elements.

map:serialize The map:serialize element defines the final stage of a pipeline because it performs actual output to a response. The type attribute determines which of the serializers is used. A map:serialize element can occur with the pipeline elements map:act, map:match, map:handle-errors, map:resource, or map:view.

`map:serializer` This element defines an individual serializer type with a name, MIME-type that the serializer generates, and the Java class that performs the operation.

`map:serializers` A first-level child of `map:components`, this element encloses one or more `map:serializer` elements. Serializers are the output stage of a pipeline. Cocoon provides a large number of serializers. This tag typically contains a `default` attribute naming the serializer to be used if a `map:serialize` tag does not contain a `type` attribute.

`map:select` The `map:select` element appears in pipelines where its `type` attribute names a selector to be executed. A `map:select` contains `map:when` elements that give values to be tested.

`map:selector` A `map:selector` element names a selector and gives the Java class that executes it. The element can contain specialized data elements that set up the selector object. In a pipeline, a selector examines sitemap data and controls flow.

`map:selectors` A first-level child of `map:components`, this element encloses one or more `map:selector` elements. Selectors are one of the components that can control which part of a pipeline is executed. Similar components are matchers and actions. Typically, this tag contains a `default` attribute naming the selector to be used if a `map:select` tag does not contain a `type` attribute.

`map:sitemap` The root element of a sitemap. An attribute declares the namespace used in the sitemap. There are five first-level child elements in a sitemap: `map:components`, `map:views`, `map:resources`, `map:action-sets`, and `map:pipelines`.

`map:transform` This element occurs in pipelines to define a transformation step anywhere there is a stream of SAX events. Optional attributes give the type, label, and a `src` source for transformers that read a file; for example, the XSL file used by the XSLT transformer. The element may contain `map:parameter` elements giving additional setup parameters.

`map:transformer` Found inside the `map:transformers` element, this defines a transformer with a name and implementing Java class. Optional attributes can define logger, label, and cache related parameters. The `map:transformer` element can contain custom elements used for the initialization of that particular kind of transformer.

`map:transformers` A first-level child of `map:components`, this element encloses one or more `map:transformer` elements. Transformers perform operations on SAX events as they flow through a pipeline. Typically, this tag contains a `default` attribute naming the transformer to be used if a `map:transform` tag does not contain a `type` attribute.

`map:view` A `map:view` is an alternate way of processing SAX events.

`map:views` This first-level child of `map:sitemap` contains one or more `map:view` elements.

`map:when` A `map:when` element appears inside a `map:select` in a pipeline, and contains pipeline elements. It has a `test` attribute that is used by the selector. If the test is satisfied, the pipeline inside the `map:when` is executed.

Glossary

100% Pure Java The designation for classes and applications that comply with Sun's criteria for total independence from the underlying operating system.

A

abstract A Java keyword describing classes or methods that define a runtime behavior but that don't provide a complete implementation. You can't create an object from an `abstract` class, but an object created from a class extending the `abstract` class can be referred to with the `abstract` class name.

action Pipeline components that can manipulate runtime parameters, such as the contents of a request. An action can also determine whether a particular pipeline segment is executed based on the parameters.

Action logicsheet A collection of custom XML tags for automating standard action operations. *See* logicsheet.

Active Server Pages (ASP) Microsoft's technology for programmatically delivering HTML pages using embedded programming code written in VBScript or JScript.

adapter Design pattern for converting or adapting one class interface to another. For example, there are classes in the `java.awt.event` package that support the creation of event listeners.

aggregation The Cocoon process for assembling a document from multiple pipelines.

algorithm A problem-solving operation that proceeds one step at a time to accomplish a specific program task.

alpha The typical designation given a program or application that is undergoing initial (internal) testing before being released for testing outside the company that developed it. *See also* beta.

American Standard Code for Information Interchange (ASCII) The ubiquitous computer industry standard for encoding text and control characters.

Apache Software Foundation The nonprofit umbrella organization for many open-source projects such as Cocoon and Tomcat. The name comes from the original informal project to build a web server.

API *See* application programming interface.

applet A Java program that operates within a Java Virtual Machine (JVM), supplied by the user's web browser. You can think of the browser as providing an applet container that lets it run on the client machine more or less independently of the underlying operating system.

application programming interface (API) Calling conventions or instruction set used by an application to access operating system and library services.

Application Service Provider (ASP) The rather general term for a service that provides access to one or more applications over the Internet.

argument Java method call data item that can designate a Java primitive or object.

array Group of data items that share the same type, in which a 32-bit integer index addresses each data item uniquely.

ASCII *See* American Standard Code for Information Interchange.

ASP *See* Active Server Pages; *see also* Application Service Provider.

attribute In XML, a name-value pair within the start tag of an element.

automatic (local) variable Variable declared inside a method to which memory is automatically allocated when the method is called.

Avalon The Apache Software Foundation project for creating a generalized Java framework for server applications. Cocoon makes extensive use of Avalon libraries.

B

bean *See* Java bean.

Bean Scripting Framework (BSF) A Java toolkit for executing programs in scripting languages. It is used in Cocoon in the `ScriptGenerator`.

beta The typical designation given a program or application that is under development and is released for testing outside the company that developed it. *See also* alpha.

block A section of Java code that is contained within matching { and } characters.

BSF *See* Bean Scripting Framework.

byte An 8-bit Java integer-type primitive that is treated as a signed integer.

C

cache As a verb, to hold in memory the contents of a resource to speed access when the resource is needed. Also, the program mechanism that performs this function. Optimized caching can significantly improve Cocoon server response.

Capture logicsheet A collection of custom XML tags performing standard operations for capturing parts of the XSP-generated XML as XML fragments or DOM nodes.

case-insensitive Naming convention that does not distinguish between upper- and lowercase letters.

case-sensitive Programming language naming convention that distinguishes between upper- and lowercase letters; in other words, "Text" and "text" are read differently. Java and XML are case-sensitive.

catch Java keyword that declares a specific exception type and creates a block of code or clause that executes when that exception contained in code with a `try` statement is thrown.

CGI *See* Common Gateway Interface.

char Java integer primitive variable that represents Unicode characters as 16-bit unsigned integers.

Character (class) The Java wrapper class for `char` values.

character data The text contents of an element or attribute.

child In the context of object-oriented programming, any object that inherits from and obtains information from another object; a Java class that inherits from another class (parent or superclass).

In the context of XML documents, an element contained immediately inside another element is called a child.

class In general context of object-oriented programming, a method for grouping objects that share some characteristic or characteristics; all Java classes descend from the `Object` class.

Class (class) The Java class (`java.lang.Class`) that indicates the runtime type of any object.

class file The result of compiling a Java class is a class file containing byte codes.

class method Java method declared `static` and attached to an entire class, rather than to objects in the class.

Collection (interface) Java interface (`java.util.Collection`) that defines basic behavior for Collections API objects.

Collections API Java 2 set of classes and interfaces that provide a number of methods for handling collections of objects.

Collections (class) Java class (`java.util.Collections`) containing `static` methods applicable to collections.

Common Gateway Interface (CGI) The conventions governing communication between web servers and external applications. This was the first technology that supported dynamic interaction between users (via browsers) and web servers.

completeness Java term denoting whether a class behavior is fully developed or requires further development by subclasses.

Component (class) Java abstract class (`java.awt.Component`) that is the parent of all screen components in the AWT graphics package except those related to menus.

components In Cocoon pipelines, components are the main processing elements. They are declared in a special section of the sitemap.

constructor Special kind of member function called on the creation of a class instance using `new`; initializes the object. Java classes can declare *none*, *one*, or *many* constructor methods.

container In Sun's terminology, the environment a Java applet, Servlet, or EJB operates in is a specialized container that is required to provide specific services.

Container (class) The Java class (`java.awt.Container`) that is the ancestor of all AWT GUI objects that contain and manage interface components.

content management A system or process to manage the creation and maintenance of web content.

controller In the Model-View-Controller design pattern, the controller provides functions or services for communicating user input to the model and view(s).

conversion A term used in describing a Java expression, `conversion` changes the expression type.

cookie A small chunk of text data stored by a web browser as a consequence of visiting a website. This data is returned to the web server on subsequent visits to the site and may be used to identify a user.

Cookie logicsheet A collection of custom XML tags for automating standard cookie operations.

D

dbXML A project to create databases holding XML data. Recently donated to the Apache Software Foundation as the Xindice project. Supports the proposed XML:DB standard.

delegation (model) Java 1.1 event model in which event-generating components transfer event handling to specific event listeners.

deprecated JDK (Java Development Kit) term that indicates a method whose use is no longer recommended. Deprecated methods might not be supported in future releases.

directives In JavaServer Pages, directives are tags that define general policies or conditions for a page or part of a page.

DLL *See* dynamic link library.

Document Object Model (DOM) An approach to processing an XML document in which the entire document is stored in memory as a parsed hierarchy of elements. Also, in web browsers, the hierarchical structure of the HTML document.

document type declaration A structure within an XML document that points to or contains markup declarations that describe a class of XML documents.

Document Type Definition (DTD) The markup declarations that describe a class of XML documents.

DOM *See* Document Object Model.

double (double precision) Java 64-bit floating-point primitive type.

Double (class) Java wrapper class for `double` primitive values.

DTD *See* Document Type Definition.

dynamic link library (DLL) Executable packages or modules that a programmer can bring into memory and link to as needed by an application.

E

element An XML structural construct consisting of a start tag, an end tag, and information between the tags (contents).

encapsulation Term used in object-oriented programming for enclosing information and behavior within an object, hiding its structure and implementation from other objects. Encapsulation allows programmers to modify the object's internal functions without affecting any other code using the object.

entity An XML structural construct that associates character data or well-formed XML with a name. An entity can be referred to using an *entity reference*.

equals Java method that compares two object references and returns `true` when both objects' contents are identical. The `Object` class default `equals` method returns `true` when both reference the same object.

Error (class) Java class (`java.lang.Error`) that is the parent class of all Java error classes and a subclass of `Throwable`. Errors are typically conditions that a program cannot recover from, such as running out of memory.

ESQL logicsheet A collection of custom XML tags that perform standard SQL queries and serialize the results as XML.

Excalibur Excalibur is a sub-project of the Apache Avalon project. It is intended to provide a number of useful components and utilities.

Exception (class) Java class (`java.lang.Exception`) that is the parent class of all Java exceptions and a subclass of `Throwable`. Exceptions generally signal conditions from which the program may be able to recover.

extends Java keyword used to define a new class that indicates the base class from which the new class will inherit.

Extensible Markup Language (XML) A simplified form of SGML that is the standard for creating custom markup languages. Its purpose is to permit the tags in a document to exactly describe the contents.

Extensible Server Pages (XSP) The Cocoon server-side programming language for mixing content and logic. XSP is similar to JSP except for one key characteristic: executing an XSP page produces XML, not HTML (in the JSP case). The resulting XML is consumed by a pipeline producing an output format, typically HTML or XHTML in web applications of XSP.

Extensible Stylesheet Language (XSL) A specification for transforming and presenting documents created with XML.

Extensible Stylesheet Language for Transformations (XSLT) One of two parts of the W3C XSL recommendation that addresses the transformation of documents from one XML language to another.

F

field Java variable that defines a particular class characteristic.

File (class) Java class (`java.io.File`) that manages file and directory pathnames instead of actual data files.

filter (file I/O sense) Package of interfaces (`java.io`) that specify filtering methods for input and output streams and filenames.

filter (image sense) The Java `java.awt.image` package provides so-called filter classes for transforming image information.

Filter (Java Servlet sense) An interface introduced with the Servlet 2.3 API used to create objects that modify a Servlet request or response.

final Java keyword that stipulates that a class cannot have subclasses. Applied to a member method, this stipulates that the method cannot be overridden by subclasses. Applied to a member variable, it stipulates that the variable is a constant whose value cannot be changed once it is set.

finalize Object method executed by the Java garbage collection process when the memory that object occupies is to be reclaimed. Typically used to ensure that system resources are recovered when an object is discarded.

float Java 32-bit floating-point primitive type.

Float (class) Java wrapper class for `float` primitive values.

FO *See* Formatting Objects.

FOP *See* Formatting Objects Processor.

form A structure used in HTML pages to create elements that can accept user input and transmit it to a web server using CGI conventions.

Formval logicsheet A collection of custom XML tags for automating browser form input validation operations.

Formatting Objects (FO) Part of the XSL standard that describes page composition. See `www.w3.org/TR/2001/xsl/` for the latest standard.

Formatting Objects Processor (FOP) The Apache Software Foundation project to create implementations of the FO standard. A number of output formats are supported and are available in Cocoon, but the emphasis is on PDF. See `http://xml.apache.org/fop` for the current status.

forwarding The process by which a Java Servlet or JSP handles an HTTP request by transparently sending it to another Servlet or JSP on the same server, which continues handling the request. This process is invisible to the requesting agent. *Contrast to* redirect.

G

Generator A Cocoon component that creates SAX events defining some content at the start of a pipeline. Also the Cocoon interface that a generator must implement.

GIF *See* Graphics Interchange Format.

graphical user interface (GUI) A computer user interface that uses graphical elements, windows, and a pointing device; Mac OS, Windows, and X11 are examples of GUIs; supported by Java.

Graphics (class) Java class (`java.awt.Graphics`) that supplies the context for drawing components and screen images.

graphics context Hardware-specific information used by an operating system in allowing applications to draw on a graphics device, such as the computer screen.

Graphics Interchange Format (GIF) Ubiquitous HTML-compressed graphics file format (.gif file extension) for inline graphical elements. Unisys owns the format's patent. *See also* Joint Photographic Experts Group (JPEG).

GUI *See* graphical user interface.

H

hashcode In a general computing context, a characteristic number derived from a data item's contents that allows a program or application to locate the item quickly by operating on the number.

hashCode The method in every Java object that generates an `int` primitive hashcode value characteristic of the object.

Hashtable (class) Java class (`java.util.Hashtable`) object that stores object references denoted by "key" objects using the key's hashcode.

hex (hexadecimal) Mathematical base-16 system used in computer programming that uses alphanumeric characters *0* through *9* and *A* through *F* or *a* through *f*.

hierarchical Logical arrangement of elements, also called a tree structure, in which every element, with the exception of the root object, has parents and might or might not have child objects (children). Examples of this structure can be found in the Java class library, XML documents, and computer file systems.

HTML *See* Hypertext Markup Language.

HTTP *See* Hypertext Transfer Protocol.

HttpServlet (class) The base class in the `javax.servlet.http` package extended by Servlets that need to respond to GET and POST operations.

Hypertext Markup Language (HTML) The document markup language used to create web pages and standardized by the W3C.

Hypertext Transfer Protocol (HTTP) The set of rules (protocols) based on TCP/IP that provides the foundation for communication between web clients and servers.

I

identifier Name given an item in a Java program or application.

Image (class) Java abstract class (`java.awt.Image`) that defines how graphics representation information is held.

implements Java keyword in class declarations that precedes a list of one or more interfaces for which the class supplies methods.

import Java source code file statement that informs the Java compiler as to which package holds classes used in the code.

inheritance In object-oriented programming, relationship among hierarchically arranged objects by which some objects (children) are granted attributes of another object (parent).

init (applet method) By convention, a method that belongs to a Java applet's initial class and that is called by a web browser's JVM after the applet object is created but before it is displayed.

init (Servlet method) A method that belongs to a Java Servlet class and that is called by the Servlet engine after the Servlet object is created but before it services any user requests.

initialize; initialization Setting a variable's starting value.

InputStream (class) Java abstract base class (`java.io.InputStream`) for various Java classes that read data as a byte stream.

instance An object created from a specific class is said to be an instance of that class.

instance variable Java variable that is part of a class instance instead of the class itself (as opposed to a class or `static` variable).

int Java 32-bit integer primitive type that is always treated as a signed integer.

Integer (class) Java wrapper class for `int` values.

interface Similar to a Java class definition, but provides only method declarations, not implementations. A Java class is free to implement as many interfaces as needed.

International Organization for Standardization (ISO) Group comprising national standards organizations from 89 countries, which establishes international standards for telecommunications and technology.

IOException (class) Java class (`java.io.Exception`) that is the parent class of all exceptions related to I/O processes; e.g., opening and reading a file.

ISO *See* International Organization for Standardization.

J

J2EE *See* Java 2 Enterprise Edition.

J2SE *See* Java 2 Standard Edition.

Jakarta The Jakarta project is a major subdivision of the Apache Software Foundation's activities. Generally sub-projects of Jakarta are concerned with server applications, but it also contains utility projects such as the Ant utility.

JAR (Java ARchive) File format similar to Zip for collecting multiple resources (such as class files and Java class libraries) in a single file.

Java 2 Enterprise Edition (J2EE) The largest of Sun's collection of Java utilities and libraries, designed for developing multi-tier enterprise applications.

Java 2 Standard Edition (J2SE) Sun's collection of Java utilities and libraries designed to fit most developers' needs.

Java API for XML Parsing (JAXP) Sun's API that provides a standardized way to specify operations on XML documents. This API is intended to be independent of the actual parser used.

Java bean *also* JavaBean Reusable software component written for a specific function or use and that meets the JavaBeans standard for getting and setting instance variable values.

Java Database Connectivity (JDBC) The collection of Java classes in the `java.sql` package that enables Java programs to connect to SQL-style databases.

Java Development Kit (JDK) Java package of development tools, utilities, a class library, and documentation, which is downloadable from the `java.sun.com` website.

Java Message Service (JMS) The Java API for transmitting application messages over a network using industry standard formats.

Java Virtual Machine (JVM) Nonphysical (virtual) computer that is part of the Java runtime environment and interprets Java bytecodes, providing the foundation for the cross-platform features of Java programs.

JavaBeans Java programming standard for components that comply with a standard interface.

javadoc Java utility that allows automatic documentation by processing source code and producing reference pages in HTML format.

JavaScript Web page scripting language developed by Netscape (originally called *LiveScript*) that controls the way in which web pages appear in browsers. It is now found in both browser-side and server-side versions. Server-side JavaScript can be executed in Cocoon through the `ScriptGenerator` class and the Bean Scripting Framework.

JavaServer Pages (JSP) The Java API that allows a programmer to combine HTML and Java code in a single document to create a dynamic web page. A JSP page is converted into a Servlet automatically. Cocoon uses the `JSPGenerator` class to execute JavaServer Pages documents.

JAXP *See* Java API for XML Parsing.

JDBC *See* Java Database Connectivity.

JDK *See* Java Development Kit.

join `Thread` class instance method for coordinating `Threads`.

Joint Photographic Experts Group (JPEG) Compressed graphics file format (.jpg file extension) supported by JVM and often found in web pages. *See also* Graphics Interchange Format (GIF).

JMS *See* Java Message Service.

JPEG *See* Joint Photographic Experts Group.

JSP *See* JavaServer Pages.

JVM *See* Java Virtual Machine.

Jython The Java version of the popular scripting language, Python.

L

label An identifier followed by a colon appended to a Java statement; used only with `break` and `continue` statements.

List (interface) Java interface (`java.util.List`) that supplies an ordered collection of object references. Not to be confused with the AWT component called List.

listener Java 1.1 event model object registered with a generating component that is informed about a particular class of events.

lock The equivalent of a variable associated with every object that controls access to the object by threads. Locks can be manipulated only by the JVM in the process of synchronizing access to the object.

Log logicsheet A collection of custom XML tags for automating standard log operations.

logicsheet A tag library made up of custom XML tags that is used to embed blocks of code into a document. A pillar of the Cocoon architecture providing separation of logic from content and presentation. Similar to a JSP taglib, a logicsheet provides a powerful abstraction mechanism by burying detailed programming code in a logicsheet while providing a simple parameterized XML tag to the nonprogramming author. Cocoon 2 has several built-in logicsheets. You can also create your own logicsheet.

long Java 64-bit integer primitive type; always treated as signed integer. *See also* double (double precision).

Long (class) Java wrapper class for `long` values.

M

matcher The Cocoon component used in sitemaps to examine the contents of a request and decide if a particular pipeline should be executed. Also the Cocoon interface that a matcher must implement.

method Java class function that is named and for which specific input parameters and return types are declared.

MIME, MIME type *See* Multipurpose Internet Mail Extensions.

modulus (modulo) Java operator (%), used with either integer or floating-point types, that divides the left operand by the right operand and returns the result.

Multipurpose Internet Mail Extensions (MIME) A standard way of denoting content type in a resource; originated for use with e-mail but now widely used in network applications, including SOAP. A MIME type is a standardized string designating a particular type.

mySQL A very popular open-source database. It is designed for power, precision, and speed in heavy load and mission-critical use. See `www.mysql.org`.

N

namespace 1. Complete set of class and method names and other program items that the Java compiler tracks to identify an item uniquely. 2. A way to resolve naming conflicts between elements from different vocabularies in an XML document.

notify Java `Object` class method that causes a `Thread` on the object's wait list to become runnable; `Thread` does not run until allowed to do so by the JVM scheduling mechanism.

null Java special literal value that is used for the value of an uninitialized reference variable.

O

object A class instance.

P

package Collection of associated Java classes and interfaces organized into distinct namespaces.

parent In a hierarchical system, any class that is the ancestor of another class.

PDF *See* Portable Document Format.

pipeline The basic Cocoon data structure for producing a document by connecting various components in a sequence of data handling functions.

pool A supply of objects that are managed by a dedicated mechanism that can supply an object to a requesting process and recover it after the process is finished. Pools of reusable objects are used to reduce Cocoon's response time.

Portable Document Format (PDF) A widely used format invented by Adobe Systems, Inc. for describing and displaying complex documents in a hardware independent fashion. Cocoon can produce PDF-formatted documents using the XSL Formatting Objects API.

portal A general term for a website designed to be a major entry point to the Web. Typically provides many functions such as news, a search engine, and links. Frequently provides the possibility of customized creation of an entry page according to a user's interest. Yahoo! is an example of a very general portal.

portlet A proposed standard API for portal building components, currently described in Java Community Process JSR 167 and 168.

PostScript (PS) A page description language originated by Adobe Systems, Inc. that is the *de facto* standard in many commercial printing organizations. It is notable for ease of scaling and portability. PostScript files have the .ps file extension.

primitive Java types (`boolean`, `char`, `byte`, `short`, `int`, `long`, `float`, and `double`) that are stored and accessed directly in binary form.

priority Value from 1 to 10 that is assigned to `Threads` and that the JVM uses in determining which `Thread` is to run next.

private Java keyword used to tag variables and methods that can be accessed only by methods declared within the same class.

profiling Gathering statistics about the amount of resources used by various processes, which is typically done to guide optimization efforts. Cocoon provides facilities for profiling pipeline operation.

protocol Rules that govern a transaction or data transmission between devices.

PS *See* PostScript.

public Java keyword for modifying visibility of classes and members, making them accessible by all objects, regardless of package boundaries.

Python A popular scripting language available in a Java version called Jython that can be executed with Cocoon's `ScriptGenerator`.

R

Reader (class) Java `abstract` base class (`java.io.Reader`) for classes that read data as a stream of 16-bit Unicode characters.

Reader (Cocoon component) In a Cocoon pipeline, a reader is used to produce an output stream efficiently by output from a resource without creating a SAX event stream. Also the Cocoon interface that readers must implement.

redirect In handling an HTTP request, a Servlet such as Cocoon may send a response that redirects to another resource. This terminates the request, and it is up to the requesting agent to generate a new request to the other resource. *Compare to* forwarding.

reference In Java, the process handled by the JVM by which a programmer works a "pointer" to an object (object reference) rather than directly with an object's physical memory address.

Regular Expression A set of formulas and patterns for matching strings and performing string operations.

Remote Method Invocation (RMI) Java communications standard for distributed computing that allows a Java program to execute a method on an object that resides on another system or JVM as if it were a local object. RMI is a core technology for J2EE-based servers.

remote procedure call (RPC) The general term for executing a method on an application that resides on another system by means of some communication protocol.

Response logicsheet A collection of custom XML tags for performing standard response operations (methods of the `HttpServerResponse` object).

Request logicsheet A collection of custom XML tags for performing standard request operations (methods of the `HttpServerRequest` object).

Rich Text Format (RTF) A widely used format for representing complex documents, roughly comparable to Microsoft Word's doc format in scope.

RMI *See* Remote Method Invocation.

RPC *See* remote procedure call.

root The one item or object from which all others descend in a hierarchical system.

RTF *See* Rich Text Format.

S

SAX *See* Simplified API for XML.

Scalable Vector Graphics (SVG) A standard for specifying graphic elements in an XML markup vocabulary. See `www.w3.org/TR/SVG/` for the latest standard.

schema A formal specification of the structure of an XML document, including information on the types of content allowed in each element.

scope The identifier attribute that controls the identifier's accessibility to other parts of a program.

scripting language Generally speaking, scripting languages are designed for rapid development by linking together components from a powerful toolkit. They tend to have weak variable typing, and are interpreted rather than compiled. Examples include JavaScript, Python, and Perl.

Sel logicsheet A collection of custom XML tags for automating the aggregation of multiple XSP pages into one.

Selector A Cocoon sitemap component that examines a request and determines if a particular pipeline should be executed. Similar to a matcher but more flexible. Also the Cocoon interface such components must implement.

serialize To convert a Java primitive value or object into a byte stream or character stream that is formatted in a way that allows reconstruction of the primitive value or object on the other end of a communication link.

Serializer A Cocoon pipeline component that converts SAX events from the pipeline into a final output format. Also the Cocoon interface such components must implement.

server Network computer that supplies resources and services to client computers.

Servlet Java program that runs in a Servlet container on a web server and processes network requests (typically HTTP requests).

Servlet container The environment in which a Servlet runs. The Servlet API defines a number of services that a Servlet container must provide.

session In Java Servlet and JSP applications, a session maintains information about a user during the course of interaction with an application.

Session logicsheet A collection of custom XML tags for performing standard session operations (methods of the `HttpSession` object).

Set (interface) Java interface (`java.util.Set`) that is an extension of the `Collection` interface that holds object references and that is restricted to prevent duplication of references; hence, every reference is unique.

setup (method) The `setup` method in Cocoon pipeline components is called when a new request must be processed, and before any content is generated. Also, the phase of pipeline operation when this is done.

SGML *See* Standard Generalized Markup Language.

short Java 16-bit integer primitive variable type; always treated as signed integer.

Short (class) Java wrapper class for `short` values.

signature Java method's name along with the type and order of parameters in its argument list.

Simple Object Access Protocol (SOAP) A standard way to transmit messages over networks using XML-formatted documents. The words "Object Access" indicate that SOAP lends itself to object-oriented programming, typically in remote procedure calls (RPCs).

Simplified API for XML (SAX) An approach to processing XML documents in which the parser identifies and parses elements as it encounters them in a single pass through the document. The user of SAX must provide methods to process the parsed elements.

singleton Design pattern that allows the creation of only one instance of a class; a `static` class method controls access to the instance.

sitemap The sitemap is the basic data structure that defines how Cocoon responds to a request. It provides the initial logic that selects a particular pipeline segment to process that request.

Slide A popular Jakarta sub-project for website content management. It is anticipated that an implementation of Slide as a Cocoon source should be available shortly.

SOAP *See* Simple Object Access Protocol.

SOAP logicsheet A collection of custom XML tags for automating standard Simple Object Access Protocol (SOAP) operations.

socket On computer networks, the combination of a computer address and a port number that provides a unique channel of communications.

Socket (class) Java class object (`java.net.Socket`) representing a single network socket connection; can supply an `InputStream` and `OutputStream` for communication.

Source The Cocoon interface that provides simple methods for getting an input stream or SAX events from an object that can serve as a source of data.

SourceForge The home of many Java- and XML-related open-source projects. The main site is at `www.sourceforge.net`, but various projects have their own URLs.

SQL *See* Structured Query Language.

stack trace Formatted text output that can provide the history of a `Thread`'s execution of a method that throws an exception or results in an error.

Standard Generalized Markup Language (SGML) A standard for annotating text documents with tags that expresses the structure of the document and how the content should be treated. SGML served as the basis for HTML and XML.

static Java method or variable tag that indicates the variable or method belongs to a class, rather than to a class instance.

stream A sequence (stream) of bytes that can be read only in sequence from start to finish.

Structured Query Language (SQL) A standard for programming and manipulating the contents of relational databases via text statements. Supported in Java by the JDBC API.

stylesheet A file that contains rules for formatting and presenting the data contained in an XML (or HTML) document. XSL is a stylesheet language based on XML. Cascading Style Sheets (CSS) are files with presentation rules that do not follow XML syntax.

subsitemap A file in the sitemap format that handles only a portion of a Cocoon website. Execution of a request is directed to a subsitemap from the main sitemap according to the request URL or other parameters.

subclass Class that extends (indirectly or directly) another class; all Java classes (except `Object`) are subclasses of the `Object` class.

SVG *See* Scalable Vector Graphics.

synchronized Java keyword that activates a method's or code block's monitor mechanism.

syntax Explicit rules for constructing code statements, including particular values and the order or placement of symbols.

System (class) Java class (`java.lang.System`) composed of `static` methods and variables that the JVM initializes when a program starts.

T

tag In markup languages such as HTML, XML, and JSP pages, a tag is a special character sequence that is not part of the document text but defines additional information.

taglib In JSP technology, a programmer can define his own library of special purpose Java functions identified by tags. A special `taglib` directive tells JSP to use a particular library. XSP also uses the term for a library of functions.

TCP/IP *See* Transmission Control Protocol/Internet Protocol.

Thread (class) Java class (`java.lang.Thread`) that encloses a single thread of control in the JVM and defines its behavior.

throw A Java statement that causes normal statement processing to halt and starts processing of an exception; must be associated with a `Throwable` object.

throws Java keyword that is employed in method declarations to introduce a list of the exceptions that method can throw.

timestamp Java `long` primitive variable that holds the system time for an event's occurrence.

Tomcat This is the Servlet container developed by the Apache Foundation. It is the Reference Implementation of the Java Servlet and Java Server Pages technologies developed by Sun Microsystems, Inc.

toString Method possessed by all Java reference types that the compiler uses to evaluate statements that include `String` objects and the + operator.

Transformer A Cocoon pipeline component that receives SAX events and carries out some transformation of the data these events represent. Also the Cocoon interface that such components must implement.

Transmission Control Protocol/Internet Protocol (TCP/IP) Suite of communications protocols developed to support mixed network environments, such as the Internet.

try Java statement that constructs a code block in which an exception can occur; must be followed by at least one associated `catch` clause and/or a `finally` clause.

type A Java object's class or interface. In object-oriented programming in general, an object's interface is sometimes considered separately from its implementation, resulting in a further division into class and type.

U

Uniform Resource Identifier (URI) The generic set of all names and addresses that refer to resources.

Uniform Resource Locator (URL) The set of URI schemes that contains explicit instructions on how to access a resource on the Internet.

URI *See* Uniform Resource Identifier.

URL *See* Uniform Resource Locator.

URL (class) Java class (`java.net.URL`) that represents a Uniform Resource Locator for a web server.

Util logicsheet A collection of custom XML tags for various standard utility operations.

V

valid XML XML that conforms to the vocabulary specified in a DTD or schema.

view An object that creates a specific model data display in the Model-View-Controller design pattern. One model may have many views, but a view is always attached to a single model.

visibility Level of access a Java class grants to other Java classes.

W

W3C *See* World Wide Web Consortium.

wait Java `Object` class method that when called by a `Thread` releases the `Thread`'s lock on the object, causes the `Thread` to become inactive, and places the `Thread` on the object's wait list.

web application A collection of Servlets, JSP pages, HTML files, image files, and other resources that exist in a structured hierarchy of directories on a server.

Web Service Definition Language (WSDL) A standard XML format for describing network services as a set of messages that can be sent to defined servers, mainly used to define SOAP services.

well formed XML XML markup that meets the requirements of the W3C Recommendation for XML 1.0.

Wireless Markup Language (WML) A simplified variant of HTML designed for small wireless device displays.

WML *See* Wireless Markup Language.

World Wide Web Consortium (W3C) The organization that creates standards for the Web (`www.w3.org`).

wrapper classes Java classes that correspond to each of the primitive types, providing related utility functions.

WSDL *See* Web Service Definition Language.

X

Xalan The Apache XSL stylesheet processor used in Cocoon. See the `xml.apache.org` website for the latest version.

Xerces The Apache XML parser used in Cocoon. See the `xml.apache.org` website for the latest version.

Xindice The Apache project for support of the proposed XML:DB standard for databases accessing XML data directly.

XML *See* Extensible Markup Language.

XMLP Title of the XML Protocol project at the W3C that has taken over development of SOAP standards.

XPath This W3C recommendation language is designed to address subparts of an XML document that can be used by XPointer and XSLT.

XPointer The XML Pointer language defines constructs that can be used to address internal sections of an XML document.

XSL *See* Extensible Stylesheet Language.

XSLT *See* Extensible Stylesheet Language for Transformations.

XSP *See* Extensible Server Pages.

Index

Note to the reader: Throughout this index **boldfaced** page numbers indicate primary discussions of a topic. *Italicized* page numbers indicate illustrations.

SYMBOLS & NUMBERS

A

B

C

D

E

F

G

H

I

J

L

M

N

O

P

Q

R

S

T

U

V

X

Z

The quotation at the bottom of the front cover is taken from Lao Tzu's Tao Te Ching, *the classic work of Taoist philosophy. These particular verses are from the translation by D. C. Lau (copyright 1963) and are part of a larger exploration of the nature of the Tao, sometimes translated as "the way."*

It is traditionally held that Lao Tzu lived in the fifth century B.C. in China, but it is unclear whether he was actually a historical figure. The concepts embodied in the Tao Te Ching *influenced religious thinking in the Far East, including Zen Buddhism in Japan. Many in the West, however, have wrongly understood the* Tao Te Ching *to be primarily a mystical work; in fact, much of the advice in the book is grounded in a practical moral philosophy governing personal conduct.*